The Post-War Generation and Establishment Religion

The Post-War Generation and Establishment Religion

Cross-Cultural Perspectives

EDITED BY

Wade Clark Roof, Jackson W. Carroll, and David A. Roozen

Westview Press

BOULDER • SAN FRANCISCO • OXFORD

Copyright © 1995 by Westview Press, Inc.

Published in 1995 in the United States of America by Westview Press, Inc., 5500 Central Avenue, Boulder, Colorado 80301-2877, and in the United Kingdom by Westview Press, 36 Lonsdale Road, Summertown, Oxford OX2 7EW

Library of Congress Cataloging-in-Publication Data
The post-war generation and establishment religion : cross- cultural
    perspectives / edited by Wade Clark Roof, Jackson W. Carroll, David
    A. Roozen.
        p.   cm.
    Includes bibliographical references.
    ISBN 0-8133-8914-3
    1. Christianity—Europe—20th century.   2. Baby boom generation—
Europe—Religious life.   I. Roof, Wade Clark.   II. Carroll,
Jackson W.   III. Roozen, David A.
BR735.P675   1995
274'.0825—dc20   94-24178
                                                                              CIP

Printed and bound in the United States of America

The paper used in this publication meets the requirements
of the American National Standard for Permanence of Paper
for Printed Library Materials Z39.48-1984.

10   9   8   7   6   5   4   3   2   1

Contents

Preface   vii
Introduction   ix

1   The Post-War Generation and Establishment
    Religion in England, *Eileen Barker*   1

2   Baby Boomers Downunder: The Case of Australia,
    Gary D. Bouma and Michael Mason   27

3   Fifty Years of Religious Change in the United States,
    David A. Roozen, Jackson W. Carroll, and Wade Clark Roof   59

4   Tradition and Change in the Nordic Countries,
    Susan Sundback   87

5   The Post-War Generations and Institutional Religion
    in Germany, *Karl Gabriel*   113

6   The Case of the Netherlands, *Leo Laeyendecker*   131

7   The Case of French Catholicism, *Danièle Hervieu-Léger*   151

8   The Surviving Dominant Catholic Church in
    Belgium: A Consequence of Its Popular Religious
    Practices? *Karel Dobbelaere*   171

9   From Institutional Catholicism to "Christian
    Inspiration": Another Look at Belgium, *Liliane Voyé*   191

10 Religion and the Post-War Generation in Italy,
    Salvatore Abbruzzese   207

11 The Orthodox Church and the Post-War Religious
    Situation in Greece, *Vasilios N. Makrides*   225

12 Conclusion: The Post-War Generation - Carriers of a
    New Spirituality, *Wade Clark Roof, Jackson W. Carroll,
    and David Roozen*   243

    About the Editors and Contributors   257
    References   259
    About the Book   291

Preface

This collection of papers presents a comparative analysis of religious trends in ten Western countries since World War II. Our intent has been to explore as systematically as possible trends in what we call "establishment religion" in ten countries. At the same time we also look at new, emergent forms of religion in each case. Our principal concern has been to consider the impact of the post-war generation--that cohort of people born in the wake of World War II--on the trends. In doing so, we have attempted to look at the big religious picture and not get lost in a myriad of smaller developments.

Plans for the project first materialized in 1987 at a meeting of the International Society for the Sociology of Religion (S.I.S.R.) in Tübingen, West Germany. The group of scholars who agreed to participate met on three subsequent occasions to present and discuss their papers. Drafts of the papers were presented at various professional meetings: at the S.I.S.R. meeting in Helsinki, Finland, in 1989; at the S.I.S.R. meeting in Maynooth, Ireland, in 1991; and at the Association for the Sociology of Religion meeting in Washington, D. C., in 1992.

The project was made possible by grants from the Lilly Endowment, Inc. to Hartford Seminary and the University of Massachusetts.

Brian Wilson and Richard Merkel read the papers and made editorial suggestions, and Paige Ann Scarlett prepared the manuscript for publication. We are most grateful for their efforts.

We also thank the chapter authors for their papers and for agreeing to a common format for discussion of themes. The project itself was an experiment in international cooperation--and proof that comparative study is not only possible but exciting and productive. Over the course of our work, we formed new scholarly and friendship ties, laughed at difficulties in cross-cultural communication, and genuinely enjoyed our work together.

Wade Clark Roof
Jackson W. Carroll
David A. Roozen

Introduction

A new world emerged after World War II, one that shaped and was shaped by a post-war generation. Those born after 1945 in the more advanced industrial countries of the West enjoyed not only a world that had returned to stability, but also unprecedented levels of technological and economic development, new standards of living and consumption, and enhanced opportunities for expressive fulfillment. They had high hopes and expectations, both materially and for a better quality of life.

They also grew up in the aftermath of "the Bomb," aware of the possibilities of nuclear annihilation. Members of this generation alternatively participated in and resisted--if not in person, then through the instantaneous and omnipresent wonder of television--ideological confrontation between communism and Western capitalism, intervention in "foreign" wars for liberation (e.g., the Vietnam War), and racial/ethnic uprisings at home. At the forefront of a gender revolution, they were aware of changing relations between men and women. They witnessed national and international terrorism, environmental disasters, and assassinations of major political figures. In addition to affluence and consumerism, there were also cycles of economic disparity and recessions. They experimented with new lifestyles, but also encountered the intolerance and rejection that often accompanies cultural experimentation. Their idealism challenged establishments of all kinds, but at least in the short term, historical entrenchment carried the day. Many became politically alienated and "turned off" to established values and lifestyles.

Indeed, for this younger generation World War II is more than just a backdrop to history; it is a marker setting off the new world with all its promise and peril from a past to which there can be no return. There were other changes of the post-war era--most notably, a changing international political and economic system, television and the growth of visual media, and widening exposure to many differing peoples and cultures as a result of broad-scale immigration--which, combined with generational changes, all led to a greater pluralism and global consciousness. And in time, all the major social spheres--family, political, educational, religious--would come to be restructured, embodying the visions and values of this younger generation.

This book explores how one of these spheres--the religious--has come to be re-patterned by these visions and values. Our approach is cross-cultural, looking at ten different countries: England, Italy, Belgium, Germany, France, Greece, the Netherlands, and the Nordic countries, plus Australia and the United States. These are among the most advanced contemporary nation-states, often described today as in a late- or post-modern phase. What happens to religion for the post-war generation in these settings is suggestive of religion's fate in other modernizing places.

Religion "Establishments"

Religion is of course a broadly based cultural phenomenon not easily captured by any single definition. We speak of "religious establishments," referring to the dominant, culturally maintained religious institutions in these countries--such as the Church of England, the Orthodox Church in Greece, the Catholic Church in France or Belgium, the Lutheran Church in Sweden, or the mainstream Protestant and Catholic churches in the United States. These are all institutions (with their constitutive sets of beliefs, rituals, moral and behavioral norms, and constituencies) which have historically enjoyed either legal or cultural establishment in their respective countries. While the two types of establishment have their own distinct dynamics, still both entail a privileged status and are closely identified with the history, values, and customs of their countries.

The role of religious establishments is important for several reasons. By virtue of their close ties to the state, they provide an overarching canopy of religious symbols, rituals, and meanings that are integral to tradition and help to shape everyday definitions of reality. Anthony Giddens (1984) describes how, through routinized practices, feelings, and beliefs, tradition (in both the religious and non-religious sense) creates a sense of what he calls "ontological security." National ceremonies and holidays, for example, help to sustain a consciousness of social order and psychological stability, even for people who claim no involvement in organized religion. Moreover, symbols, myths, and rituals all make up a crucial part of the political culture known as civil religion. If, as Ninian Smart suggests, it is impossible to take religion seriously without trying to understand how religious symbols work--the "vocabulary of mythic thinking" as he puts it (1987: 14)--then it follows that we cannot really understand nation-states without considering the myths and symbols that legitimate them. Myths and symbols are fundamental to national consciousness, and thus they can, and often do, evoke deep emotional reactions. And in yet another way as well, religious establishments serve a crucial function even in the most secular societies:

they constitute the "official" religion, i.e., the institutionalized norms of belief and practice, against which other forms of religious belief and practice are defined. The terms used to describe alternative religious groups in the various countries, for example, all reflect their non-official status: "dissenters," "separatists," "sects," "cults," and "religious fringe."

The privileges of establishment vary depending upon circumstance and patterns of church-state relations. Greece, for example, maintains an established church (the Orthodox Church in Greece), which both politically and culturally commands strong support. The Church of England is still officially the established church in England, yet culturally much of its influence has eroded. The Anglican Church in Australia, while established during the colonial period, never enjoyed political support after independence, although it did, for a time, exert considerable influence in the culture. In the Nordic countries (Lutheran Church) and in France and Belgium (Catholic Church) the situations were roughly analogous to that of Australia: while the established churches in these countries had enjoyed cultural dominance, they lost their political status during the late nineteenth and early twentieth centuries. The Netherlands is different still since historically there have been multiple, established denominations. And, of course, the denominationalism of the United States, with its vaguely Judeo-Christian "civil religion," represents yet another pattern. Today, the regulatory patterns having evolved between church and state have led to many churches in many European countries becoming more involved in social support services. In Italy, the state has moved in the direction of supporting the clergy; in France, the state assumes the cost of instruction in Catholic schools; in Germany, church-run hospitals and other charities are funded by the state. Despite their low levels of religious attendance, the churches have assumed public roles with the blessings of the state, especially in education, charity, health care, and national commentary (see Francis 1992).

In the United States, by contrast, a much different situation exists. Levels of religious involvement are higher, and churches cannot receive support from the state for their activities. The heritage of religious freedom and absence of a legal establishment of religion means that religious groups function in a more open and competitive environment. From colonial times to the present there have been, as Finke and Stark (1992) say, "winners" and "losers," churches that have enjoyed widespread influence through their close association with the culture and others whose significance has waned over time. There have long been so-called mainstream churches with strong followings, although the particular churches making up this normative core at any given time has varied.

Religious establishments have their privileges. They also have their downside. Their fates often follow those of nation-states. Periods of national dominance in the world order tend to be periods of religious vibrancy. Correspondingly, with loss of national dominance, religious establishments frequently decline in significance (Smith 1986; Burdick and Hammond 1991). The ties of nation-states to the larger international system are complex and shaped by a myriad of particular factors. Nevertheless there are linkages between the political and economic structure, on the one hand, and the cultural and religious life, on the other hand.

Within national cultures as well, value shifts and popular sentiments have religious reverberations. Especially in periods of great social and cultural change, established religions experience strain and are easily disadvantaged, if not marginalized or even singled out for attack. Martin E. Marty (1976: 71) writes: "Mainline churches suffer in times of cultural crisis and disintegration, when they receive blame for what goes wrong in society, but are bypassed when people look for new ways to achieve social identity and location." While his comments are specifically addressed to the religious situation in the United States, his double-edged observation applies more generally. In times when the culture is undergoing rapid change and is not very supportive of the establishment, people often turn elsewhere in their religious and spiritual quests. And the "new" quests often, though not always, stand in striking, even opposite, relation to the "older," more established faiths, as when Catholic dropouts turn to something very different like neo-paganism or Goddess worship. Both of these aspects of religious change are of interest to us in this volume, i.e., how religious establishments have suffered from their close cultural ties *and* in what ways and to what extent people have sought other religious expressions.

Generational Change

Why so much attention to generational change? Quite simply, generations are carriers of culture--including religious and spiritual ideas. They are major social units, bound together by age-related experiences and a common outlook on life, and an integral part of every society. This being the case, it is surprising that so little attention has been given to generational patterns of beliefs, practices, and symbols.

Karl Mannheim's notion of a "generation unit" is fundamental to our consideration. In Mannheim's terms, a generation unit is more than just an age cohort; it is a group that shares a "common location in the social and historical process" which limits it to "a specific range of potential experience, predisposing it for a certain characteristic mode of thought and experience, and a characteristic type of historically relevant action" (Mannheim 1952; also see Wuthnow 1978: 125). Hence, members of a generation are influenced in their formative years by a particular set of social experiences; and, to an extent, they share a common culture and are self-conscious of themselves as having a distinctive outlook and identity. This outlook and identity tend to remain with them throughout their lives despite life-cycle changes as well as shifts in societal context.

Generational cultures emerge especially in times when social and cultural changes affect some age strata more than others. And given the pace of innovation in technological and material culture in all the advanced societies since World War II, the possibilities for such distinctive experiences and outlook were, and still are, great indeed. Television's role since World War II in defining and solidifying opinion about political events and value shifts, and thereby helping to shape a generational consciousness in many differing national settings, was itself incalculable. The women's movement which radically altered opportunity structures and power relations between men and women cut across national boundaries. So did fears of nuclear war and concerns about the environment. For the post-war generation, there were widespread disjunctures in experience, values, and outlook that registered across societies. The youth counterculture that drew so much attention in the United States, to cite an obvious example, led to student protests against the Vietnam War during the late 1960s and early 1970s not just in places like Washington and San Francisco but in London, Bonn, Copenhagen, and Paris as well.

The sheer size of the post-war age cohorts is a factor. Birth rates rose in the aftermath of World War II, decisively so in countries such as the United States and Australia where the term "baby boom generation" caught on and remained as a label. Members of the post-war generation were conscious of themselves as a *large* group, as children in school, and then later as youth both in universities and in the larger cities. Their peer-related experiences during their teenage and early adult years helped to shape radical political ideologies, alternative ways of living, and a global consciousness. Isolated into large student populations during a time of economic expansion, on the one hand, and social and political unrest, on the other--Vietnam War, East-West tensions, environmental crises, lifestyle and sexual experimentation--it is not surprising that youth countercultures became highly visible.

But even more important than demography were the cultural conflicts themselves. Youth broke with their parents' generation in basic values across a wide spectrum--concerning politics, work, family, sexuality, leisure, and religion. The most comprehensive, well-documented study describing such a break is that put forth by Ronald Inglehart (1990). Based upon examination of trends in more than a dozen advanced industrial societies, he refers to a "culture shift," arguing that the basic value priorities of Western nations have been shifting over the past several decades from materialist to post-materialist. He describes this shift as one "from giving top priority to physical sustenance and safety toward heavier emphasis on belonging, self-expression, and the quality of life" (1990: 66). His argument rests on psychologist Abraham Maslow's assumption about the "hierarchy of needs," which in this instance translates: because large portions of the young adult Western populations were raised under conditions of economic expansion and security, there has been a corresponding shift in values--away from attention to high salaries, job security, and national defense toward greater emphasis on environmental protection, women's rights, opportunities for personal fulfillment, and the priority of ideas over money.

What is striking about Inglehart's analysis is that he is able, as best one can, to sort out the generational (or "cohort" effects) from "period" and "aging" effects. Period effects have to do with value changes that presumably influence all age groups. Aging effects refer to changes in values over time due to the life-cycle. His conclusion is that there has been an inter-generational shift in values as members of the post-war generation over time have replaced older citizens in their societies, or more exactly, a combination of generational change combined with period effects (1990: 103). Gradually the older, more materialist values are being replaced by post-materialist values, themselves rather broadly based in the societies to begin with. This diffusion of cultural values holds for European countries and for the United States, though the latter appears to be experiencing these changes more slowly than the Northern European countries such as the Netherlands, Denmark, and Sweden.

The religious changes that Inglehart uncovers are particularly interesting and bear directly upon our concerns in this volume. Using a battery of questions on belief in God, the importance of belief in God, religious practices, and the meaning and purpose of life, he offers the following interpretation of generational religious change:

> It would be a serious oversimplification to describe this process as the decline of religion. In some respects, the emerging generation seems to have a *heightened* sensitivity to spiritual concerns, by comparison with older groups. But the worldview espoused by most of the established religious denominations seems increasingly out of touch with the perceptions and priorities of the younger generation. Thus, we simultaneously find indications of a heightened reverence for nature and an increased concern for the meaning and purpose of life among postmaterialists together with much weaker support for traditional religious norms (1990: 187).

Elsewhere he writes:

> Post-materialists may have *more* potential interest in religion
> than Materialists do. A religious message based on economic
> and physical insecurity finds little resonance among Post-
> materialists--but one that conveyed a sense of meaning and
> purpose in contemporary society might fill a need that is
> becoming increasingly widespread (1990: 211).

Chapter Themes

In this volume, we explore the post-war generation's involvement with religion in far greater depth than does Inglehart, yet like him, we look at what is happening both to their participation in the established religion and to their more personal spiritual concerns. Our approach is both cross-cultural and historical, which allows us to chart some of the major religious and spiritual changes that have occurred across a range of societies. Some of the themes found in the papers are well-known in the sociology of religion, such as functional differentiation, secularization, privatization, and greater individualism. Generational changes in religion are less well-understood, and it is to these, and specifically to the post-war generation, that all the papers here are addressed. The oldest members of this generation are now approaching fifty years of age, and great numbers of them in all the countries are now in their forties; thus, we are able to examine how their religious beliefs and practices have evolved over a significant portion of the life-span, from youth through marriage and parenting and into mid-life.

We begin with England, the first of three countries we examine that have an Anglo-Saxon Protestant heritage and that are quite pluralist religiously. England is in some respects highly secularized, yet as Eileen Barker points out, there remains "a still-recognizable sacred canopy of British society" which is symbolically affirmed and celebrated by the Church of England. Despite liturgical changes and efforts at making the Church more of a social and political force, however, members of the post-war generation are less involved within it and other mainstream churches than are those born into preceding generations. Family changes, religious education in the schools, the media, and a more pluralist culture brought on by the influx of immigrants are all factors leading Barker to suggest that the post-war generation feels less obligation to have contact with establishment churches. At the same time, she observes that the period since the 1970s has been a time of considerable religious and spiritual ferment among young people, as evidenced in the growth of house churches, evangelical Christianity, new religious and human potential movements, and New Age consciousness.

In Australia, historically Anglican and Catholic, but now with near equal proportions of Catholics, Anglicans, other Protestants, and non-affiliated, we find post-war generation declines in institutional religious participation similar to those in England. Overall levels of church involvement are higher in Australia than in England, partly because of the Catholic presence, but the patterns of change are fundamentally the same. Gary D. Bouma and Michael Mason argue that the declines in religious identification, practice, and belief among Australians are a result largely of cohort and period effects. "Now," as they say, "affiliation as well as participation has become increasingly optional." Cohort changes are also evident in belief in God, in imageries from God as creator to God as friend, in reliance upon faith, and in keeping the Ten Commandments. Australian boomers increasingly opt out of religious participation altogether and join the ranks of those having "no religion"; far fewer it seems leave the establishment churches for new religious movements. They suggest that while secularizing trends and reduced religious inter-group hostility have affected all age groups, they have disproportionately influenced the post-war generation.

In the case of the denominationally diverse United States, patterns for religion are both different and similar to those of England and Australia. David A. Roozen, Jackson W. Carroll, and Wade Clark Roof trace fifty years of religious change through the experience of the baby boom generation. The boomers were born during a time of religious vitality and church growth, fostered by economic expansion and post-war ideological climate. Beginning in the mid-1960s, national surveys show a downward trend in religious life, and particularly so for the young adult cohort deeply touched by an expressive, highly subjective culture. By the late 1970s, overall declines are less apparent than a "restructuring" of the religious: the old established Protestant churches continued to lose members and support, evangelical and charismatic Christianity continued to grow, post-Vatican II Catholicism accommodated norms of openness and personal freedom, new religious and human potential movements flourished. Today, many in the baby boom generation who dropped out are "returning" to churches. However, even greater numbers appear to turn to the churches only for rites of passage or are exploring alternative spiritualities outside of the religious establishment. Over time American religious institutions have become more de-centralized, in keeping with the diverse interests of participants and a climate of greater religious choice.

Next, we look at three non-Anglo settings that were all shaped historically by core Protestant cultures: the Scandinavian countries, Germany, and the Netherlands. Susan Sundback describes recent trends in

Denmark, Iceland, Finland, Norway, and Sweden where increasing religious pluralism resulting from immigration, movement from rural to urban areas, greater choice on the part of individuals, and secularization generally has eroded the influence of the Lutheran state church (except in Finland, which has both Lutheran and Orthodox churches). She observes that for the post-war generation there were high rates of withdrawal from the religious institutions and a weakening of adherence to church teachings, beliefs, and morals. Open critique of church teachings, free-thinking and acceptance of alternative religions all became more popular after the 1960s. She views these changes in an ideological context of the end of the cold war, the collapse of the Soviet superpower, and the building of a global world, all of which leads Sundback to conclude that the post-war generation's experience in the Scandinavian countries is crucially different in that it was "the first to have been forced to consider its relation to the church and religion in a conscious way."

The case of Germany is complex given its historic separation into eastern and western states and recent re-unification. As Karl Gabriel observes, religious observance declined significantly after World War II in East Germany where atheism, not the churches, was the official religion; in West Germany, levels of religious involvement remained relatively high during the 1950s and early 1960s, but toward the end of the 1960s there were substantial declines. He attributes the declines in West Germany to the post-war generation, who, in their attitudes toward church membership and worship attendance, in matters of faith and values, and in ethical stance, as he says, "display marked differences from the preceding generations." Gabriel argues that this generational shift in beliefs and values came about as a late phase in the historic process of modernization. In earlier times establishment churches were aligned with those segments of the population that were less affected by modernization; however, with the extraordinary economic success and expansion of the industrial, market-oriented sectors after the war newer ideologies won out. Similar changes were brought about by more coercive political means in eastern Germany.

In the Netherlands, where historically there have been three major denominations--the Roman Catholic Church, the Netherlands Reformed Church, and the Neo-Calvinist Church--there have also long been large numbers of non-affiliates. But as Leo Laeyendecker points out, since the early 1970s non-affiliates have increased for the population in general and among the younger Dutch in particular. This defection affected all religious groups, and especially the Roman Catholics who up to that time formed a closed community, or "pillar," with its own social and political organizations. "De-pillarization" led to a decline in the cohesiveness of religious communities as well as other kinds of religious changes, such as declining participation in worship services, erosion of traditional beliefs, and lower levels of confidence in the churches. Laeyendecker links these changes with the expectations generated by Vatican Council II and subsequent efforts by Rome to set limits on the movement toward church renewal--which led to strong protests on the part of a post-war generation optimistic about social change, committed to new moral values, and believing in radical democracy. He also provides an extensive and helpful perspective on the generational concept, suggesting that three "layers of time" shape a generation's experiences: long-term societal processes (e.g., increasing individualism), short-term fluctuations (e.g., economic and business cycles), and major events (e.g., Vatican Council II).

Turning to countries where Roman Catholicism has been the historically dominant religious establishment, we look first at France. Danièle Hervieu-Léger argues that the religious foundations for an older "parochial civilization" in France have crumbled and are being replaced by a more diffuse and private style of religiosity. The latter is oriented to the psychological needs of individuals and is expressed in many ways: in the recomposition of beliefs drawing off of science and other religious traditions, in the rise of small groups where people share experiences and personal stories, and in the emergence of "festive religion" related to peak experiences and significant moments in a person's life. This new "religion of emotional communities," she reports, is especially strong among the post-war generation. She suggests there is an affinity between the psychological culture in which members of this generation were reared after the 1960s and the shift from an older, officially sanctioned mode of Christianity to these more informal, individually constructed forms of religion incorporating a mix of themes and elements (texts, beliefs, rituals) that serve the expressive and affective needs of individuals.

Similar trends are reported in Belgium. Karel Dobbelaere's chapter provides a broad perspective on recent religious changes in that country, including a description of how conceptions of the supernatural have been changing. He suggests that many of the older views about God no longer fit very neatly in a world, both physical and social, where people think more and more in terms of knowledge, control, and planning--precisely that world in which the post-war generation is most at home. His data suggest that for this younger generation of Belgians there have been precipitous declines in traditional Catholic beliefs and practices, yet he also observes other, more accommodating types of religious changes: ritual as celebration and incantation rather than as community of believers, with more attention to the festive and familial aspects of life; *bricolage*, or pulling together various elements drawn from a variety of sources to create one's own religious views; and popular styles of religion, such as pilgrimages and blessings. Dobbelaere interprets these trends not as the vanishing of the sacred but as expression of a post-modern style of spirituality, more subjective and more open to individualistic interpretation than the official beliefs and practices of the Church.

In a second paper on Belgium, Liliane Voyé offers a more detailed description of the new spirituality as found among small voluntary groups of young, middle-class adults. Her title--"From Institutional Catholicism to 'Christian Inspiration'"--is itself suggestive. She identifies four characteristics of these new groups: (1) attention to specific life experiences, such as the loss of a child or choice of a lifestyle; (2) concern with personal spiritual growth, i.e., "seeking" and "learning"; (3) diverse means and gestures, such as mixing Bible readings with scientific texts; and (4) distancing from the institutional Church. These are all features of post-modernity, she argues, characterized by the end of the Great Narratives, the mixing of codes, and the voluntary nature of the religious bonds. Undermined as well is the traditional hierarchical relationship of the cleric over the laity, and the superior claims of Catholicism over other religions or science. Voyé goes further than most other contributors in the volume toward describing the new religious and spiritual styles now taking shape among many young adults.

In Italy, which has had a peculiar and somewhat conflicted history of social development since World War II, the religious changes are somewhat distinctive as well. The modernization process entailed "anti-modern" contradictions, particularly discrepancies between political and economic change on the one hand, and traditional work and family patterns on the other, which, as Salvatore Abbruzzese points out, shaped the post-war generation's views in that country toward both modernity and religion. Young Italians grew disillusioned with modernity's promises of unlimited well-being as well as with the Church's positions on sexuality, abortion, and divorce in the period after Vatican Council II when there were heightened expectations of social and cultural accommodation. But as Abbruzzese makes clear, this younger generation is characterized "more by a simple discordance rather than a true opposition to religion." It is an opposition to an institution and not a decline of the sacred itself, and it is an expression of greater individualism in matters of belief and morals and strong reliance upon an inner spirituality. Having exhausted modernity's ethical potential, this generation embraces ethical relativism and a more practical stance toward the religious establishment, emphasizing that this establishment should be judged on the basis of its actions and contributions to a better society and not by its normative statements of belief and practice necessary to spiritual well-being.

Finally, we look at Greece, where, compared to other European countries, culture and religion remain closely related. Despite current trends of urbanization and exposure to new cultures, as Vasilios N.

Makrides describes, "being Greek" and "being Orthodox" are still inextricably intertwined. Greece has been spared many of the secular challenges and anti-religious protests that other countries have experienced. However, there have been important trends for the post-war generation--opposition to conventional religion in the direction of spiritual renewal on the one hand, and movement toward the intensification of Orthodox fundamentalism on the other. The major trend Makrides describes as a "multi-faceted distancing from religion," by which he refers to a growing individualism and exercise of choice in religious matters, among people who yet remain aligned with the Greek Orthodox tradition. What has emerged is a more "diffused religion" that is subjective, syncretistic, and more voluntaristic, but at the same time continues to be loosely bounded by the Orthodox tradition. Where all of this may lead in the future and whether Orthodoxy will be able to contain popular religious trends and a growing pluralism are open to speculation, although clearly a younger generation of Greeks is reshaping that country's religious life.

Following the chapters on the various countries, we offer a brief conclusion. Here we take stock of the generational changes as found in these settings and offer further interpretation of the religious and spiritual patterns now in the making.

1

The Post-War Generation and Establishment Religion in England

Eileen Barker

The General Context

This portrayal of the English post-war generation with respect to establishment religion is to be located within the context of a society which has had an established church for more than four centuries, and which now entertains what might be termed a gentle, secularizing pluralism. Over half the 48 million or so people living in England have a loose affiliation with the Church of England, but around 5 million are associated with both the Nonconformist and Catholic churches; also, there are now well over a million Muslims, and several hundreds of thousands who belong to the Jewish, Hindu and Sikh traditions. It is possible to list over a thousand other religious institutions in England, some of which may have several thousands of members, while others will have no more than a score or so.

The gentleness of English pluralism may sometimes express itself in indifference or apathy; but the adjective has been chosen to evoke a relative absence of embattled positions. England has enjoyed, on the one hand, a relative absence of virulent antagonisms (there is little of the anti-clericalism that has been evident in some, mainly Catholic, parts of Europe) and, on the other hand, a relative absence of frenetic enthusiasms (as are evident in segments of the United States).

The secularization manifested in twentieth-century England is not unlike the secularization that was anticipated by Weber and Durkheim, and which has been variously described in neo-classic form by Wilson (1966b), Dobbelaere (1981), Westley (1983) and many others. It is a secularization that is intrinsically tied to social variables such as industrialization, modernity, urbanization, rationalization, bureaucratization, and societalization and to both structural and functional differentiation. It is a "process whereby religious thinking, practice and institutions lose social significance" (Wilson 1966b:14). It is, concurrently, a process by which religion has become increasingly a leisure pursuit, privatized and/or individualized in, to some extent, the apparently opposing, but basically compatible, processes that are described by Luckmann (1967; 1977) and Berger (1969) and, indeed, somewhat more provocatively, by Wilson:

> In this private sphere, religion often continues, and even acquires new forms of expression, many of them much less related to other aspects of culture than were the religions of the past. . . . religion remains an alternative culture, observed as unthreatening to the modern system, in much the same way that entertainment is seen as unthreatening. It offers another world to explore as an escape from the rigors of technological order and the ennui that is the incidental by-product of an increasingly programmed world (Wilson 1985:20).

The pluralism is contained, rather than actively restrained or encouraged, by an established church which, in some ways, has gradually become marginalized from an historically evolved, but ever-more shifting establishment. It is not a pluralism of fierce competition, nor yet is it one of utter *laissez faire*. It is not a pluralism devoid of tension, nor yet is it one fundamentally undermined by tension. While it is a pluralism in which the dice may be historically or economically loaded, it is, nonetheless, a genuine pluralism in that it is one in which the question "who's going to win?" is not a pressing question for English society, despite the fact that it may be such for some of the society's constituents.

It is a pluralism that tallies well with the familiar metaphor of the supermarket. It is one in which geographical, occupational, and social mobility have contributed to the erosion of the ties of family and tradition. It is a pluralism that is fed by the media and the educational system, both of which, while embracing homogenizing tendencies towards a monolithic culture, also encourage seekership, the questioning, even ridiculing, of authority, and an emphasis upon the primacy of individual freedom and choice. It is a pluralism that extends, beyond a multitude of religious, spiritual, political and/or ideological choices, to a possibly more fundamental pluralism of identity.

But, while there are undoubted differences and divisions within and between the different generations of English society, there is no great fragmentation, and, except, perhaps, among the immigrant Muslim populations, there is little in the culture or the structure of contemporary England that resembles the pillarization of social life such as one would find in Holland, and, to some extent, in Northern Ireland. English Anglicans may go to Catholic convent schools, Methodists and Muslims to Church of England schools, but the vast majority of children born in post-war England have attended state schools.

There lingers, furthermore, a still-recognizable sacred canopy of British society that transcends denominational labels. While the establishment embraces Nonconformity and the Catholic church, Britons do not generally articulate their common identity as "One Nation under God"--although such rhetoric is sometimes drawn upon. Rather, the Church of England is understood as part of something else--an unarticulated jumble of 1066 and 1215, of Shakespeare and Wordsworth, of Waterloo and Dunkirk, of Celtic mysteries and vague memories of a colonial past. In a delicate tension with the pluralism, there lurks a shared culture, a shared history that defines as a single and a separate entity the island Kingdom, which is both small enough and large enough to have a dozen national *Dailies*. While internationalism spreads and pluralism proliferates (and the post-war generation has done much to promote such changes), establishment religions take their place as *partial* upholders of a wider *British* sacred identity that may be symbolically affirmed and celebrated at Royal Weddings, in a Falklands War[1], through Elgar at a last night of the Proms,[2] or in the solemn aftermath of a Hillsborough disaster.[3]

The Demographic Context

Given that the concept "baby boomers" is sometimes used interchangeably with "post-war generation", a brief demographic account of the crude birth-rate in the United Kingdom should be given. The generation referred to as the "baby boomers" were born in Britain not so much during a peak in the birth-rate as between two peaks (one of 20.7 per thousand of population in 1947 and another of 18.8 in 1964) which fall either side of a trough of about 15.6 in 1953. Since then, the rate has continued a long-term fall, reaching 13.4 by the late 1980s (Central Office of Information 1967:9; Economist 1990:20; and Sillitoe 1971:20). The rates have been consistently slightly lower for England and Wales, slightly higher for Scotland and considerably higher for Northern Ireland (Central Statistical Office 1972:25).

Limitations of the Data

While the main thrust of this paper concerns England, some of the data to which I shall be referring apply to Britain (including Scotland and Wales), or the United Kingdom (including Northern Ireland) as a whole. No systematic study of the religious attitudes, beliefs and practices of the post-war generation in Britain has been conducted, although there are several sources providing partial information. Unfortunately, the sources tend to use different years of birth for dividing age cohorts, so precise comparisons over time are difficult, and sometimes it is not possible to separate out the whole of the post-war generation (presuming this to consist of those born between 1945 and 1965) from earlier or later generations. A further limitation in the data is due to the fact that the only occasion on which the decennial population census of the U.K. inquired about religious beliefs was in 1851.

Continuing Decline or Revitalization?

The so-called "secularization debate" seems to have been taking on a new life in England in the past few years. There has been a certain amount of speculation that the post-war generation might be returning to established religion, or at least becoming more religious in some ill-defined form. A recent television series stated that:

> New evidence suggests that our religious belief, ritual and experiences are as persistent and widespread as ever and ready for a comeback.[4]

The new evidence does not, however, appear to be all that evident! Indeed, the only evidence would seem to be that some commentators have come to recognize that religion among the young is not as dead as it has sometimes been thought to be--which is doubtless true. But the fact that there are enthusiastic Pentecostalists, charismatics and evangelicals, and that there is a healthy interest in the New Age, is hardly proof that church-going or even religiosity is about to undergo a spectacular revival.

The optimism that an increase in church attendance could be around the corner is hinted at even by Peter Brierley, who, in his work for the Evangelical Alliance, the Bible Society and Marc Europe, has possibly done more than anyone to keep track of U.K. church-going figures. *Prima facie*, Brierley's figures (see Tables 1.2-1.4 below) would seem to point in a contrary direction, yet he writes that:

> Some research has shown that these ["baby boomers"] return to churches after years away because they want to give their children a religious education and value system (Brierley 1991a:88).

What Brierley does not point out in the text, however, is that this research was conducted in the United States--and, to confuse matters somewhat further, a few pages later he quotes the same researcher as saying that he (George Barna) believes that baby boomers "will be the first generation in the twentieth century to break the pattern in which people increasingly embrace the church as they age" (Brierley 1991a:95).

Roof (1990:17) tells us that of the two-thirds of American baby boomers who had dropped out of religious institutions for at least two years (at an average age of 19), about a third have returned (at an average age of 28, often when they have school-age children). Recently there has been some evidence that very slightly (but hardly significantly) more Americans aged between 30 and 49 are increasing their frequency of church attendance (34 percent) than are decreasing it (33 percent) (Princeton Religion Research Center 1991:3), and several of those who are increasing their attendance are quite likely to give "for our children" (18 percent) or "worship as a family" as their reason (PRRC 1991:2).

But that is America. If a similar pattern exists in England, it appears still to be statistically swamped by a continuing exodus from the mainstream churches. It seems, moreover, that the British population has its doubts about the future of religion. In the 1981 European Value Survey, only 21 percent of the British respondents thought that religion would become more important in the future, compared to 40 percent (the European average was 34 percent) who thought it would become less important (Gerard 1985:61). And it is clear that, according to a number of criteria, post-war generations in England have been, and appear progressively to be, less involved with establishment religion than are those born into preceding generations.

Some Statistics

The latest (1990) European Value Survey clearly indicates that the proportion of those who were brought up religiously has fallen dramatically since pre-war times, with the vast majority of those over 65, two-thirds of those aged 35-64, two-fifths of the 25-34 year-olds and only a third of the 18-24 year-olds saying that they had been brought up religiously at home (Gallup 1990:Table 27).[5]

Currie et al. (1977:114-5) note that the Second World War broke pre-war customs of Sunday School attendance, and that it appears that:

> [although] parents partly re-established Sunday-School attendace among their younger children after 1943, older children never regained ties with the church lost after 1939. In consequence, full membership continued to fall after 1943.

They went on to speculate that:

> If wartime disturbance of established religious practices did thus break certain habits of religious observance permanently, the effects of war would, to this extent at least, make themselves felt

TABLE 1.1: Denomination by Church Members[a] and Adult Church-goers in England in 1989 and by Community in the U. K. in 1987

	Church members	Church-goers	Community
Methodist	422,200	396,100	1,300,000
Baptist	170,600	199,400	600,000
United Reformed/Presbyterian	119,900	114,000	1,700,000
Independent Afro-Carribean	68,200	68,500	
Pentecostal	68,000	95,200	
Other Free Churches	103,200	83,000	1,300,000
Total Free Churches	1,174,200	1,249,000	4,900,000
Anglican	1,559,000	1,143,900	26,900,000[b]
Roman Catholic	4,197,100[c]	1,304,600	5,200,000[b]
Orthodox	232,100	9,400	500,000
Total Trinitarian Churches	7,162,400	3,706,900	37,500,000
Non-Trinitarian Churches			800,000
Jews			300,000
Hindus			300,000
Muslims			1,500,000
Sikhs			500,000
Other religions			300,000
Total all religions			41,200,000[d]

(Brierley 1991a:57; 1991b:20; 1988:151).

[a] "It is important to note that the definitions being used are different and so the table could therefore be misleading. The Free Churches keep membership rolls in various ways. Baptists normally expect members to be baptised as believers, Pentecostalist for them to speak in tongues. The Anglican figures used in the Census - because they were readily available - are those for the Electoral Roll, not strictly membership at all since anyone over 16 and living in a parish for at least six months can apply. Roman Catholic figures are for those christened or otherwise admitted to the church through their first Communion . . . They have no equivalent of the Anglican Electoral Roll or Free Church membership" (Brierley 1991a:55-6).
[b] Baptised membership.
[c] The membership figure given for 1985 in Brierley (1988:150) was 1,342,547, which might be more useful for some comparative purposes.
[d] For reasons discussed in Barker 1989a:152, I have not included the 600,000 members of the Church of Scientology that Brierley includes.

over the long-term. But the significance of the generation that grew up in the war years must diminish as the churches seek to recruit the generations born in the post-war years, and the effects of war must therefore decrease over time as other exogenous factors become more powerful (1977:115).

In fact, whatever the reasons, while in 1949, over 30 percent of the child population (under the age of 15) attended church (Brierley 1980:25), by 1979--and again in 1989--only 14 percent did so (Brierley 1991a:100). The fall was especially severe among the mainstream Protestant churches, and, moreover, among those denominations in which a tradition of Sunday School attendance had been particularly strong.

According to Brierley (1988:144), total U.K. church membership as a percentage of the adult population fell from 20.7 percent in 1970, to 18.6 percent in 1975, to 16.9 percent in 1980, to 15.3 percent in 1985, and to 15.0 percent in 1987. More recently, the 1990 European Values Survey shows a strong inverse relationship between age and church-attendance, with around a third of people aged 65 or older attending at least once a month, but only a sixth of adults under 35 doing so. The proportions of those saying that they attended weekly more than halved with the same age drop--this time from just under a quarter to less than one in ten (Gallup 1990:Table 27).

The Church Census, carried out to see how many people were at church on a particular Sunday in 1989, concluded that, so far as religious commitment was concerned (as defined on a combined scale), age was more important than education, class or location-- indeed, when the influence of age was accounted for, other differences tended to disappear (Brierley 1991a:1991:67-8). Tables 1.2-1.5 indicate some of the age-related differences that emerged from this and the earlier European Values Study, and that have been confirmed by numerous smaller-scale studies around the country.

The Established and Establishment Churches in England

General Background
An organized Church in England can be traced to early in the fourth century. Following the Norman Conquest in 1066, the introduction of Roman canon law opened the way for papal control, which had become very powerful by the thirteenth century. By the sixteenth century, there was considerable dissatisfaction with the Papacy for a number of reasons-- financial, theological and plain power politics (Livingstone 1977:109-10). As every English schoolchild knows, the occasion of England's Reformation and repudiation of the supremacy of the Pope began when, in 1527, Henry VIII started taking steps to divorce his first wife. In 1533, Cranmer (whom Henry had appointed Archbishop of Canterbury) pronounced the marriage to Catherine of Aragon invalid and, a few days later, pronounced him married to Anne Boleyn. The following year,

TABLE 1.2:   Overall Religious Commitment (combined scale) (Brierley 1991a:70).

	low	*low-medium*	*medium*	*med-high*	*high*	*N*
Age:	%	%	%	%	%	
18-24	39	27	15	11	9	193
25-44	24	31	16	16	14	446
45-64	14	21	19	20	27	335
65 and over	14	11	18	28	28	202

Parliament passed the series of Acts which severed financial, judicial and administrative links with Rome. Since 1559, the Church of England has been "by law established" in England. (There is also an established church in Scotland; the Church of Ireland was disestablished in 1869, and the Church of Wales was disestablished in 1920.)

Since the Restoration of the Monarchy, neither the throne nor the established church has enjoyed the kind of power that they had previously wielded over the English population--or, indeed, that the Catholic church continued to hold well into modern times in parts of continental Europe and elsewhere. None the less, it took some time for the rights enjoyed by members of the Church of England to be extended to those of other faiths: it was not until the nineteenth century that Nonconformists (1828), Roman Catholics (1829) and Jews (1858) could hold political office; and religious tests for students and academic staff at the ancient universities were abolished just over 100 years ago. There is still doubt as to whether the office of Lord Chancellor can be held by a Roman Catholic. While voluntary schools of any Christian denomination may now be wholly or partly maintained by public funds, Muslims are unable to receive state

TABLE 1.3: Age and Gender of Church-goers 1979 and 1989 Compared with General Population 1989 (Brierley 1991b:21).

	Church-goers '79			Pop.n			Church-goers '89				Population in '89		
	men	*women*	*total*	*1979*			*men*	*women*	*total*		*men*	*women*	*total*
Age	%	%	%	%			%	%	%		%	%	%
00-15	13	3	26	21			12	13	25		10	9	19
15-19	4	5	9	8			3	4	7		4	4	8
20-29	5	6	11	14			4	6	10		8	8	16
30-44	7	9	16	19			7	10	17		10	10	20
45-64	9	11	20	23			9	13	22		11	11	22
65+	7	11	18	15			7	12	19		6	9	15
all ages	45	55	100	100			42	58	100		49	51	100

TABLE 1.4: Net Change in Church-goers and in Population 1979-1989 by Age and Gender (Brierley 1991a:82 & 84).

Age	Church-goers			Population		
	men	*women*	*total*	*men*	*women*	*total*
00-15	-124,000	-70,000	-194,000	-198,000	-206,000	-404,000
15-19	-64,000	-91,000	-155,000	-435,000	-426,000	-861,000
20-29	-52,000	-43,000	-95,000	+504,000	+448,000	+952,000
30-44	**-56,000**	**-19,000**	**-75,000**[a]	**+464,000**	**+497,000**	**+961,000**
45-64	-29,000	+43,000	+14,000	+34,000	-92,000	-58,000
65+	-35,000	+27,000	-8,000	+260,000	+226,000	+486,000
all ages	-360,000	-153,000	-513,000	+629,000	+447,000	+1,076,000

[a] Note that this table does not mean that 75,000 baby boomers stopped going to church in the ten year period, but that 75,000 less of those who were aged 30-44 in 1989 went to church than those who were aged 30-44 in 1979, despite the fact that there were 961,000 more in the former category than in the latter.

funding for their schools. Discrimination on grounds of sex or race became illegal in the 1970s, but Northern Ireland is the only part of the U.K. in which discrimination on religious grounds is an offence. The law on blasphemy, which has been under renewed scrutiny since the publication of Salman Rushdie's *Satanic Verses*, defends only the Church of England-- one may still attack the Roman Catholic church with legal impunity (Barker 1987:273).

The Church of England is uniquely related to the Crown in that the Sovereign, who must be a member of the Church of England, is called "Defender of the Faith" and must promise on his or her accession to uphold it. Church of England archbishops, bishops and deans are appointed by the sovereign on the advice of the prime minister. The Church of England (but not the other established churches) is also linked to the State through the House of Lords, in which the Archbishops of Canterbury and York and 24 senior diocesan bishops have seats.

So far as other religions are concerned, it is now quite possible to speak of the United Reformed church (created out of a union between the English Presbyterians and Congregationalists in 1972), the Methodists and some Baptist churches as mainstream, and possibly even establishment. The Roman Catholic church and Judaism would generally be regarded as mainstream, with several of their members occupying establishment positions within the society. Nineteenth-century sects such as the Mormons, Jehovah's Witnesses, Seventh-Day Adventists, Christadelphians and Christian Scientists would certainly not be considered mainstream, let alone establishment, although they are treated with varying degrees of

TABLE 1.5: Selected Indicators of Religious Disposition, Belief and Institutional attachment by Age, Sex and Working Status of Women (Gerard 1985:72-3).

Indicator	Sex/status	Age			
		30 yrs & under	*Over 30 & not retired*	*Retired*	**Total**
Often think about	male	29	34	48	*35
meaning & purpose	w/female	24	37	36	*34
to life	non-w/f	31	31	--	*32
God important in life	male	17	39	57	36
	w/female	28	52	70	44
	non-w/f	27	64	57	--
Belief in God	male	53	75	80	70
	w/female	73	80	89	*77
	non-w/f	67	91	--	--
Belief in personal God	male	23	27	32	*26
	w/female	33	36	41	*35
	non-w/f	--	28	43	39
Belief in Hell	male	25	22	26	*24
	w/female	26	24	34	*25
	non-w/f	21	39	*33	--
Fully accept first	male	24	49	61	44
commandments	w/female	33	57	70	49
	non-w/f	29	64	58	--
Fully accept third	male	9	23	46	23
commandment	w/female	16	23	47	*21
	non-w/f	12	36	34	--
Attend church	male	16	14	17	15
monthly	w/female	25	33	40	*30
	non-w/f	6	36	29	
N		**333**	**688**	**191**	**12129**

* not significant for age

respect--usually far more than that accorded to the "cults" or new religious movements which have become visible since World War II. Religions in the non-Judaeo-Christian tradition, such as Islam, Hinduism and Buddhism are tolerated, sometimes with respect, sometimes with suspicion.

The Image of the Church of England from World War II Until the 1960s
The Church of England had been losing members throughout the century (as had the Free Churches), but, contrary to the oft-stated expectation that people will flock to the churches at time of war, there is little evidence that the British population did so during either the First or the Second World Wars. Indeed, it appears that both active communicants

and recruitment into all the mainstream churches fell from the onset of war. By the mid-fifties, they had recovered some of their lost ground, but, as indicated earlier, the war seemed to have shaken some loyalties permanently (Currie 1977:113-5).

So far as its place in English culture was concerned, the established church appeared to continue much as it had before World War II; that is, it continued as part of the general backdrop of English society. It was not expected to interfere, and it did not interfere very much. It was just part of the establishment. The Church of England was, indeed, frequently described as the Conservative Party at prayer. One commentator felt moved to write:

> The history of the Church of England over the last three hundred years has been one of a gradual movement away from the center of national and social life....

> In recent years the Church of England has become very concerned about its declining position within national society. Reports have been published, and big changes instituted. Unfortunately they are concerned almost exclusively with internal reorganization. The real problem is that the Church of England is still geared to a stable and static pre-industrial and pre-urban society (Gay 1971:80).

In England, unlike, for example, France and Italy, there was no anti-clericalism--or practically none. At the same time, there was little in the way of passionate religiosity. This is not to deny that a considerable proportion of the English population, indeed the majority of the English population, was not a member of the Church of England; those who identified themselves with the church accounted for a little more than two-thirds of the English population (Martin 1967:36). But, generally speaking, to be a member of the Church of England was not a religious statement. It was a cultural assumption.

The Free Churches were by now fully part of the establishment (with a small e); and there was also a sizeable proportion of Catholics and Jews who had been in the country for generations--Catholicism had, of course, been "the Church of England" until Tudor times. Nevertheless, there lingered in certain post-war circles a sort of feeling that Catholics and Jews were not *quite* English.

While a variety of different beliefs and practices certainly existed, the shared culture, in so far as such a thing existed (consciously or unconsciously) in such matters, was that there *was* a shared culture. Atheists, Buddhists, Jews and communists were known to exist ("some of our best friends" might belong to their number), but they tended not to be

TABLE 1.6: Rate of Change of Membership (Brierley 1988:144).

	1970-1980	1980-1990	1990-2000 estimated
Anglican	-1.7	-1.7	-1.6
Methodist	-2.2	-0.9	-0.6
Baptist	-2.1	+0.2	-1.3
Other	0.0	+2.0	+1.8
Total Protestant	-1.6	-1.0	-0.7
RC	-1.5	-1.8	-1.6
Orthodox	+0.8	+1.1	+0.8
Total Christian	-1.5	-1.2	-0.9

considered part of *real* English culture--even, perhaps, by the atheists, Buddhists, Jews and communists themselves.

As the 1950s progressed, however, a gradual change could be detected. Instead of remaining an unquestioned and respected part of the English cultural heritage, establishment churches came to be more the object of apathy and disinterest. Vicars came to be depicted in the media as slightly ridiculous figures of fun-- bumbling idiots who usually meant well, but did not really have their finger on the pulse of society and were, on the whole, seen to be fulfilling their role at garden fêtes or becoming rather disingenuously embarrassed by the "modern" approach to life of their younger parishioners.

The first visible crack in the theological armor of the traditionalism and uniformity that the Church of England was assumed to uphold came with the publication, in 1963, of the Bishop of Woolwich, John Robinson's *Honest to God*. The book gave rise to an unprecedented amount of discussion in the media, and a flood of correspondence--mostly from people who had not read the book but felt the necessity to tell the bishop what their religion meant to them and therefore, almost by definition, what they would expect it ought to mean to a bishop of the Church of England. Robert Towler (1985), when he analysed the 4,000 letters sent to the bishop, discovered a motley assortment of beliefs that were sitting side by side in the same church on a Sunday. For years, it seemed, these beliefs had co-existed without very much friction between them--possibly because nobody had known what the person in the next pew was thinking.

The Establishment Churches Since 1970

The 1970s offered little hope for the mainstream churches. Membership continued to fall at a far greater rate than that at which the population was declining. By 1979, 89 percent of the population was *not* in church on a typical Sunday, and on the day of the U.K. Church Census, 15 October 1989, 90 percent had other things to do (Brierley 1991a:95). As suggested above, in accounting (in so far as accounting has been done) for the membership loss, the most significant variable has been age.

As can be seen in Table 1.6, the only churches that were increasing were the non-establishment ones: Pentecostal, African Independent churches, and a few national churches (Orthodox or State Lutheran). The membership of new religious movements was also increasing; but, although the percentage rate of increase of these non-establishment churches was enormous, the actual numbers involved were very small (Barker 1989a:145-55). According to one calculation that I carried out, the more successful "alternative" religions between them gained, in the period 1975-1980, about 20,000 members--no more than 4 percent of the loss of roughly half a million persons from the mainstream religions (Barker 1989b:191).

And, on the whole, the mainstream churches displayed little in the way of reaction to what was going on so far as these unconventional explorations by youth were concerned. They tended rather to be somewhat bemused whenever they noticed--which was only occasionally. The cries by the anti-cultists that the churches ought to *do* something went almost unheeded, although, by the late 1980s, the Archbishop of Canterbury and leaders of the other mainstream religions were relieved to find that they could "do something" by offering their support to INFORM, an independent charity, funded by the Home Office, that was established with the aim of offering anxious parents and other inquirers help by providing them with accurate and up-to-date information about the new religions (Barker 1989a:141-4).

But while the new religions did not seem to have significantly affected the mainstream religions, there were some signs of revitalization within or overlapping the Church of England and other mainstream religions (most notably the Baptist church). There developed in the late 1970s, and continued to grow in the 1980s, pockets of house churches, which came to be known as the Restoration movement (Walker 1988), the charismatic movement (in both Protestantism and Catholicism) and other enthusiastic, evangelical Christian movements. Some of these developments were considered "respectable"; others have been more controversial. All of them, in their own way, offered young seekers meaning, direction and a religious life within the Christian tradition.

At the same time, one could find what England had probably always had: the invisible, privatized, implicit, folk, and/or common religions. And one could find people just not giving very much thought to religion at all. Melanie Cottrell (1986), for example, asked people for their life history and found less than one in ten bringing up God or religion at all. She did not uncover an antagonism towards religion; her respondents just seemed to get on quite happily without it.

In a study of young people's beliefs carried out from 1974-5, when the younger baby boomers were still at school, Martin and Pluck (1976:17, 19) described the widespread lack of church-going among the children-- how, in fact, it was a universal point made in both individual and group interviews that an adolescent who went to church would be unmercifully teased and probably rejected: "Anyone who used to go to Sunday School at that time used to be a sissy" (Boy, 17). "If anyone started on about church, I doubt if we'd want to know them" (Boy, 14). Yet, at the same time, not only those with no habit of religious practice, but even those with no discernible belief "of even the vaguest deism", would claim adherence to the Church of England. "You'd have to put C. of E. [on an official form] because if you did go to church it would be C. of E." "It's like this, see. Say if this Jamaican bird came over here and had a baby, *they'd* say it was British but really it's Jamaican. Same as us; we're *born* C. of E" (Group interview, Boys, 16-18). The authors concluded:

> For all the erosion of religious practice and amorphous belief it would be wrong to assume total, contextless privatization. Institutions, even churches, do still play a part, however equivocal, in the acquisition of identity for large numbers of people. Symbols of belonging, especially to the *national, established* church [are] part of the sense that this is your society (1976:19).

Towards the end of the 1970s, however, the Church of England started to change. It started trying in a number of ways to make itself more relevant (through the introduction of new forms of liturgy, or the attempted introduction of women priests), and more of a social and even political force in the land. While such attempts have been welcomed in some quarters, they have been received with shock and consternation in others. The warning sentiment that "This is *England* that you're destroying", has often been more vocal than any theological objections. There was, for example, the "Crisis for Cranmer and King James" when an impressively large number of establishment persons declared themselves to be:

> concerned for the wellsprings of expressive power contained in the Authorised Version of the Bible and the Book of Common Prayer. They are the great originals of English life and language, informing piety and inspiring justice. (*PN Review* 1979, 6(5):back cover)

If one examined the signatories to the petitions presented to "the Right Reverend Fathers-in-God, the Clergy, and Laity of the General Synod of the Church of England", it was possible to observe that a sizeable proportion were not members of the Church of England in any except a purely nominal sense--some were publicly avowed atheists. The point was that an important part of English tradition was disappearing and had to be held on to; the church, by introducing new versions of the Bible and "Alternative" prayer books and liturgies, was risking not merely the religious but the cultural heritage of the post-war and subsequent generations.

Another interesting fact is that, when asked in 1984 "Which version of the service would you prefer for the main service on a Sunday?", only 9 percent of the bishops, and 14 percent of full-time clergy, but 42 percent of retired clergy, chose the Book of Common Prayer, which had been only minimally altered since Cranmer's sixteenth century editions (Gallup 1984, Table 26).

As the 1980s progressed, religion started to become something of a front-page phenomenon: as the result of a number of incidents, it emerged from the Court Circular page and hit the headlines. There were *theological* pronouncements. David Jenkins was made Bishop of Durham. A former academic, he has very liberal, modernist views which he was not reticent about explaining when questioned. This created quite an uproar and it appeared that God was not very happy either, because on the day after he was installed as bishop, York Minster (where the ceremony had taken place) was struck by lightning and its roof burnt down! Clearly, such a bishop was not meant to be part of the Church of England!

There were further theological disturbances on television, such as Don Cupitt's *The Sea of Faith*.[6] The "coming out" of liberal theologians among the Anglican clergy has also been accompanied by a growing unease among some of their number about the established nature of the church. In a 1984 Gallup Poll, in answer to the question "Do you think the Church of England should remain as the "established church" within England and therefore keep its association with the state, or not?", 81 percent of the bishops, 85 percent retired clergy, but only 57 percent of full-time clergy answered "yes" (Gallup 1984, Table 30).

Stirrings on the *political-social* front were also connected with the Bishop of Durham, but perhaps the greatest controversy arose when the Church of England (1985) produced a report called "Faith in the City." Briefly, the report exposed inner city areas to be an absolute disgrace, whereupon the Government said that it was a Marxist report, and there was a big row. But, while sections of the Conservative Government seemed to think that the Church of England had become irredeemably socialist, actually it had by now become, at least according to statistics, the Social Democratic Party at prayer.

Another straining of relations had occurred between the Government (then represented by Mrs. Thatcher) and the Church of England (as represented by the then Archbishop of Canterbury, Robert Runcie) at the end of the Falklands War when Dr. Runcie prayed in an official Memorial service, not merely for the British casualties, but for those on both sides of the conflict.

In 1988, the Home Secretary gave a speech to the governing body of the Church of England, the General Synod, which was markedly Durkheimian in tone. He told the church that really it ought to keep out of politics and see what was happening to the younger generation; there was an increase in crime, morals were in decline, the family was falling apart, and if only the Church of England would do what it was meant to do, then England could regain its former strength. The real, old England needed to be preserved.

Youth

While the late 1940s was a time of rebuilding, recovery and ration books, the post-war generation was the first to be born into a welfare state, with a national health service and the 1944 Butler Act ensuring a minimal, universal standard of education for all. It was also the first British generation of the century that was not to experience directly the hardships of either war or a severe economic depression.

Before the 1950s, the social status of youth hardly existed. One had progressed without noticeable interruption from the status of childhood to that of adulthood. Toward the end of the 1950s, however, young people had begun to enjoy a new economic independence, unencumbered by responsibilities. The youth of England started to develop a culture of their own--or, rather, a number of cultures were developed in a number of different ways as the post-war generation entered its adolescence.

Working-Class Youth. Thanks to extensive coverage in the media, the emerging cultures among working-class youth were particularly visible. Consumer products played an important role in separating the Teds (Teddy Boys), the Mods, the Rockers and then, later, the Punks from the rest of society. Dress and music in particular were used by "the younger generation" to symbolize a rejection of the establishment. Despite the media coverage, it was more of a symbolic rejection than an outright attack on the establishment. The mainstream churches received relatively little attention. They were not attacked, except perhaps as part of the establishment--probably because it was not thought worth attacking them because nobody, least of all working-class youth, was noticing them very much.

Later, in the 1970s, economic changes and, in particular, high rates of unemployment heralded a growing apathy and disillusionment among working-class youths, especially among those whose expectations of expressing their identity rested upon a consumer-power that was now greatly diminished (Barker 1985:74-80). Interestingly, it was among the most disadvantaged--the urban black youth--that a new sub-culture emerged that took a religious form in the growth of the Rastafarian movement. And, while working-class youth culture has never had much to do with the establishment churches, one of the most visible of the evangelistic Christian groups, the Jesus Army, has, since the late 1980s, had growing success in extending its outreach to working-class youth; although, even here, we are talking in terms of at most a few thousand individuals. It might also be mentioned that the Jesus Army was expelled from the Baptist Union of Great Britain.

Middle-Class Youth. Middle-class youth followed much the same pattern as that exhibited in the States and parts of continental Europe. First of all, in the 1960s, there were the street demonstrations and sit-ins by the post-war generation students. The new, politically conscious generation was going to change the structures and overthrow bourgeois everything. Then, when the demonstrations did not noticeably result in a change in the structures, all structures and materialism had to be rejected and there emerged the Hippie flower-power, the drug culture, and the early stirrings of a New Age consciousness. With the rejection of materialism and structure, however, one could observe a classic situation of anomie. Then there followed, in part as a backlash, a move to recreate structures, but this time without overt materialism; in certain quarters, there was a growth in authoritarian, totalitarian-type new religious movements offering The Truth and certainties, as opposed to the many ways which were co-existing in apparent confusion. At the same time, English youth was discovering the Human Potential movement. The Church of Scientology and T.M. in Britain can account for about half a million people having taken at least one of their courses at some point or another. Witches crept out of and into covens, and neo-paganism and the occult started, in a modest way, to flourish.

In fact, there are relatively few people who have stayed for any length of time as hard-core members of any of the new religions or the Human Potential movement. Nonetheless, the general cultural milieu became, as in parts of America, infused with ideas promoted by the movements. Indeed, what knowledge we have of the beliefs of the post-war generation suggests that these beliefs are moving away from traditional "established" beliefs, with the increase in acceptance of beliefs in, for example, God as a non-personal life-force and/or reincarnation: while just under a third of the British population say that they believe in the resurrection of the dead, almost one quarter (24 percent) say they believe in reincarnation. Interestingly, the categories of people reporting greatest belief in reincarnation included those who said God was very important in their lives (37 percent), church-goers (32 percent), Catholics (32 percent), women (29 percent), those aged 45-54 (30 percent) and aged 25-34 (28 percent), students (32 percent), the most politically right-wing (33 percent), the unemployed (30 percent), those with the lowest socio-economic status (28 percent) and those living in Scotland (31 percent), while belief in reincarnation was least among men (19 percent), farmers (17 percent), the most politically left-wing (18 percent), those who said they had no religion (19 percent), those who claimed to be unhappy (17 percent), convinced atheists (9 percent), and 18-24-year olds. Among the variables that did not seem to be particularly significant with respect to belief in reincarnation were marital status (23-25 percent), level of income (23-26 percent), age at completion of education (23-26 percent), and (except for the farmers) socio-economic status (23-24 percent) (Gallup 1990, Table 32).

There can be little doubt that, despite their attempts to come to terms with the changing requirements of the post-war generation, increasing numbers of young people are looking outside establishment religion to find their answers to questions that the churches have traditionally claimed to answer. The 1990 European Values Study indicated that there was general dissatisfaction with the church in that the majority of Britons did not feel that the church was providing adequate answers to the moral problems and needs of the individual, the problems of the family, and the social problems facing the country. The dissatisfaction was greatest among the 25-34 year-olds. Only just over a half the respondents felt that the church was providing an adequate answer to people's spiritual needs (Gallup 1990:Table 28).

Factors Involved in the Relationship
Between the Post-War Generation and Establishment Religion

A number of variables might explain the lack of enthusiasm to be found among the post-war generation for establishment religion in contemporary Britain. In this section, four threads will be selected from the complex tapestry of changes occurring in English society and an attempt will be made to indicate how these could have a bearing on the situation.

The Family

As a direct result of the war, a large number of children (who were to become the parents of the post-war generation) were evacuated from their homes; many women entered employment for the first time, and many men changed their employment and often their residence (Currie et al. 1977:113). The disruption to family life in the immediate aftermath of the war was considerable in terms of economic, political and social change, but also through the redefinition of relationships that had been brought about by both temporary and permanent separations.

In 1929, three quarters of marriages in England and Wales were celebrated with some religious ceremony. In the 1950s and early 1960s, when the majority of the post-war generation was born, roughly two thirds of marriages were "religious." In the 1970s, when the post-war generation was itself getting married, only half the marriages were "religious" (Currie 1977:224). By the time the 1981 European Value Survey was conducted, only 14 percent of the British respondents (16 percent of the Europeans) considered religious faith an important value to develop in children (Gerard 1985:61).

Homosexual law reform[7] and the growth of single-parent families (now 17 percent of all households in England and Wales) symbolize just two of the changes in attitudes about family life and sexual morality for which the churches have been blamed. But obviously this has been a two-way process: One could indeed argue that the Church of England is more likely to have itself changed because of alterations in the family and family attitudes than to have brought these about.

Education

The 1944 Butler Education Act decreed that religious education must be given in the schools. There was a sort of paradox here because, in religious education classes, what has tended to happen is that there is a discussion about whether one should sleep with one's boyfriend before one is married, or perhaps the class will learn about Ramadan or Diwali, especially if the school is in an area with a high concentration of immigrants. Except in Church of England schools, the pupils are unlikely to learn a great deal about the Church of England. Religious education tends to be fairly sanitized.

Furthermore, educational philosophies changed so that, from around the late 1950s and early 1960s, possibly even before, far less emphasis was laid on learning by rote. "Progressive" ideas that had been developed by earlier generations of educationalists such as Maria Montessori or Rudolf Steiner, and, later, A. S. Neil at Summerhill, began to infiltrate the general educational system. The student was taught to explore, to question and to develop his or her own potential. It would be surprising if this increasing individualism and questioning of authority, undoubtedly fostered in the English education system, were not related to the general withdrawal from the traditional, establishment religion.

Even if there is no direct evidence that the changing values within the British educational system were directly responsible for many of the changes in the post-war generation's relationship to establishment religion, they are at least compatible with many of the trends and could well have played quite an important contributory role. Michael Hornsby-Smith (1991:118) found that only 43 percent of Catholics aged 15-24 believed that "under certain conditions, when he speaks on matters of faith and morals the pope is infallible," while 83 percent of the over-65s accepted papal infallibility. Clearly Vatican II and other factors (see, for example, the section on the media below) have had an enormous influence on the post-war generation's understanding of authority. It is difficult to believe, however, that this change would be so pronounced without the radical change that has taken place in attitudes to education.

Immigration

From about the mid-1950s, England had been host to a significant influx of immigrants: first West Indians, and then Asians. Religious pluralism became far more visible than it ever had been before and, indeed, far more of a fact. The significance of this for the concerns of this paper is that it has become increasingly common for a post-war generation to be brought up alongside people who did not take it for granted that the chances were that if you were born in England you would identify with the Church of England, or, at least, with one of the small-e-established churches. This is particularly significant so far as the non Judaeo-Christian groups that have entered the country in the post-war period are concerned. Some of these immigrants are lobbying to have their own schools, a situation that has given rise to considerable debate about the nature of a pluralistic culture.

Furthermore, the very fact that the immigrants and their children were becoming, in at least certain parts of the country, important and highly conspicuous members of the community was almost bound to increase relativism in religious outlooks--even when the relativism produced the reaction of strongly stated Christianity. That Christianity had to be not only mentioned, but also defended, is in itself a marked break with the past. One manifestation of this change was a recent report that recommended that Christian Religious Education should continue to be taught in the British schools. This, as should be obvious at this stage in the argument, was not the result of there having been a great surge of belief in the Church of England or even in Christianity. On the contrary, it was a consequence of the fact that the question had never before been seriously considered. It had just been assumed that Religious Education meant Christian Education. Upholders of the establishment, such as the Baroness Cox, became extremely upset when it became clear that this was no longer a reliable assumption. The fact that it was now questionable meant that it had to be affirmed that Britain was still a Christian nation.

The Media

The media in England have had both a homogenizing and a diversifying influence. In this, their role is unlikely to be significantly different from the role they play in most democracies, so this topic will not be elaborated beyond the point of stating that they have obviously had an enormous effect on the culture of the young. The post-war generation is the first generation in which a television set is an expected part of socialization--and socialization by the media, as by the formal educational system, means the transmission of both information and attitudes.

Each new idea becomes a potential resource--many of the ideas may have been around elsewhere for centuries, but what is new is that a single individual, without studying theology or philosophy, history or anthropology, without reading the literature of the world, can have a sip--an aperitif, a sniff--of what is on offer. It is not merely the innovators who produce new gestalts, new packages; each individual is invited to choose his or her own ingredients--or none at all--and the new mixtures create new tastes, new creations, new wholes. One may be attracted by a part of a package and find oneself accepting the rest, or one may put together the parts, piece by piece--serially or at the same time.

Just as the post-war generation was reaching adolescence, a cultural explosion of young men and women was questioning--even mocking and ridiculing--all aspects of the British establishment with plays such as John Osborne's *Look Back in Anger*, revues such as *Beyond the Fringe*, and periodicals such as *Private Eye*. There had certainly been satirical plays for the middle classes and Music Hall acts for the workers--each, in its own ways criticizing the establishment long before the Second World War (and it is 100 years since *Punch* first hit the streets of London). The scale, however, on which the establishment was attacked and undermined in the late 1950s and early 1960s was without precedent in twentieth century Britain. A television series such as *That Was The Week That Was* could and did reach an audience whose size and social diversity would have been unimaginable in pre-war days. Nothing seemed to be held sacred any longer--certainly not the established church. By the early 1970s, the post-war generation was itself carrying on the tradition of youthful irreverences with *Monty Python's Flying Circus* and *The Life of Brian*.[8]

Concluding Remarks

These (and other) threads of the English tapestry need to be explored in far greater depth if we want to understand further the changing patterns of association between establishment religion and the post-war generation. In summary, however, it has been suggested that there has been a significant decline in involvement in mainstream religion among the post-war generation in England; that this has not taken a particularly strident path, the mainstream religions having suffered not so much from active opposition as from increasing marginalization. But there are signs that the post-war generation has become increasingly disillusioned with the establishment churches. A March 1991 Gallup poll found that only about one Briton in three has "a great deal" (11 percent) or "quite a bit" (25 percent) of confidence in the church--the total of 36 percent expressing confidence was significantly different from the 56 percent of Americans who expressed confidence in a similar poll around the same time (Princeton Religion Research Center, vol. 13, no. 5, May 1991:5).

The drift (rather than mass exodus) from mainstream, organized religion is explicable partly in terms of general secularizing trends in the social structure, coupled with a post-war culture in which families are less likely to socialize their children into "C of E" membership, and in which changes in education and the media play an important role reflecting and reinforcing a cultural pluralization, which is, in turn, reinforced by the influx of non-Christian migrants and their children.

There are two final points that I would like to underline with respect to the general "secularization thesis": First, as was intimated earlier, one can legitimately argue that the data are not sufficiently detailed to tell us whether, by describing the involvement of the post-war generation with the mainstream churches, they are reflecting a phenomenon related to the *age* of the generation, rather than the generation *per se*. Nonetheless, what data there are do suggest that members of the post-war generation are not becoming as involved as their parents were at a comparable age. Even more significantly, the fact that there has been a change in the importance accorded to the religious socialization of children suggests that the trends that are being observed are unlikely to be as temporary as the "young people go back to the churches as they get older" hypothesis might have us believe.

It has been commented in the USA that many baby boomers "believe no institution deserves their total loyalty," and that they "choose which church to attend on the basis of which one will address their most keenly-felt needs" (Barna 1990:27-8, quoted in Brierley, 1991a:95). If this is correct for England (and I suspect it may be), it could well be that the relationship of the post-war generation to establishment religion is turning out to be radically different from that of previous generations. The Bishop of Southwark recently remarked, "We have moved from where Christianity is a culture to where Christianity is a choice" (quoted in Brierley 1991a:95). Those who are uninterested in religious questions no longer feel any obligation to have contact with establishment churches for social reasons, although the church may still be expected to provide services such as celebrating rites of passage. But even here the statistics show that the numbers getting married in church have been dropping, as, to a lesser extent, has the baptism of babies. In fact, the 1990 European Value Survey found that the 25-34 age group was the one least likely to believe that holding a religious service for birth, marriage or death was important; only just over half of that age group thought it was important for a birth, but just under three-quarters still thought it important for marriage and over three-quarters thought it important for death (Gallup 1990:Table 27).

A second, related, point has been articulated by Grace Davie with the phrase that English religiosity is "more believing than belonging" (Davie 1990a). This, I think, carries a considerable amount of truth—at least in urban areas;[9] but it is also true that the data with respect to age indicate that the believing in God (however understood), as well as the belonging (to the established churches), has been becoming less pronounced among England's youth. The 1990 European Value Survey indicates a dramatic inverse relationship between age and those who, independent of whether or not they went to church, would call themselves a religious person. While three-quarters of the over-65s and about three-fifths of those aged 35-65 would describe themselves as religious, less than two-fifths of 25-34 year-olds, and only just over a quarter of 18-24 year-olds would do so (Gallup 1990:Table 28). The 1981 European Value Survey also showed that those under 30 were unlikely to call themselves religious, 35 percent of men and 47 percent of working women under 30 (compared to 60 percent of men and 72 percent of women over 30 but below retiring age) called themselves religious (Gerard 1985:68, 72).

A discussion of the constituent ingredients, attractions (and disappointments) of the many alternatives on offer in contemporary Britain is beyond the scope of this chapter. What is clear, however, is that for the inhabitants of England, establishment churches no longer stand for what they were once taken to stand for. For a post-war generation, to have an English identity is no longer equivalent to being a member of the Church of England. To reiterate the point made at the beginning of this paper: a more helpful way of understanding the religious, and non-religious beliefs and practices of England's post-war generations is as a gentle, secularizing pluralism.

Perhaps I could end by recounting an incident which might epitomize the type of pluralism one can find in contemporary England. It was no great surprise to be told by the chatty young girl who cut my hair that she believed in reincarnation *and* enjoyed going to Mass most Sundays--"if me boyfriend hasn't arranged anything else." Her reasons for this apparent inconsistency were that (a) she liked feeling at home in the church, and (b) she sometimes had *deja vu* feelings, and reincarnation seemed to be a natural explanation for this. What did her Catholic parents think? Then came what for me *was* a surprise: "My mother brought in the Jehovah's Witnesses to help me when I was asking questions, because she thought they might be able to help, knowing such a lot about the Bible like they do." It was not that her mother (presumably a baby boomer) was in the slightest way antagonistic to her daughter's seekership, or, indeed, to her conclusions--she just wanted to help the girl have access to the best resources available in the cultural supermarket.

Notes

1. But see below for a description of how the Archbishop of Canterbury was perceived as endangering this celebration of English unity.

2. Each year, songs such as "Rule Britannia" and Blake's "Jerusalem" are sung by the audience at the last night of the Henry Wod Promenade Concerts at the Royal Albert Hall, and watched by millions on BBC television.

3. This was the tragic accident in April, 1989 at which 95 Liverpool supporters were crushed to death at the Hillsborough football stadium in Sheffield. In the aftermath, rituals were performed, the community was celebrated; sacred objects (scarves, mascots, caps etc) were laid in memory of the dead (Davie, forthcoming).

4. *Radio Times* entry for *Faith in the Future*, London Weekend Television, 4 August 1991.

5. The Gallup, 1990 figures reported in this paper are not yet officially released, so I am grateful for permission to reproduce them. They should not, however, be reproduced elsewhere without written permission.

6. Don Cupitt's *Sea of Faith: Christianity in Change* was originally a BBC television series and published by the British Broadcasting Corporation in 1984. By 1989, the ideas embodied in Cupitt's book had led to the establishment of an organisation calling itself *Sea of Faith: a network for exploring and promoting religious faith as a human creation*. The network has regular conferences and publishes a magazine.

7. The 1957 Wolfenden Report recommended that homosexual acts between consenting adults over 21 and in private be decriminalised. It was not until 10 years later that this was actually enacted.

8. Unlike the situation in predominantly Catholic countries, the Church of England has not had a direct role in censorship of the media. What censorship there has been in Britain has been carried out by the Lord Chamberlain and the courts.

9. Michael Winter has found that people in rural areas have both high levels of belief and a sense of belonging to a denomination, despite their formal observance being minimal (*British Journal of Sociology*, forthcoming).

2

Baby Boomers Downunder:
The Case of Australia

Gary D. Bouma
and
Michael Mason

Introduction

The "baby boomers," as they are popularly called, have been held responsible for everything from the rise and fall of the baby food industry, a massive expansion in education facilities, the rise of certain forms of popular music and now, as they enter middle age, the growing conservatism of the societies they have come to dominate. One of the demographic sequels of World War II for Western industrial societies has been the creation of this cohort which due to its size and concentration has come to influence many features of these societies. What has been their impact on Australia's mainstream religious institutions?

Although there has been a recent resurgence of research on religion in Australia (Black 1990, 1991; Blombery 1989a, 1989b; Bouma 1983, 1988, 1992; Hughes 1989; Hughes and Blombery 1990; Kaldor 1987; Mason 1991; Mol 1985), the sociological data available for the pursuit of an answer to this question are limited. We have the incomparable advantage of a question on religious affiliation in federal government censuses, conducted usually at five-year intervals, throughout the entire period. The only other resource covering this span of years is opinion poll data on weekly church attendance. A major survey on religion was conducted in 1966 (Mol 1971), but there is nothing further of this kind until the eighties. A major source utilized in this chapter is data from a national sample of 4,500 Australians collected in 1989 by the National Social Science Survey team at the Australian National University.[1]

The issues addressed in our analysis are: How do baby boomers compare with others in retention of identification, rates of participation, religious beliefs and the relationship between levels of belief and practice and other attitudes? After an overview of the three major phases in the life of the Australian post-war generation, we will analyse the contemporary data to compare the "early" and "late" baby boomer groups with each other and with the cohorts which precede and follow them, concluding with reflections on the variety of interpretations which have been or can be applied to these phenomena.

Other demographic and religious features of Australian society must be borne in mind when assessing post-war trends. Any analysis of post-war changes in Australian society must take into account the fact that in addition to the baby boom there was massive immigration from Europe and Asia. Between 1947 and 1986 Australia's population doubled from 7.5 million to over 15 million. The population of Australia in 1989 was 23% foreign-born. Our analyses were controlled for the effects of birthplace, which turned out to be smaller than expected.

Australia's religious composition reflects the historical patterns of immigration. Two groups, the Anglicans and the Catholics, have comprised over half the population since the beginning of European settlement in 1788. Two other major groups are Protestants,[2] and those who say they have no religious denomination. Within the three religious groups, only a minority have been regular church-attenders. Each of the four groups embraces a wide range of diversity: Anglicans range from evangelical to high-church, "Catholic" includes Eastern "uniate" rites (Eastern churches in communion with the Latin rite Western church), charismatics, liberals, Tridentine conservatives, etc. The Protestant group includes liberal mainstream denominations like the Uniting Church, but also Evangelicals, Pentecostals and sects like the Brethren; the "No religion" group is also varied, ranging from atheists to those who retain Christian beliefs but are not actively affiliated with any denomination.[3]

As the established church of the mother country, the Church of England enjoyed the same status in the colony of New South Wales until 1836, when financial support for schools, clergy and church-building was extended to the major denominations on a more equal basis. Later in the nineteenth century, all of this support, which had occasioned much denominational rivalry, was withdrawn (Hogan 1987). In the Constitution adopted at Federation in 1901, the principle of establishment of religion was expressly repudiated. There were both secularist and religious proponents of this provision: the former drew their strength from the tide of liberal free-thought that swept both Europe and Australia in the late nineteenth century, the latter were influenced by the desire to keep religion free from state interference--more an American sentiment. Nonetheless, a powerful Anglican ascendancy remained in place; in the 1933 census, 39% of the population indicated affiliation with the Church of England; Catholics were about half as numerous.

There has been considerable change in the nature and shape of Australia's religious life since the end of World War II. Some of these changes will be described in their broader political, social and institutional contexts, and then the role of the post-war generation in establishment religions during this era will be examined.

Three Periods Since World War II

For our purposes, the social history of Australia since World War II can be divided into three periods.

1) 1947-65 was a time of quiet economic growth, low inflation and a genuine spread of affluence through a society which had felt severely, well into World War II, the privations of the depression of the thirties. As a nation, Australia, led by Prime Minister Robert Menzies, looked to England for leadership, investment and innovation. A colonial mentality prevailed which defined standards in British terms. The United Kingdom was Australia's largest trading partner in a set of economic ties which favored members of the British Commonwealth of Nations. The education system was based largely on English models and the universities looked towards Oxford and Cambridge. There was a strong pro-family ideology, a high rate of marriage, a relatively low rate of female participation in the labor force, and a high birth rate. The bulk of migration earlier in this period came from the United Kingdom and northern Europe. Later, the primary source shifted to southern Europe.

In this context Australian religious life was quietly confident and enjoyed a period of growth and institutional expansion. Its state mirrored that of the society prior to World War II. The long-maintained Anglican hegemony in numbers (still 39% in 1947) and social influence continued. The Catholics, although they had constituted over 20% of the population since the mid-nineteenth century, continued to define themselves as Irish, independent and non-mainstream.

Sectarian strife reached a peak in the mid-1950s when the largely Catholic, anti-communist "Industrial Group" members left the Labor Party to form what eventually became the Democratic Labor Party. Two state Labor Governments lost office, the party (except in New South Wales) was delivered to the control of the Left, and the Liberal-Country Party coalition government was able, with the help of DLP preference votes, to hold

TABLE 2.1a: Religious Denominations, Australia: Census 1947-66

Denomination	1947 N	%	1954 %	% INCR	1961 %	% INCR	1966 %	% INCR
Christian								
Anglican	2,957032	39.0	37.9	15	34.9	8	33.5	6
Baptist	113,527	1.5	1.4	12	1.4	18	1.4	11
Brethren	13,002	0.2	0.2	26	0.1	-5	0.1	0.1
Catholic	1,586,768	20.9	22.9	30	24.9	27	26.2	16
Churches of Christ	71,771	0.9	0.9	12	0.9	19	0.9	8
Congregational	63,243	0.8	0.8	10	0.7	6	0.7	4
Jehovah's Witness								
Latter Day Saints								
Lutheran	66,891	0.9	1.3	74	1.5	38	1.6	12
Methodist	871,425	11.5	10.9	12	10.2	10	9.7	5
Oriental Christian								
Orthodox		0.8	1.5	107			2.2	65
Pentecostal								
Presbyterian	743,540	9.8	9.7	17	9.3	12	9.0	7
Salvation Army	37,572	0.5	0.5	14	0.5	19	0.5	11
7th Day Adventist	17,550	0.2	0.3	44	0.3	25	0.3	20
Uniting Church								
Other Protestant	73,270	1.0	1.1	0.9				
Other Christian	57,375	0.8	0.8	1.0				
Total Christian	6,672,936	88.0	89.4	20	88.3	16	88.2	10
(Mcpu)*	1,678,208	22.1	21.3	14	20.2	11	19.4	6
Other religions								
Buddhist								
Hindu								
Jewish	32,019	0.4	0.5	51	0.6	23	0.5	7
Muslim								
Other Non-Christian	4,543	0.1	0.1	0.1			0.1	
Total Other Religion	36,562	0.5	0.6	48	0.7	36	0.7	5
Other groups								
Non Theistic								
Inadeq. Described	18,708	0.2	0.2	-4	0.2	17	0.3	74
No Religion	26,328	0.3	0.3	-10	0.4	59	0.8	156
Not Stated	824,824	9.5	9.5	4	10.5	29	10.0	5
Total Pop.	7,579,358	100.0	100.0	19	100.0	17	100.0	10

power until 1972, a total of 23 years. Both the labor movement and the Catholic church were rent with bitter recriminations.

By this time, Anglicans and Catholics between them made up over 60 percent of the population, with Methodists and Presbyterians, the only other major denominations, accounting for about half the remainder (see Tables 2.1 and 2.2). That religion was a family affair is supported by Mol's (1971:34-40) 1966 survey, which found no marked age differences in religious participation. Poll data echo this conclusion from 1946 until 1970.[4]

Table 2.1 shows a wide range of denominations as recorded in the census over a forty year period.[5]

This was the childhood world of the baby boomers. They can be defined as the cohort born between 1947 and 1961. The phenomenon commenced with the return of those who had been away during World War II and whose family formation had been delayed. The children produced by these parents overlapped those births which would normally have occurred in the years following 1945. In addition, the pro-familist ideologies, promoted in part to legitimate the return to the home (and motherhood) of women who had been employed during the war, promoted an increase in overall fertility. Finally, a high rate of marriage combined with these factors to produce a significant bulge in the population structures of Western societies.

There is disagreement about the end of the baby boom. We have selected 1961 because that was the last year of high fertility in Australia and was followed by a significant decline. The oral contraceptive became generally available from 1961. This combined with the decline of pro-familist ideology, the rise of a new wave of feminist writing and the increased labor force participation of women, including mothers, to change the socio-cultural context in which fertility decisions were made. Others pick an earlier date, such as 1955.

Since the baby boomers have affected every other aspect of society, it is also likely that they have had an impact on religion. They accounted for a high incidence of baptism. They occasioned a higher rate of church attendance as those who would not otherwise have attended accompanied their children through various stages of Christian initiation. The baby boomers filled Sunday schools, and required great expansion of both the public and private primary and secondary school systems. Was this positive impact sustained when the time came for the baby boomers to take responsibility for the religious dimensions of their lives?

2) The next period, from 1966 till 1980, saw major disruptions to this placid pattern. The pace of social change quickened in

TABLE 2.1b: Religious Denominations, Australia: Census 1971-76

Denomination	1971 N	%	%INCR	1976 N	%	%INCR
Christian						
Anglican	3,953,204	31.0	2	3,752,222	27.7	-5
Baptist	175,969	1.4	6	174,151	1.3	-1
Brethren	22,963	0.2	47	20,719	0.2	-10
Catholic	3,442,634	27.0	13	3,482,847	25.7	1
Churches of Christ	97,423	0.8	-6	86,850	0.6	-11
Congregational	68,159	0.5	-11	53,444	0.4	-22
Jehovah's Witness	35,752	0.3	--	41,359	0.3	16
Latter Day Saints						
Lutheran	196,847	1.5	10	191,548	1.4	-3
Methodist	1,099,019	8.6	-3	983,240	7.3	-11
Oriental Christian						
Orthodox	338,632	2.7	33	372,234	2.7	10
Pentecostal				38,393	0.3	--
Presbyterian	1,028,581	8.1	-2	899,950	6.6	-13
Salvation Army	65,831	0.5	16	63,335	0.5	-4
7th Day Adventist	41,617	0.3	9	41,471	0.3	0
Uniting Church						
Other Protestant	243,202	1.9		206,160	1.5	
Other Christian	180,546	1.4		236,928	1.7	
Total Christian	10,990,379	86.2	7	10,644,851	78.6	-3
(Mcpu)*	2,195,759	17.2	-2	1,963,634	14.3	-12
Other religions						
Buddhist						
Hindu						
Jewish	62,208	0.5	-2	53,441	0.4	-14
Muslim	22,311	0.2	--	45,205	0.3	103
Other Non-Christian	14,404	0.1	--	30,422	0.2	
Total Other Religion	98,923	0.8	29	129,068	1.0	31
Other groups						
Non Theistic						
Inadeq. Described	29,413	0.2	-20	51,271	0.4	74
No Religion	855,676	6.7	790	1,130,300	8.3	32
Not Stated	781,247	6.1	-33	1,592,959	11.8	104
Total Population	12,755,638	100.0	10	13,548,488	100.0	6

Australia, as in many Western countries. From 1963 to 1971 there was an economic springtime of growth and full employment. The post-war generation were coming of age--the eldest of them turned 19 in 1966.[6] They were numerous, relatively more affluent and better educated than their parents had been. They did not easily accept the authority of traditional norms in any sphere--cultural, social, political or economic--and swelled the constituency in favor of change. Political conflict over the Vietnam war and conscription both expressed and sharpened the polarization. In Australia as elsewhere, it was an era of student unrest, of social, sexual and artistic experimentation.

Britain gave up the fight to maintain her colonies in Malaysia and withdrew the fleet from Singapore, leaving Australia alone and unprotected in Asia. This severing of colonial ties was more a British than an Australian initiative. It dawned on some Australians that the center of the cultural and intellectual world could no longer be assumed to be England; but where it should now be located was unclear--some looked to the United States, others to Europe, and still others to Asia.

By the late 1960s, the electoral power of the DLP had begun to wane, and Labor leader Gough Whitlam, ignoring the traditional Catholic Labor base and appealing to the new middle class (Hogan 1987), rose dramatically to power in 1972 with a program of radical social change. In the ensuing three-year term of Labor government, Australia's participation in the Vietnam war was ended, a range of new universities and colleges of advanced education were opened, the welfare sector was greatly expanded, "no-fault" divorce legislation was passed and de-facto relationships recognized.

The introduction of the contraceptive pill and increased female participation in the labor force brought the fertility rate down to nearly zero-growth level. Reduction in the size of the family, and in its centrality to social life, was partly offset by the traditional family patterns of new migrants coming largely from southern Europe. This shift in the origin of migration produced very rapid growth for a time in the numbers of Orthodox Christians. The brief reign of triumphant socialism under Labor, filled (especially for the young) with a sense of liberation from an era of conservative politics which had lasted as long as they could remember, engendered a climate of exuberant optimism in the pursuit of a secular utopia. The universities, secular since their foundation, began to produce a generation of teachers and civil servants who no longer saw Australia as a Christian country.

If the start of the decade had seemed to some like a new dawn, the storm clouds soon gathered. The economy suffered a series of setbacks: the oil shock, increased inflation, reduced economic growth and higher

TABLE 2.1c: Religious Denominations, Australia: Census 1981-86

Denomination	1981 N	%	%INCR	1986 N	%	%INCR
Christian						
Anglican	3,810,469	26.1	2	3,723,419	2.39	-2
Baptist	190,259	1.3	9	196,782	1.3	3
Brethren	21,489	0.1	4	23,164	0.1	8
Catholic	3,786,505	26.0	9	4,064,413	26.1	7
Churches Of Christ	89,424	0.6	3	88,511	0.6	-1
Congregational	23,071	0.2	-57	16,616	0.1	-28
Jehovah's Witness	51,815	0.4	25	66,496	0.4	28
Latter Day Saints	32,444	0.2	--	35,490	0.2	9
Lutheran	199,760	1.4	4	208,304	1.3	4
Methodist	490,797	3.4	-50	NA		
Oriental Christian				10,374	0.1	--
Orthodox	421,281	2.9	13	427,445	2.7	2
Pentecostal	72,148	0.5	88	107,007	0.7	48
Presbyterian	637,818	4.4	-29	560,025	3.6	-12
Salvation Army	71,570	0.5	13	77,771	0.5	9
7th Day Adventist	47,474	0.3	15	47,981	0.3	1
Uniting Church	712,609	4.9	--	1,182,310	7.6	66
Other Protestant	220,679	1.5		199,446	1.3	
Other Christian	253,770	1.7		346,345	2.2	
Total Christian	11,133,298	76.4	5	11,381,908	73.0	2
(Mcpu)*	1,864,211	12.8	-4	1,742,335	11.2	-7
Other Religions						
Buddhist	35,073	0.2	--	80,387	0.5	129
Hindu				21,454	0.1	--
Jewish	62,126	0.4	16	69,087	0.4	11
Muslim	76,792	0.5	70	109,523	0.7	43
Other Non-Christian	23,577	0.2		35,742	0.2	
Total Other Religion	197,568	1.4	53	316,193	2.0	60
Other Groups						
Non Theistic				4,909	0.0	
Inadeq. Described	73,551	0.5	44	58,040	0.4	-21
No Religion	1,576,718	10.8	40	1,977,464	12.7	25
Not Stated	1,595,195	10.9	0	1,863,342	11.9	17
Total Population	14,576,330	100.0	8	15,602,156	100.0	7

unemployment. In a major constitutional crisis, the Whitlam government was dismissed from office by the Governor-General in 1975 after prolonged failure to get its supply bills through the federal Senate. The Liberals were returned to power for eight years.

Developments in the nation's religious institutions during these turbulent years were just as dramatic as those in the political, social and economic spheres. As Table 2.1 shows, nearly every religious group in Australia suffered an actual numerical decline in adherents between the censuses of 1971 and 1976. Almost all had previously shown a regular increase in numbers at each census.

In the case of Catholics, for instance, about a quarter of a million people who described themselves as Catholic in 1971 did not do so in 1976. This phenomenon was particularly strong among those born between 1946 and 1958 (Mason 1983:34-35). Five years later, disaffiliation was seen to be continuing among the younger members of this cohort, but some of those born in the 1940s were actually changing again, and re-identifying as Catholics. So the Catholic sense of identity retains some durability--even resilience. Two things remain unclear: whether those born in the sixties and later will follow the same pattern of disaffiliating during their twenties, and whether the "fifties generation" will reassert their former denominational allegiance when they move into their forties. Census results from 1991 and 1996 will show whether this is true.

Since most denominations lost adherents between 1971 and 1976, no explanation that applies uniquely to Catholics seems called for. But there was also a sharp decline in Catholic church attendance, particularly marked from the late sixties onwards, not matched in severity in other denominations. This was not systematically explored at the time, but can be presumed to have been influenced by factors which have been shown to have affected Catholics in other Western societies over the same period, such as the Second Vatican Council, the 1968 papal document on contraception, and, at root, a decline in the authority of tradition among Catholics (cf. Greeley 1976, Mason 1991 and in press).

Table 2.2 summarizes the pattern of religious affiliation and church attendance for Catholics and Anglicans over the whole period from World War II to the present. Participation in religious activities became less a family affair and increasingly, for the baby boomers, a matter of individual choice: poll data on church attendance began to display an age gradient from 1970; by the end of the decade this had become quite marked: only 14% of those in their twenties (the last of the baby boomers) were now weekly attenders, compared with 28% of those aged 50-69, and 36% of those 70 and over.[7]

TABLE 2.2: Catholic and Anglican Affiliation as a Percentage of the Australian Population, Percentage of Adherents Attending Church Weekly, and Percentage of Total Australian Population Attending Church Weekly, 1950-89.*

Year	Catholic		Anglican		Aus.pop.
	Affiliation	Attendance	Affil.	Attnd.	Attnd.
1950	23	62	38	6	23
1961	25	54	35	13	27
1966	26	**61	34	*14	27
1972	27	42	31	9	21
1976	26	42	28	9	20
1981	26	37	26	12	22
1989	26	29	24	9	17

* Sources: data on religious affiliation are from the censuses of these years, or, in the case of 1950, from the 1954 census; for 1972, from the 1971 census, and in the case of 1989, from the 1986 census. Data on church attendance 1950 and 1961 are from bulletins issued throughout these years by Australian Gallup Polls; for 1966, from Mol's *Religion in Australia* survey (Mol 1971:15); for 1972, 1976 and 1981, from Morgan Gallup Polls conducted by Roy Morgan Research Centre, for 1989, from the NSSS. Categories of frequency of attendance in this survey included `Nearly every week'; respondents who chose this answer have been included in this table (the category `weekly' should thus be understood to mean `Nearly every week or more often'), so that the decline in attendance is conservatively calculated.

There are no easily comparable affiliation or attendance statistics for Protestants which cover the entire period. Only Methodist and Presbyterian, among Protestants, were singled out for attention in many of the polls, and with the formation of the Uniting Church in the early seventies, members of these two denominations merged with Congregationalists.

* The asterisked figures are probably overestimates; Mol's sample included young children, and was confined to the states of Victoria, New South Wales and Tasmania. Some of the states not represented have been found in other surveys to have lower rates of church attendance.

The inability of the economy to deliver the new heaven on earth, regardless of the good intentions of political leaders, was all too evident by the time the seventies came to an end. The grand designs had proven inadequate; social reforms had been found often too difficult or too costly. What now?

3) The 1980s reflected this post-modern condition. The lines of political demarcation became blurred as congeries of interest groups struggled to secure partisan objectives; minority governments became increasingly common. The resources boom did not live up to its promise, and the economy entered a phase in which the norm was a combination of stagnation and inflation--near-depression punctuated by several short-lived boomlets based on speculation rather than productive investment. Most Australians were less well-off at the end of the decade than they were

at its start, despite the return of the Labor party to power from 1983 under the leadership of Bob Hawke.

Multiculturalism was embraced as official policy as it became clear that the migrants have more to offer Australian culture and society than just a broader range of cuisine. During the 1980s the source of immigration shifted to Asia and the Middle East, sharply increasing the range of cultural and religious diversity. The number of Muslims recorded in the 1986 census increased to nearly 110,000, with probably many others not stating this religious affiliation (Table 2.1). A single paradigm of education no longer seemed possible, and private schools, many of them "church schools," flourished as parents sought to find (or found) schools which designed curricula according to their values. Australia struggled to overcome its "cultural cringe"--to regard itself as a legitimate focus of cultural life.

If it was the rise of secular optimism which caused the decline in institutional religion, then the dashing of these same hopes did not inspire any wholesale return to traditional forms. Some of the more resilient institutions resumed a modest rate of growth, as recorded in the 1981 and 1986 censuses; others continued to decline (Tables 2.1 and 2.2). Charismatic and evangelical wings of mainline denominations have enjoyed some growth, but high growth rates are achieved only by numerically small groups--especially Evangelical and Pentecostal groups outside the Christian mainstream. The only small religious group ever to break the "1% of the population" barrier were the Orthodox, during the sixties; the next will probably be the Muslims. The major change in this decade was the final passing of the Anglican hegemony. If "multiculturalism" implies that "Englishness" is no longer normative, then it may be symbolic that at the 1986 census Catholics slightly outnumbered Anglicans for the first time, holding steady at 26% of the population, while Anglican numbers were reduced to 24%.

As Table 2.1 shows, Catholics found themselves in the position of being the largest denomination, not by increasing as a proportion of the population, but by retaining their proportionate size while the previously larger Anglican group declined in the census count. Nor does this indicate that the Catholic group is unaffected by decline. Since the birthrate among Catholics is still higher than average, and Catholics have made up a higher than average proportion of immigrants, one would expect an increase in the Catholic proportion of the population. The fact that this is not taking place indicates that despite numerous baptisms, there is a counterbalancing loss by the departure of older members.

Many denominations continued liturgical changes during this decade, and Anglicans struggled over the issue of the ordination of women. Conservative emphases in theology and social policy regained some purchase in most denominations, tempering enthusiasm for social reform, and promoting a concern with issues of "spirituality," worship and meaning. Religious identification and participation are increasingly seen as individual, optional concerns, so that even the more "churchly" institutions, usually despite themselves, take on the character of voluntary associations.

One of the major changes which has occurred in Australian religious life since World War II is the rapid increase in those who respond to the census question on religious identification by declaring that they have "no religion" (0.3% in 1947, 7% in 1971 (when the instruction "If no religion, write None" was placed after the question), and 13% in 1986).[8] No doubt many non-participants who had retained some vestigial sense of denominational identity are deciding that they no longer regard themselves as affiliated with their denomination even in terms of sharing its beliefs, and find that in today's secular climate it is quite acceptable to declare such a position. This census statistic may thus represent more an increase in honesty--acknowledging an established state of affairs--than any recent profound change of heart (Bouma 1983, 1992); or it may be argued that the acknowledgement and reporting of the "fact" is itself significant evidence of secularization (McCallum 1987). Most likely both interpretations are valid.

Because the census question on religion is optional, there are many who do not answer it at all--almost 2 million in 1986. Survey interviewers get a higher rate of response when they ask the same question, so we can use their results to make a reliable estimate of the religion of those who do not reply to the census question. It appears that most of the census non-respondents have no denominational affiliation, (bringing the "nones" up to about 20% of the population) and the remainder belong to non-Christian religions or various Other Christian or Protestant denominations. The four principal groups: Catholic, Anglican, Protestant and No Religion, are comparable in size and include nearly 90% of the population.[9]

Contrasts Between Australia and the United States

While in some of these post-war changes Australia resembles the United States, it is important to note some marked differences. First, the distribution of religious groups is very different. As has been seen, Anglicans and Catholics have dominated the country's religious life since the beginning of European settlement. In 1986, no other group attracted more than 8% of the population except those who claim no religious identification (13%). The Uniting Church (an amalgam of former Methodists, Congregationalists and Presbyterians) accounted for 8% and the Presbyterian and Reformed churches (enumerated together) for 4%. Orthodox stood at 3%, and no other Christian denomination or non-

Christian religion attracted more than about 1% of the population. Together, the Protestant[10] denominations amounted to 17%. Hence mainline religion in Australia has always been, and still is, predominantly Catholic and Anglican, with a significant minority of Protestants, a marked contrast with the United States, which has almost as many Mormons as Anglicans (Episcopalians).

A second major contrast with the United States arises when characterizations of American society such as the following by Andrew Greeley are considered:

> Their children remain Catholic because in our society you have to be something and Catholicism seems to them the most rational choice (Greeley 1990:7).

> Assimilation into American society would have weakened the religious commitment of American Catholics if, and only if America were not a religious society (1990:20).

In Australia, as in some parts of Europe, it has not been necessary for a long time to "be something." Former Prime Minister Hawke, like many leading figures in political and cultural life, is an avowed agnostic. And around 20% of the population, as measured by surveys, declare that they have no religious denomination, although in the past many of these would have declared at least nominal adherence to the "C of E" (Church of England) or one of the other major groups.

A third distinction is the lack of an association between socio-economic status and religious affiliation. The two main denominations attract people from across the spectrum roughly in proportion to their numbers in the population. In Australia there is no detectable pattern of changing religious identification as part of upward social mobility. The commonest type of change of affiliation is for people to drop their former Christian denomination and merge into the "No religion" category.

The Post-War Generation in Australia in 1989
In 1989, the boomers[11] constituted 35% of the population, and a similar proportion of each of the four religious groups except the last: 36% of Catholics, 31% of Anglicans, 30% of Protestants, but 45% of the "No religion" category. The Anglicans had the highest proportion of pre-boomers (27%) and the "nones" the lowest (14%). The Anglicans had the lowest proportion of post-boomers (13%) and the "nones" had the most (22%).

Affiliation with Mainstream Religious Denominations

Because the NSSS included the question "what was your religious denomination when you were growing up" as well as "what is your denomination now," we can observe the proportion of members retained by each group, and the direction of changes in affiliation.

Most of the respondents claimed not to have changed their affiliation.[12]   Retention was highest among Catholics, followed by Protestants and Anglicans. Sixty-five percent of the changes were from one of the Christian denominations to No Religion; 32% were between the Catholic, Protestant and Anglican groups. About 3% of those raised as Methodist or Presbyterian later joined Pentecostal churches, together with about 2% of former Anglicans and 1% of Catholics--most Pentecostalists, as of 1989, were formerly affiliated with one of these four denominations. The number who indicated that they had changed from mainstream denominations to the smaller sects and cults was too slight for reliable measurement in the NSSS. Referring back for a moment to Table 2.1, we see that the categories "Other Protestant," "Other Christian" and "Other non-Christian," which contain such groups, amount to only 3.7% of the population. It is evident that there has been no major outflow from the establishment churches to such groups. Nor do "New Age" religious movements compete with mainstream groups for formal affiliation, although they exist, are well-publicized, and doubtless attract some interest from members of traditional churches.

Eighty-one percent of those brought up without any religious affiliation still had none in 1989, but by then they comprised only 18% of the nones. As can be seen from the last line of row percentages in Table 2.3, most nones are former Anglicans, Protestants or Catholics.

Next, the focus is narrowed to those who retained their childhood denominational affiliation, and the four age cohorts are compared.

As Table 2.4 shows, the "retention rate" varied across cohorts in a similar manner for the Christian groups. The boomers were less retentive than the generations before and after them. (The contrast is even more marked if those born before 1925 are included in the analysis: those over 60 in 1989 are only half as likely (12%) to have abandoned their Christian affiliation as those in their thirties (24%), despite having had twice the length of time in which to do so.) Most of those who changed did so between the ages of 14 and 29. This may explain in part why the percentage of post-boomers who have changed is lower; they are all still within this age range. Much denominational change happens in the context of marriage, where one partner changes to the religious identification of the other. Respondents are more likely to report identifying with their mother's denomination (when they were growing up) than with their father's.

TABLE 2.3: Denomination When Growing Up Compared to Denomination Now, 1989.

Denomination--when growing up:				
	Cath.	Prot.	Angl.	No rel.	Row Total
Denomination--now					
Catholic (Row%)	91.9	2.6	4.8	0.7	25.9
(Col%)	83.2	2.1	3.6	3.9	
Protestant (Row%)	3.1	83.9	11.2	1.7	27.1
(Col%)	3.0	71.2	8.7	10.5	
Anglican (Row%)	0.8	8.5	89.9	0.7	26.7
(Col%)	.08	7.1	68.8	4.4	
No religion (Row%)	18.4	31.0	32.6	18.1	20.3
(Col%)	13.0	19.6	18.9	81.2	
Total	28.6	32.0	34.9	4.5	100.0
(N = 4018)					

SOURCE: 1989 National Social Science Survey, Australia National University, Canberra

The boomers also have a higher proportion indicating no religious identification in 1989 than those who were born before or after them.

Church Attendance

Australian rates of church attendance as measured by responses to social surveys tend to be between American and British rates. Although the opinion poll questions on attendance are seldom strictly comparable across time because of changes in wording, there has been a decline in the overall rate of regular (monthly or more) attendance from about 36% in 1950 to 24% in 1989. Within denominations there is greater variation: Catholic regular attendance has declined from over 63% to 39%; Anglicans have registered a slight decline from 19% to 15%.

Of pre-boomers 28% claimed to attend church monthly or more, 19% for early and late boomers and 16% for post-boomers. Of pre-boomers 70% claimed they attended church frequently when they were aged 14; 67%, 64% and 56% for early, late and post-boomers. The mother's pattern of attendance when the respondent was growing up is more likely to be reflected in the attendance of children while growing up than the father's. However church attendance later in life, as measured at the time of the survey, was closer to that of the father, both for frequent and infrequent attenders.

The effect of cohort on pattern of church-attendance persisted when controlled for gender and female labor force status. More women claimed to attend frequently than men and fewer working women attended frequently than women not employed outside the home. Female

TABLE 2.4: Percentage of Those Belonging to Each Christian Group When Growing Up, Who had Retained Their Affiliation in 1989, by Cohort.

	Denomination			
Cohort	Catholic	Protestant	Anglican	Total
Pre-boom (1925-40)	88.6	75.6	76.8	79.5
Boomers (1947-53)	81.5	63.1	61.9	68.3
Boomers (1954-61)	77.0	66.2	61.8	68.6
Post-boom (1962-71) (N = 3837)	83.8	75.6	70.7	77.2

SOURCE: 1989 National Social Science Survey, Australia National University, Canberra.

labor force status was in fact more influential than gender for all but the post-boomers, where both have only slight effect. However, for men, working women and women not employed there was a marked decline in reported rates of church attendance in all denominations from the pre-boomers to the post-boomers. Birthplace (Australian vs. foreign) had no effect on rates of attendance.

Denomination, cohort, gender and women's occupational status all showed independent effects on the decline in church attendance; the contrast between attendance when growing up and later, and the dip in the twenties followed by a degree of recovery, show traces of the usual age effects. The overall attendance rates, when compared with those from earlier dates, and the emergence of cohort differences not seen twenty years before, also give evidence of a period trend independent of age. Birthplace had no effect. We shall discuss possible interpretations in a later section.

Religious Beliefs

The NSSS had several questions related to religious belief. Each will be examined in turn for "boomer" effects. The first such question concerned belief in God.

Those born before World War II were more likely to believe with no doubts, and slightly less likely to affirm weaker belief statements, but there were few differences between the other three groups.[13] This pattern persisted when controls for gender and female labor force status were introduced. Once again gender and women's labor force status also patterned belief in God in the ways one would expect. Church attendance was strongly associated with belief in God--presumably they reinforce each other--with regular attenders two to four times more likely to affirm belief

TABLE 2.5: Monthly or More Frequent Church Attendance by Denomination and Cohort, 1989.

	Denomination			
	Catholic	Protestant	Anglican	Total
Cohort				
Pre-boom (1925-40)	46.0	38.7	15.1	28.3
Boomers (1947-53)	37.4	28.5	12.9	19.3
Boomers (1954-61)	29.9	26.8	14.4	18.8
Post-boom (1962-71)	26.0	23.2	11.9	16.1
(N = 3072)				

SOURCE: 1989 National Social Science Survey, Australia National University, Canberra.

without doubts. Denomination also had an effect; regularly attending Catholics, Protestants and Anglicans were ranked in that order in the proportion who believe, followed by irregularly attending members of the same denominations in the same order. Interestingly, 23% of those with no religious denomination indicated belief in God (with either no doubts, or some doubts, or at least some of the time), and a further 21% believed in a "Higher power."

The NSSS included several questions about what happens after death. Forty-eight percent of Australians believe in a life after death, 47% in heaven, 35% in the Day of Judgement, 29% in Hell, and 28% in the devil. The order of denominations was as given above, except that practising Protestants, especially the post-boomers, affirmed these beliefs in larger proportion than their Catholic counterparts, especially belief in the Day of Judgment, Hell and the devil. Women, regardless of labor force status, had a somewhat higher rate of belief than men.[14]

Responses to these questions were influenced by age in a complex manner: the proportion of those who believe was inversely related to age, (not among practising Catholics), especially among infrequent attenders; there were no current signs of a generational decline (lower rates of belief among younger cohorts) except in the case of practising Catholics, whose post-boomer group, educated after the Second Vatican Council, are less likely to accept these beliefs than their forebears. Without knowing what today's pre-boomers believed when they were younger, we cannot interpret either finding with certainty as a result of age, cohort experience, or the temper of the times. One possibility is that regular attendance maintains the beliefs of Catholics against the advancing scepticism of age, but not against generational decline, except in the case of the belief in Heaven.

TABLE 2.6: Belief in God by Cohort (Percentages)

Cohort	Preboom 1925-40	Boomers 1947-53	Boomers 1954-61	Postboom 1962-75	Total
Belief in God					
Believe with no doubts	37	24	25	26	29
Doubts but believe	25	25	24	25	25
Believe some of time	9	12	14	12	13
Believe in "higher power"	14	16	11	11	13
Agnostic	12	14	16	13	13
Don't believe	4	9	9	10	8
TOTAL	100	100	100	100	100

SOURCE: 1989 National Social Science Survey, Australia National University, Canberra.

Images of God

Respondents were asked how important certain images of God were to them. "Friend" was the image preferred by the largest proportion, 46%; then "creator," 44%; "ever-present helper," 41%; "indefinable spiritual being," 39% and finally "redeemer," 36%. More of the pre-boomers, and the Protestant and Anglican (but not Catholic) post-boomers considered these images "important" to them than did boomers. The same is true of regular vs. irregular church attenders; the percentage of the first group rating an item "very important" was typically double that of the latter group. There was variation among the cohorts in the way these images were ranked. The pre-boomers ranked "creator" first; later cohorts preferred "friend" except among regularly attending Anglicans, where "redeemer" was ranked equal with "friend." Most boomers rated "creator" second, while post-boomers tended to rate "helper" second with creator third. All regular attenders rated "indefinable spiritual being" as least important, while infrequent attenders invariably rated "redeemer" lowest, with "helper" usually not far above.

The major difference among the cohorts is the shift from God as creator among the pre-boomers to God as friend among the rest.[15]

Value of Faith to Everyday Life

Respondents were asked to indicate whether their faith helped them in everyday life by providing any of the following, and how important this was to them. Fifty-two percent indicated that their faith's provision of "moral standards" was very important to them; "values to live by," 47%; "inner strength and peace," 39%; "a sense of purpose in life," 39%;

and "access to God who helps you," 34%. In this case the pre-boomers were more likely to rate each of these as more important than were the rest, and as before, practicing members of a given denomination and cohort were twice as likely to rate items important as their non-practicing counterparts. The decline was about 20 percentage points from the pre-boomer rating to the ratings of the rest.

Marks of a Good Christian

When asked how important was each of the following "in being a good Christian," 60% of respondents indicated that "keeping the Ten Commandments" was very important; "belief in God," 58%; "following the teachings of Jesus," 48%; "having a personal relationship with God," 45%; "attending church regularly," 24%. There tended to be a decline in the ratings of each item with each cohort except for the post-boomers who nearly tied the pre-boomers on the rating of the importance of "belief in God." There was considerable variation among the cohorts in the ranking of these "marks of being a Christian." The pre-boomers ranked "keeping the Ten Commandments" first, and "belief in God" second; boomers rated them close together, and post-boomers reversed the order.

The pre-boomers view God as creator, and place more emphasis on keeping the Ten Commandments. The post-boomers have learned, and prefer, a less transcendent image of God, and a stronger emphasis on belief than on moral demands.

Other Attitudes

The NSSS questionnaire explored a wide range of other attitudes. There were strong cohort effects on attitudes towards public spending, with the pre-boomers favoring cuts to social welfare, increased law and order, less spending on the environment, less spending on Aborigines, and more on the old age pension. The reverse of this was true for post-boomers with the boomers in between. The older were more conservative and the younger more in favor of social justice and environment issues.

Discussion

There are clear differences among the three cohorts. The baby boomers are different from those who were born just before and after them. In assessing these data it is important to remember that the pre-boomer cohort we chose from the larger sample[16] are only just beginning to retire; they are not the retired and the elderly but people between 49 and 64 years of age at the time of the survey. The pre-boomers were consistently more religious: more likely to identify, to attend, to believe, more likely to say that faith was important; they tended to see God more as creator and religion more in terms of moral rules; were more likely to take a pro-familist viewpoint and were more conservative and less "green" on social issues. The post-boomers were in some respects more religious than the boomers, but have not yet passed through the period when disaffiliation and lapsation from practice are most likely. They were not as religious as the pre-boomers. They were the most "green" and the most likely to support social and economic polices which provided freedom to the individual and redistributed income in favor of the disadvantaged.

The fundamental question to be asked is whether the differences among the cohorts reflect different life-stages ("age" effects), represent intergenerational differences ("cohort" effects) reflecting the different socio-cultural exposures of these groups, or are readings on a longer-term trend line affecting all cohorts ("period effects").[17] Some interpretations have in the past taken almost any downturn as *prima facie* evidence of secularization, that is, as evidence of a long-term decline in the influence of religion in social and individual life. It is important to look first at possible alternative explanations: at effects attributable to age or cohort experience. We will then consider period effects, remembering that the nature of religious life has changed and its intensity has varied both up and down from epoch to epoch and generation to generation--period effects may be multiple and have no concerted secularising direction.

Age Effects

Effects of this kind are familiar and popularly recognized. Most discussions of the religious "revival" of the fifties took into account the fact that a numerous generation of post-war children were being christened, later entering Sunday schools or church schools, receiving First Communion, and, in a kind of ripple effect, drawing with them into at least a temporary resumption of religious practice, parents and other relatives. There may have been nothing unique about the participation rates of either the children or their parents, compared with former cohorts. Young people whose participation declines in their early twenties have in the past often resumed closer involvement with their churches at the time of marriage, or on the occasions just mentioned.

The reassertion of Catholic identity in the 1981 and 1986 censuses on the part of a proportion of those Australian Catholics who in 1976, when they were predominantly in their twenties and early thirties, had omitted this claim, should probably be viewed in the same light.

Those measures of religiosity (not including church attendance) on which our post-boomers show an increase from the late boomers rather than a continued decline, need not be interpreted as a cohort "recovery," but as consequences of the life-stage of the post-boomers at the time of the survey: many would still have been living at home; they have not yet passed through the period when some changes (such as disaffiliation) are most likely to occur. Post-boom Catholics show less of this trend, and Protestants more, perhaps owing to the influence of small conservative groups.

Cohort Effects

Other differences between the cohorts seem not to be explained by different locations in the life-span. The overall extent of disaffiliation among the baby boomers seems unprecedented in Australian history, and not to be merely a "wild oats" age fluctuation, (and so likely to be reversed by aging) since it has been maintained for twenty years by most of the earlier members of the cohort. Now, affiliation as well as participation has become increasingly optional.

Further evidence that we are not dealing here only with age effects comes from a consideration of an earlier period: the census and poll data that have already been cited show higher affiliation and attendance levels for former generations in their twenties and thirties than our boomers and post-boomers manifest now.[18]   And the indications are that belief and religiously-influenced attitudes were stronger for the same age groups immediately after World War II, although data on this point are neither abundant nor clear.

The boomers evidence decline in religious identification, practice and belief. The decline may also reflect a change in the *quality* of the religious practice and involvement among the boomers. There has been a lessening of the sense of religion as duty, the right thing, something done to maintain decency, order and civilization. Religious practice has become more relational rather than legalistic in spirit in its approach to God and the religious life. This change can be interpreted as a reflection of the different child-rearing styles more commonly in use for baby boomers than pre-boomers (Lambert et al. 1959). Baby boomers were raised to a far greater extent in a context of unconditional acceptance, rather than under the conditional and punitive child-rearing orientations of those who parented pre-boomers. Freedom of choice on moral issues, and self-affirmation were much more the style for boomers in comparison with the duty and self-denial orientation of the pre-boomers. In so far as religion was a duty to the pre-boomers, something that the boomers could opt out of, and something the post-boomers had to opt into, the quality of involvement may have changed considerably. Whether perceived as improvement or merely change, this trend needs more careful analysis before its consequences are accepted as permanent.

Attendance, and some other indicators, show also a differential impact on cohorts, increasing with time. This needs to be interpreted in terms of the different social and cultural context in which each cohort spends its formative years, and hence of their different experiences of the world, and of the different worldviews and values which they both bring to these experiences, and which are further shaped through them. The three cohorts have had very different life-histories.

The baby boomers would seem to have had a smoother ride than their predecessors. They enjoyed rising prosperity, better health than any previous generation, a period of relative peace (the Korean conflict was too early to affect them and the Vietnam conflict directly involved relatively few, although the Cold War cast a dark cloud over their future); the sacrifices of the baby boomers were the sacrifices of the protester rather than the defender of the hearth; the joys of the baby boomers were hedonistic and sensual. Religion, especially mainline religion, represented the establishment, and was condemned for its association, on the one hand, with the powerful and wealthy, and on the other, with the forces of repression which were "overcome," in the popular mentality of the time, through free speech and sexual liberation. As the baby boomers reached middle age their security was more deeply threatened; they encountered problems with their own children (of whom they had relatively fewer than previous generations), the threat of AIDS and the collapse of the stock market. These disruptions are recent; so far the style of religiosity characteristic of this cohort has manifested the selectivity and subjectivization which European observers have commented on in their own scene.[19]

The life experiences of the pre-boomers--those born between 1925 and 1940--were very different. The children of the depression had far fewer material, educational, or health resources. Most escaped direct involvement in World War II, but would have suffered privations during the war and grew up in the shadow of the massive Australian losses in World War I. Religion was part of decency, honor and dignity--civilization as they knew it. Rules represented order; order was desirable, gave safety and predictability. For most Australians of this generation the center of power, culture, education was England. According to Swanson (1960) and Bouma (1992) this state of affairs would have been conducive to an image of God as distant but potentially powerful, a remote guarantor of order. Religion could legitimate the sacrifices family members made, could be relied on to provide order, to support the right action (made known in rules) and to uphold confidence that effort would be rewarded. The maintenance of this faith did not require a high level of attendance at services of worship but did require nominal affiliation with the right team, or at least one of the teams.

The post-boomers are different again. They have been raised in the shadow of the boomers. They have received the cultural and social "hand-me-downs" of the boomers. They have experienced the turmoil of marital breakdown, family dissolution and *laissez-faire* educational policies. The economic realities are harsh for the post-boomers. Jobs are hard to get, housing unaffordable, marriage is occurring later and loneliness is a much more common reality. This group is fighting to get its start in adult life under very adverse conditions. While the boomers rejoiced in the removal of control from afar and of the rigors of decency, the post-boomers seek their fortunes in a cold, uncontrolled, unpredictable, cynical world which offers them neither engrossing causes for which to sacrifice nor the comfort of strong legitimations for the conditions of their lives. The 15-30 year old group is often the least religious in terms of participation. This suggests that the style of religiosity characteristic of this cohort may be more conducive to a searching for religious meaning than to active involvement.

The cohort differences in preferred images of God, the value of faith in everyday life, and "marks of a good Christian" are quite small, and may well indicate both a theological liberalization and a loss of transcendence and moral fortitude. Similarly, the changes of attitude to social issues such as the redistribution of wealth, and public spending on the environment or Aborigines, may be due to liberalized church agendas, but could just as easily be influenced by secular sources.

Religious *beliefs* about life after death do not seem to have declined markedly, except in terms of their salience in everyday life. Our data show that they have not so much been abandoned by later cohorts, as seen as less important. Perhaps because of this lack of salience, they may be slower to decay. By contrast, we see significant changes, again especially among Catholics, in *moral* values which are invoked in everyday life decisions, such as on issues of contraception, abortion and divorce. These developments among Catholics have the effect of reducing the differences between them, Anglicans and Protestants, a change which has occurred during the lifetime of the baby boomers.

What predictions for the future of religion can be made on the basis of the above data? If these cohorts are treated as simply different groups of people with differing experiences and hence different patterns of involvement and meaning then any predictions would be based on some assumption about trends in the socio-cultural backgrounds within which successive generations have been and will be raised. Such assumptions are well beyond these data. If the differences among the cohorts are also indicators of longer-term secularizing trends then further decline can be predicted.

Period Effects

Other aspects of our findings may be explained in terms of theories of secularization. (See, for example, the work of Dobbelaere (1981, 1985, 1987), and for a recent review of this area, Ireland (1988)). One general definition is that of Berger (1979:26): secularization is the process "in which religion loses its hold on the level both of institutions and of human consciousness." As a long-term historical process, secularization includes the emancipation of political and economic institutions from religious control (e.g. disestablishment), the removal of major social institutions and processes such as education, health care and social welfare from religious auspices, and the emergence of an autonomous culture appealing to reason rather than faith as its foundation (e.g. in science and philosophy) (Chadwick 1975). Luckmann (1967) described the impact of "functionally rational" institutions on the secularization of consciousness through the involvement of individuals in activities in the "public sphere," especially through work, and the retreat of religion to a "private sphere" whose only major institutional structure was the family, and whose dominant themes were self-development and self-realization.

Of course, there have been considerable historical fluctuations in measures of religiosity such as affiliation and attendance. Not all of these changes have proved to be part of a long-term historical process. Nor is secularization itself necessarily either inevitable or irreversible, once it is stripped of its anti-religious ideological connotations. Simple unidirectional models of secularization are now being increasingly abandoned in the face of the persistence, and periodic revivals, of religion in developed societies.[20] Not only have the major secularizations--those of nature, human institutions and knowledge--in Ancient Israel, the Reformation, and the Enlightenment respectively, been shown to have religious roots, but the major changes in social structure implicit in such processes as urbanization, industrialization, and the combination of bureaucratization and the application of technology characteristic of modernization, while presumably irreversible, have not been found to lead, with the inevitability that was once supposed, to a world without religion. "Traditional" societies may be changed out of all recognition by such processes, but communal structures adapt, re-emerge and thrive, and modern societies do not at all seem to be inherently incapable of supporting manifold forms of religion. "Traditional" religion is seen more clearly as but one historically conditioned form of religion--it has often been presented as normative for the survival of Christianity when in fact the world of the latter's own origins manifests much of the religious pluralism, confusion, and outright unbelief sometimes supposed to be uniquely characteristic of the present (Mason in press).

Secularization implies that more than short-term changes are involved: it postulates some qualitatively new developments not likely to be quickly reversed; but any theory likely to be accepted today will also have to accommodate period effects which, although long-term, do not prove irreversible. For instance, O'Dea's (1970) celebrated "dilemmas in the institutionalization of religion" need to be understood as cyclical processes: as the recent reviviscence of Protestant and Catholic religious denominations in Latin America and Africa shows, new challenges can inspire the sloughing off of institutionally encrusted structures of religious law, belief, ritual and motivation, and the emergence of novel forms of religious spontaneity and community.

In the Australian situation, both the Anglican and Catholic churches can be seen as suffering, in different forms, from a long-term crisis affecting the legitimacy of religious authority (Carroll 1991; Bouma 1991, 1992; Mason in press). In the Catholic case, some aspects of this crisis, flowing especially from papal teaching on contraception, are shared with the rest of the developed world, but others, particularly the sense of a lack of access to, a voice in, and influence over the organization, appear to have a unique local character not identical with the situation in, for example, the United States. Whatever the extent of the alienation caused by this crisis, and however severe the effects on participation, the crisis is not in principle irreversible, and only a primitive theory of secularization would be discomfited by a Catholic revival, should conditions change.

The significantly lower levels of religiosity manifested in the post-war generation in Australia show period effects of these kinds. Some of the patterns of decline, such as those in affiliation and attendance, appear to affect all age-groups, and so to transcend cohort effect alone. At their onset, period effects may have a differential impact on cohorts, (for instance, a major change in the process or content of religious socialization), but may then become entrenched, and proceed to affect subsequent cohorts with equal or greater severity. One must observe the development of these successor cohorts; if they follow the patterns of their immediate predecessors, a longer-term change may have occurred. But if they revert to established norms for their age, the farther boundary of the cohort effect becomes visible.

A second qualitative shift in the religious life of Australia which has occurred during the time of the boomers is a marked reduction in religious inter-group hostility (Hogan 1987). The religious identification of the boomers has less tribal and more cultural significance. That is, the meaning of religious identification has shifted from being a marker of a person's place in the social structure to a marker of her/his general cultural ethos (Bouma 1992). During the lifetime of the boomers the number of ethoi has increased with the arrival of migrants, and the acceptability of a variety of ethoi has increased as Anglican hegemony has declined and an official policy of multi-culturalism has taken hold. Australian Catholics, the group among whom many of the indicators of decline are strongest, and extend more clearly to the post-boomers, could be argued to have had far less exposure, prior to the time of the Second Vatican Council, to the secularizing effects of religious pluralism because of the degree to which they were insulated within ethnic lifestyle enclaves. Since the Council, this solidarity has deteriorated, and the results are now evident (Mason 1983, 1991).

The effect of gender on church attendance and some other indicators has almost been extinguished, while female labor force status is an important predictor. A plausible explanation is that firstly, gender role socialization, particularly of women, is changing as a result of ideological pressures. Former gender roles are seen by feminists as oppressive, and women are being urged, in pursuit of equality, towards a role profile much more similar to that of men. Child-rearing practices may be undergoing significant alterations in the light of such beliefs. Economic and occupational changes, not necessarily under the impulse of ideology, may have had just as much influence. De Vaus and McAllister (1987) point out that for Australian women, labor-force involvement decreases religious participation to a greater extent than for American women, because of the more strongly secular workplace culture of Australian society. There is abundant evidence that there is less difference now between women and men in schooling, length of education, access to tertiary education, pattern of leisure activities, likelihood of a substantial period of paid employment after completing education, and of return to the workforce after childbearing. The theories of secularization to which we have referred above would predict that such increased involvement in a "public" sphere dominated by functional rationality would bring about the kind of changes in women's religious attitudes and behavior that we are in fact observing. One current finding which appears to confirm this explanation is that the attendance rates for women who work are closer to those of men than to the higher levels of women not in paid employment.[21]

Because of the relatively more important role that women have played in the past in the religious socialization of children, both boys and girls (note the findings reported above on children's tendency to follow during childhood the mother's denomination and the mother's pattern of church attendance), we can also expect the decline in women's religious affiliation, beliefs or behavior to make a major negative impact on the next generation.

Conclusion

The baby boomers have had an effect on the religious life of Australia. They have been significantly less religious than the generation preceding them and have shifted toward a more relational and less legalistic style of religiosity. What effect will these changes have on the churches? Those who do participate in religious organizations now do so more out of choice than habit or duty and may take a more active role in the construction and application of religious meaning than their forbears. On the other hand, many baby boomers have opted out of formal religious identification or have reduced their participation. Most, however, would continue to see themselves as religious people. Those who do not participate regularly but continue to identify with a religious group may well be decreasing their use of formal religion to the celebration of rites of passage only. This will put pressure on many clergy and religious groups to decide whether they are willing to provide chaplaincy-style religious services (Bouma 1992) to those who otherwise do not attend, contribute, or support the institution. While Anglicans have had a long tradition of doing this, having a history of being an established church elsewhere, there is a strong reaction against continuing to do so, and some clergy, both Anglican and Catholic, are insisting that people participate in order to "qualify" for baptism, marriage or burial. This reaction to both the qualitative change in the nature of participation among those who do participate and the processes of secularization, may be seen to be forcing some church-like institutions, such as the Anglican and the Catholic to decide whether to become more sect-like by imposing membership and performance criteria on those who request their services. The institutional reactions to the changes which are associated with the baby boomers have only begun to surface.

Establishment religion in Australia, under the impact of the post-war generation, continues to be predominantly Catholic and Anglican, as before. Both of these groups show signs of decline, but from a large base. Mainstream Protestant groups are declining, while there is still growth among evangelicals, Pentecostals and smaller sects. The next decade will reveal whether the post-boom generation retain their low rate of practice, and continue to disaffiliate at the same rate as those ahead of them. The baby boomers themselves have shown markedly less enthusiasm for religion than their parents, and have demonstrated the qualitative changes in their style of religiosity that one would expect as a consequence of the social and cultural context in which they grew up.

Notes

1. National Social Science Survey 1989 (preliminary data release), directed by Jonathan Kelley, Department of Sociology, Research School of Social Sciences, Australian National University. The authors wish to thank Dr. Kelley for making the data available and the Christian Research Association and the Faculty of Arts, Monash University for their contributions toward the cost of data collection.

2. Some members of the Anglican communion consider themselves and their church to be Protestant; some do not. Here they are grouped separately from the Protestant denominations.

3. This shows that there is a confusion inherent in the label "No religion." We use it here only because it is so familiar, deriving from the way the response is labeled in the Census; but recall that the census question is: "What is this person's religious *denomination*? If no religion, write `None'." Those who write "None," intending to indicate that they belong to no denomination, are then labeled in the census results as "No religion." But "religion" includes more than belonging to a religious denomination. Some religious beliefs are retained by many who do not belong. In the 1989 National Social Science Survey, 23% of those who stated that they had no religious denomination expressed belief in God, and a further 21% believed in a "Higher power." 26% believed in life after death. In short, wherever the familiar phrase "No religion," is used here (the quotation marks are used to indicate its special sense), it means only that the person states that he or she belongs to no religious denomination, and leaves open the question of what other religious attributes the individual may retain.

In contrast to inclusive churches like the Catholic, Anglican and Orthodox, many Protestant churches require a high level of commitment and active participation for a person to retain membership of a local church, and regularly purge their rolls of inactive members. So inactive Protestants not formally enrolled can become "unchurched" in a manner impossible for members of churches in which baptism is the only required qualification for membership. It is likely that some of them, although still believers, act on this understanding and declare that they have no religious denomination.

4. Australian Gallup Polls, <u>Bulletins</u> (irregular), 1946-1970.

5. Notes to Table 2.1: Religious Denominations, Australia, Censuses 1947-86:

Format:

The table presents data on religious denominations collected at 8 successive censuses, 1947-86. Data from the 1991 census are not yet available.

The column headed "N" contains the actual number of members of each denomination who answered the question.

The "%" column expresses the number to its left as a percentage of the total Australian population.

"% Incr" denotes percentage increase (or, when preceded by a minus sign, percentage decrease), between that census and the previous one. It expresses the increase as a proportion of the former size of the group.

Sources:

1947-1961: Commonwealth Bureau of Census and Statistics ([1965]).
1966 & 1971: Commonwealth Bureau of Census and Statistics ([1974]).
1976: Australian Bureau of Statistics (ABS) ([1980]).
1981: ABS ([1983]).
1986: ABS ([1988]).

Errors:

Small errors of 2-3 (units) are not uncommon, particularly in the 1976 *totals*, since the census that year was a sample, not a full enumeration. These errors derive from the ABS source tables, are presumably due to the method of processing, and have been left as they stand in the present table.

Comparability of these statistics across the different censuses:

1) Beginning in 1966, population totals and tables include Aborigines and Torres Strait Islanders.

2) "No religion" and "Not stated":

In 1966, immediately following the question on religious denomination were the words: "There is no penalty for failure to answer this question."

In 1971 and 1976, these words were omitted, but the front page of the census schedule stated: "There is no penalty for omitting information on a person's religious denomination." And after the question on religious denomination were inserted the words: "If no religion, write `none'." Hence the categories "No religion" and "Not stated" for 1966 and 1971 are not comparable.

In 1981, the words quoted above were omitted from the front page of the schedule, and the question was changed to read: `What is each person's religious denomination? This question is optional. If no religion, write `None'." This probably had some further effect on the responses, so the "No religion" and "Not stated" categories for 1981 cannot confidently be compared with earlier years.

3) "Anglican"

The church formerly known as "Church of England in Australia" changed its name to "Anglican Church in Australia" by act of parliament prior to the 1986 census. This name is the one used across the whole table.

4) "Uniting Church"

"Congregational," "Methodist" and "Presbyterian" figures for 1981 cannot be compared with earlier years because of the introduction of "Uniting Church." Little reliance can be placed on figures for this latter category, at least in 1981, because of the recency of the merger (some Uniting Church members may still have entered their former denomination name) and the way responses were coded by ABS (e.g. the responses "Methodist," "Wesleyan Methodist," etc. were left as "Methodist," but "Methodist Church of Australasia" was coded as "Uniting Church." "Presbyterian" was not changed to "Uniting Church."

In 1986, the category "Methodist" was abolished, and responses beginning with this word were coded as "Uniting Church"; however "Wesleyan Methodist" was coded as "Other Protestant"; "Congregational" was left as a separate category, as was "Presbyterian." (see ABS Religion Index, 1981 & 1986).

The artificial category "MPCU" (consisting of the total of "Methodist," "Presbyterian," "Congregational" and "Uniting Church" has been constructed to allow some comparisons, but note that it is not the same as "Uniting Church" in reality--i.e. "MPCU includes Continuing Presbyterians, etc.

6. Any attempt to track the post-war generation through this period, when they began to come within the age range of surveys, is hampered by a lack of data; apart from Mol's survey in 1966, which found no marked age differences in religious participation, there were no further large-scale surveys including significant data on religion until the eighties. All we have are opinion poll data, which however do provide age breakdowns from 1970 on.

7. Roy Morgan Research Centre, Gallup poll *Bulletins*, 1970, 1972, 1976, 1981.

8. Given the large component of "Not stated" in the census, and the high proportion of these who appear, from surveys, to be in the "No religion" category, all of these percentages are significantly biased downwards by the non-response.

9. We have drawn these inferences from the 1989 NSSS. The remaining 12 percent would be made up of Orthodox (3 percent) and other Christian groups, Muslims and other non-Christians.

10. The category Protestant includes those who identified themselves as Methodist, Uniting, Presbyterian, Reformed, Baptist, Lutheran, Churches of Christ, Congregational, Lutheran, Pentecostal, Salvation Army, Seventh-Day Adventist, or Other Protestant and excludes the Orthodox, Jehovah's Witnesses, Latter Day Saints, and Other Christian categories.

11. "Boomers" are those born between 1947 and 1961, a 15 year span; they constituted 35% (N=1561) of the sample.

"Pre-boomers" are those who were born between 1925 and 1940, a 16 year span; 22% (N=970) of the sample.

"Post-boomers" are those born between 1962 and 1975, a 14 year span; 18% (N=805) of the sample.

Those born before 1925, and between 1941 and 1946, are not included in the cohort comparisons, but remain part of the base to which whole-sample statistics refer.

12. For the purposes of this broad analysis, a change from one Protestant denomination to another is counted as retention of one's Protestant identity.

13. The results are the same if the first three categories of response are combined. When the effect of birthplace is removed, the percentage of both early-boomers and post-boomers who believe with no doubts is somewhat reduced.

14. Birthplace had no significant effect on responses to these questions.

15. On these items, as with belief in God, a consistently higher percentage of overseas-born early boomers and post-boomers rated the item important. Birthplace is thus the source of some of the upturn in the youngest cohort. When its influence is removed, the early boomers are more similar to the late boomers, and the post-boomers fall closer to the declining trend line.

16. So as to compare the boomer cohort (which was itself defined, as noted before, on demographic criteria), with an earlier group of similar age range, we selected as pre-boomers an age cohort (1925-40) of approximately the same width as the boomer group (1947-61).

17. The terminology "age, period, cohort" is commonly used, following Ryder (1965) to distinguish these three effects. Since we do not have comparably detailed data for different periods, age cannot be held constant so as to observe different cohorts at the same age; our single detailed snapshot takes in different cohorts at the same point in time. Hence the present study is limited in the inferences that can be drawn to distinguish cohort and age effects. Nonetheless, we have some data relevant to earlier periods--for instance the testimony of Mol (1971) for 1966 and of various polls for earlier and later periods up till 1970, that church attendance did not vary significantly by age.

18. If affiliation and attendance are considered to form a continuum, all three of the religious groups have shown significant decline on that continuum: Catholics have maintained affiliation relatively better, but have had significant losses in membership and a severe and continuing downturn in attendance; Protestants have declined in both; Anglican attendance, never very high, has not clearly fallen off when measured as a percentage of members attending weekly, but disaffiliation has taken place on a large scale.

19. See the essays by Hervieu-Léger and Dobbelaere in the present volume.

20. See sections I and V of the essay by Roozen, Carroll and Roof in the present volume.

21. Karel Dobbelaere, in his essay in this volume, (Table 8.1 and later discussion) reports similar findings in Belgium. But see, by contrast, the startling evidence presented in the chapter by Eileen Barker (Table 1.5) showing exactly the opposite in the case of women in the United Kingdom who are not in the labor force: a lower level of belief and practice than found among those in paid employment.

3

Fifty Years of Religious Change in the United States

David A. Roozen, Jackson W. Carroll,
and Wade Clark Roof

Introduction

For social scientists who postulate an incongruence between religion and modernity, the immediate post-World War II period in the United States provides a creative challenge. Individual religious participation and the institutional vitality of the United States' denominational religious establishment surged upward, as did all measures of modernity. Sharp declines in religious participation and belief beginning in the early 1960s proved more fertile ground for secularization advocates. But by the mid-1970s it was the secularization boom that had gone bust. Since that time all aggregate, national levels of individual religiosity have either inched upward or remained unchanged. Renewal movements are present in all major denominations. And while the political voice of liberal Protestantism has muted, evangelical Protestantism is riding the wave of 15 years of political activism, and the United States Roman Catholic hierarchy has attained high national visibility for its liberal social pronouncements on peace and the economy. Additionally, out of the dissipating wake of the new religious movements, an eclectic mixture of Eastern and ecological consciousness has loosely coalesced in the "New Age" movement.

Given the persistence, reformulation and vitality in religion in the United States since the mid-1970s linear notions of decline prominent in secularization theory have given way to more complex notions of "restructuring" that combine arguments of differentiation between and within all levels of society with arguments of segmental innovation and adaptation. *We believe the latter perspective is especially appropriate to the*

59

situation in the United States in the last half of the 20th century, and the purpose of this paper is to use the experience of the post-war cohort to examine this possibility. By "post-war cohort" we mean what is commonly referred to in the United States as the "baby-boom generation," namely those born between the years 1946 and 1965. The sheer size of the cohort--the largest 20 year cohort in U.S. history, today roughly one third of the entire population--guaranteed their disproportionate influence not only in the religious sphere but in all sectors of society. They therefore provide an especially appropriate window through which to examine the changing nature of religion in the United States. The fact that they were the first generation to grow up in the electronic age of television and sustained, pervasive economic affluence; and the first wherein a near majority participated in some form of post-secondary education further suggests that they are an appropriate window for viewing possible changes related to the movement from modern to "post-modern" socio-cultural patterns.

Our particular interest is using the experience of this cohort to examine: (1) changes in individual religious belief and expression; (2) changes in the institutions which comprise the United States' religious establishment (by which we mean, in particular, the major oldline and evangelical Protestant denominations and Roman Catholicism); and (3) the interrelationship between the two. We begin with a descriptive account of these for each of the historical periods corresponding to the above noted three movements in U.S. religion over the last 50 years--the "revival" of the 1950s; the "declines" of the late 1960s and early 1970s; and the "renewal and stability" of the last 15 years. We then conclude with a discussion of the implications of our analysis for theoretical interpretations of religion in modern and emerging "post-modern" societies.

The "Revival" of the 1950s

Individual Involvement and Commitment
National survey and denominational yearbook data consistently show that religious membership and participation surged upward during the 1950s; that the increases outpaced population growth; that all establishment denominations shared in the increase (although evangelical Protestantism disproportionately so); and that the increases were evident for all age groups (for thorough reviews see Glock and Stark 1965; Hoge and Roozen 1979). Trend data is not available to chart possible changes in religious belief and devotional practice into and through this period. However, cross-sectional national survey data from the 1950s show that traditional belief and practice were pervasive (e.g., Marty et al. 1968). It

also shows that to the extent age differences were evident at all, it was the youngest adults (the immediate pre-baby boom cohort) who were most traditional. One of the common explanations offered for the 50s revival was the affinity between family--particularly parenting--and establishment religion. This was the period of extra-ordinarily high birthrates that produced the "baby boom" cohort, and many argue that it was parents seeking religious instruction for their children that filled church pews. National survey data does show that the vast majority, upwards to 95 percent, of the children born during this period participated in traditional religious instruction. However, direct empirical support for the claim that this was the major causal factor in the "revival" is, at best, ambiguous, as it is for other common demographic explanations (see Roozen 1979; Hoge and Roozen 1979).

In the absence of convincing demographic explanations for the religious vitality of 1950s, a variety of cultural and social-psychological explanations gained saliency. Hoge's personal investment model (1974) is representative and particularly relevant to the purposes of this paper. He argues that "adequate interpretation and explanation of religious change must work from the total meaning-commitment system of the individual" (1974: 180). This system is, for Hoge, inclusive of the values, attitudes, commitments and behavior of any individual; its structure is vaguely hierarchical, but not tightly unified, more like a network than a rigid structure; and it is subject to change due to inputs from one value area or another. Religious commitments, accordingly, are linked to others, and may change indirectly when the other commitments change.

Applying this theoretical framework to several college student surveys, Hoge consistently found that sexual and family values were most closely tied to traditional religious values; political and economic values less so, with the major exception of a fear of communism which was as strongly related as sexual and family values. Additionally, his collection of religious and value indicators gathered sporadically from 1920 to 1960 showed that, in fact, periods of high traditional religious commitment among college students (the 1920s and 1950s) were associated with periods of high conservatism and conformity in all attitude realms, and with high levels of personal and privatistic commitments not oriented to social change.

Hoge's model and conclusions are, as he notes, consistent with several other explanations of the 50s revival. These include Parsons (1960) structural differentiation thesis, Riesman's (1950) argument concerning shifts from inner-direction to out-direction, Lipset's (1959, 1963) suggestion as to the critical importance of changing political sentiments, and at least those portions of Herberg (1960) and Lenski (1963) that relate the religious revival and familial values as common derivatives of a felt need for security during a period of rapid social change. Hoge's work is also suggestive in its critique of broad ranging, linear theories for understanding religious change in the United States in the first half of the twentieth century. His principal point in this regard is that while one may be able to make the case that the explanatory mechanisms--secularization, individualism, educational attainment, mobility, urbanization, the breakdown of community, etc.--have a linear trend, the trend in traditional religious participation and commitment in the United States has been cyclical.

Preceding Hoge in the latter regard, Lipset (1959) was particularly direct in his attack on those who saw the continuing corrosive effects of secularization on individual religious commitments during the 1950s, despite the apparent increase in religious participation. Specifically Lipset argued that the secularization advocates ignored two things. One was the disproportionate growth of evangelical Christian groups. The second was the possibility that "the secularized religion which these observers see as distinctly modern may have been characteristic of American believers in the past."

In response to the apparent impasse between advocates of secularization and their critics, Glock and Stark (1965: 84) suggested that both kinds of changes may be occurring simultaneously:

> that, while the more evangelical and fundamentalist churches may be gaining new converts from certain sectors of the American public, the major denominations may be undergoing a transformation of their theology towards an increasingly less orthodox and more secularized faith.

Religious Institutions: Denominationalism in the 1950s

The distinctive institutional character of the United States' religious heritage has been "denominational" ever since the nation's founding. However, the centralized bureaucratization of denominations is a more recent phenomena and generally limited to mainline Protestantism and Roman Catholicism. At the beginning of the nineteenth century, little denominational structure existed beyond the local level. By the 1880s most oldline denominations had developed one or more nationally centralized agencies, and during the ensuing 20 years of economic growth in the nation as a whole, coupled with ever increasing memberships, full scale, complex, central bureaucracies emerged within all oldline Protestant denominations (Wuthnow 1988: 23). After the turn of the century, the initiation of apportionment plans for denominational support further consolidated the grip of national bureaucracies, and allowed for the development of new types of programs and functions which depended on more predictable sources of income. By the end of World War I the denominational bureaucracies--both oldline Protestant and Roman Catholic--were solidly entrenched and a major force toward continued denominational expansion. As Douglass and Brunner (1939: 147) note: "Like it or not, denominations have come to mean more than they used to. They exercise wider functions and their functioning is more necessary to the well-being of the local churches than ever before."

The depression of the 1930s and then World War II blunted the expansionary momentum built up over the previous century and a half of growth. But when the war ended, religious organizations, with considerable financial equity built up during the war, faced a pent-up demand for religious construction dating back to the depression. Additionally, during the favorable economic and religious climate following the war, the overall population of the country not only grew rapidly, but also shifted in location--from rural to urban, from city to suburb, from East to West. Not surprisingly, the late 1940s and entire 1950s were characterized by a tremendous growth in religious construction of all kinds (Wuthnow 1988).

The mood of church leaders was understandably optimistic, and the sense of a "new beginning" characterized not only numerical growth but theological discussion as well. Theological arguments conceived at the turn of the century and increasingly dominant through the depression, seemed naive to many after World War II. Within conservative Protestantism even the emergent National Association of Evangelicals, most prominently visible in the person of Billy Graham, found fundamentalism to be overly narrow, negative and separatist. And as the evangelicals ascended toward the mainstream of society, the old-line fundamentalists of the American Council of Christian Churches retreated further into the isolation of their Americanized version of a pillarized, fundamentalist subculture (McLoughlin 1966; Hunter 1983).

Within liberal Protestantism the modernistic and optimistic assumptions of Social Gospel idealism were displaced by Barthian neo-orthodoxy and the Christian realism of its most prominent American spokesperson, Reinhold Neibuhr--although most popular advocates stripped the latter of its radical socialistic political ethic. Gone was the modernists' amorphus theology of divine immanence, replaced by a re-emphasis of the transcendent mystery of God, the dual, sinful and irrational nature of "man," and insoluble riddle of human destiny (McLoughlin 1966).

The sharp distinction between the transcendent and worldly realms in the neo-orthodoxy which dominated mainline Protestant theology during the 1950s provided a relatively comfortable point of accommodation with the evangelicals who had come to dominate the conservative side of Protestantism. It also provided considerable affinity with the general mood of the populace caught up in the cultural and economic optimism of the 1950s, but with strong undercurrents of concern that peace and economic prosperity might not last, and about the destructive threat of the atomic bomb, "godless" communism and an unbridled, individualistic quest for material pleasure.

Further solidifying the comfortable public consensus which emerged in American Protestantism during the 1950s was the emphasis all parties placed on biblical authority. On the one hand, faith was inevitably personal, but subjectivism was constrained by a revelation of divine will that was generally understood to have been codified in the scriptural canon. On the other hand, religion had a necessarily organizational base, but it also, as a cultural embodiment, stood under the continual judgment of the over againstness of the kingdom as revealed in the scriptures.

Another point helping to solidify the rapproachment of left and right in the American Protestantism of the 1950s was the shared assumption that religion was necessarily a collective endeavor. Faith was only partially discoverable by individuals; it required the support and inspiration of a community of believers. Religious commitment was, in theory, communal, not a life of mystical isolation. Religious communities were, in a clear sense, moral communities--communities of moral obligation, defined by shared expectations, and sustained by social interaction (Wuthnow 1988).

But an emerging theme of the Protestant mainstream during the 1950s provided a peculiar twist to the communitarian ideal. That theme was an awakened sense of "the infinite worth of the individual." The twist was that fellowship became increasingly a derivative of individual devotion. How to empower the individual to be morally committed became more the issue than how to construct moral community itself; and the corporate body became subtly shifted toward a service agency for the spiritual growth of its individual members.

Despite the overt, public calm of the emerging Protestant consensus, denominational divisions related to theological, ecclesiastical, ethnic, and subcultural differences persisted as, if nothing else, sturdy social barriers. A 1955 Gallup poll, for example, showed that only one in 25 adults no longer adhered to the faith of their childhood. Such divisions within the Protestant house, however, did not erupt into major sources of social conflict or define the major sources of religious tension during the 1950s. Rather, the most visible and significant religious tension during the period was that between Protestants and Catholics.

Roman Catholicism in the 1950s was, of course, thoroughly "pre-Vatican" with all the religio-ethnic, coercive-authoritarian-hierarchical, ritualistically-mediated other-worldly, and anti-modern characteristics so aptly described by Neal (1966), Hornsby-Smith (1989) and a host of others. Pressures toward the changes to be unleased by the Vatican Council were building, to be sure; but as Hoge (1986) describes it the immigrant American Catholic church was still characterized by a "siege mentality" that included the development of its own system of organizations, publications, schools, hospitals, social service agencies, etc. to protect its people from the inhospital Protestant surroundings. And within their pillarized subculture, Roman Catholicism experienced the same kind of membership and institutional expansion as did the Protestants, which resulted in a similar optimism, only slightly muted by undercurrents of concern and anxiety.

1963-1975: The Post-War Generation Comes of Age

Individual Involvement and Commitment

The leading edge of the post-war cohort turned 18 in 1963. Symbolic of the social ethos at the time, 1963 was also the year of the first civil rights march on the nation's capital, led by the Reverend Martin Luther King, Jr. By 1965 national surveys showed a down turn in religious belief and practice. Although some downward drift was evident in all age groups, it was particularly dramatic among the then young adult, post-war cohort. Levels of participation and belief among the post-war cohort as young adults in the 1960s were not only significantly lower than that of older cohorts in the 1960s, but also significantly lower than that of the immediate pre-baby boom cohort when they were young adults during the 1950s (Wuthnow 1978; Carroll et al. 1979; Hoge and Roozen 1979).

Protestant and Catholic trends were similar, except that declines in worship attendance were more pronounced for Catholics. Greeley et al. (1976) also report significant declines in Roman Catholic acceptance of papal authority.

One area in which the "religious" practice of the young adult baby-boomers surpassed that of older cohorts was involvement in the new religious movements and the newly promoted "technologies of inner experience." Although trend data on such involvement is not available, a 1975 Gallup survey shows that adults under 30 were more than twice as likely to be involved in yoga, transcendental meditation and Eastern religions than older age groups. Nevertheless, even young adult involvement was, at best, modest--ranging from a high of 7 percent for transcendental meditation down to 3 percent for Eastern religions.

Explanations for the pattern of decline in traditional religious commitment were nearly as consistent as the data documenting them. The following summary by Hoge (1979: 120) is typical:

> Changes in church commitment are part of a broader pattern of value changes. All data supports this view. Other areas in the overall cluster undergoing change are attitudes about sex and family, birth control, ideal family size, civil liberties, legalization of marijuana, and (among Catholics) political party identification. In all these areas, change since the 1950s has taken the same pattern. It has been in the direction of individualism, personal freedom, and tolerance of diversity. The change has been much greater among young adults, especially the college educated young adults, than among any other persons. It took place mostly after 1960.

Why a new set of values took hold among the post-war cohort remains debatable. But that they took hold and that they were a major departure from previous generations in the United States seems incontestable. The specific nature of the "new values" is particularly well articulated in Yankelovich's (1974), *The New Morality: A Profile of American Youth in the 70's.* He sees them as a cluster of three sub-categories. The first category has to do with "new moral norms" including changes in sexual morality in a liberal direction and a lessening of automatic respect for and obedience to established institutional authority. The second category relates to social values, including a decreasing affirmation of the work ethic, marriage and family, and the importance of money in defining success. The third category concerns "the vague concept of self-fulfillment." For the young adults of the late 60s and early 70s, according to Yankelovich:

> Self-fulfillment is usually defined in opposition to concern with economic security. . . Once a person feels that he can take some degree of economic security for granted, he begins to look forward to relief from the discipline of a constant preoccupation with economic security, and he starts to search for forms of self-fulfillment that go beyond the daily routine. . . The self-fulfillment concept also implies a greater preoccupation with self at the expense of sacrificing one's self for family, employer and community (1974: 6).

Both the analyses of religion and of values among the youth culture of the late 60s and early 70s emphasized change. From the tone of the discussion one might conclude that nothing remained of the past. This was not the case. Despite the title of "Decline in Traditional American Beliefs" announcing one section of Yankelovich's above noted work, for example, the text and data indicate that in 1973 the large majority of young adults continued to believe in "most aspects of the puritan ethic"--thrift, the sacredness of private property, hard work always paying off and competition encouraging excellence. Additionally, the national survey data on religion which consistently pointed to some decline in traditional religion among the post-war cohort, nevertheless pointed to considerable persistence. Nine in ten young adults retained a religious preference; more than two-thirds were certain there was a God, believed in the Trinity, believed Jesus was God, and believed in life after death; and more than a third prayed daily, attended worship weekly, felt religion to be "very" important in their lives, and believed the Bible to be the actual word of God.

Unfortunately, there is relatively little empirical basis for speculating about how the persistent fragments of religiosity might have been embedded in varying and larger value constellations. Wuthnow's (1976), *The Consciousness Reformation*, is the most explicit effort in this regard. Using a 1973 survey of San Francisco Bay area adults he constructs seven different meaning systems and shows that 28 percent of respondents under the age of 30 have meaning systems that incorporate traditional religious beliefs (his "traditional," "theistic" and "transitional" types). This is in contrast to 41 percent of respondents over 30. Wuthnow's analysis further shows that 7 percent of respondents under 30 have a "traditional individualistic" meaning system, 22 percent have a "social" meaning system, 21 percent have a "mystical" meaning system and 21 percent a "modern" meaning system (which is a mix of the social and mystical). How representative Wuthnow's San Francisco Bay area data may be of the nation as a whole is difficult to judge, but all national survey data indicate that the West coast is the least traditionally religious region of the United States.

Religious Institutions: Divergent Patterns of Denominational Vitality
        The magnitude of change in America's denominational establishment during the 1960s is succinctly summarized in observations from two prominent historians of American religion. In *A Religious History of the American People*, Sydney Ahlstrom (1972: 599) states:

> It may even have ended a distinct quadricentennium--a unified four hundred-year period--in the Anglo-American experience. A Great Puritan Epoch can be seen as beginning in 1558 with the death of Mary Tudor, the last monarch to rule over an officially Roman Catholic England, and ending in 1960 with the election

of John Fitzgerald Kennedy, the first Roman Catholic president
of the United States.

Writing seven years later about mainline decline amidst continued
evangelical growth, Martin Marty (1979: 10) declares that: "A seismic shift
has been occurring and continues in American religion."

The former points to the assimilation of Roman Catholicism into
the mainstream of U.S. culture; the latter to the ascendancy of conservative
Protestantism. The base of comparison for both is the alternatively labeled
mainline, oldline, liberal or ecumenical Protestant denominations, which
during the late 60s and early 70s found themselves besieged by a variety of
internal and external pressures.

Symbolic of the mainline denominations' plight was a 10 percent
decline in adult membership and 30 percent decline in baptisms from 1965
to 1975. Demographic and religious changes related to the baby boom
cohort were an obvious contributing factor; as were a historical legacy of
local congregations heavily concentrated in areas of stagnant population
growth--especially inner cities and rural communities, and a virtual stop in
new church development.

The latter was not for lack of funds. Rather, it was a consequence
of a shift in national denominational priorities related to an equally
profound shift in the theological assumptions of denominational leaders
(Carroll et al. 1979; Greer 1993). The paradoxical relationship between
"Christ and culture" in the neo-orthodoxy that dominated mainline
theology during the 1950s and that was operationalized for the public good
through evangelism and the Christian nurture of individual conscience,
gave way to a reemphasis on immanence. This reemphasis had strong
transformational connotations that demanded direct participation in
structural reform--the latter more commonly referred to as "social action."

In addition to effecting a massive shift in denominational funding
away from evangelism and new church development into social action, the
highly visible social justice involvements of denominational leaders and
some local clergy alienated a wide spectrum of members who either
disagreed with the specific political goals of the social action, or more
likely, disagreed that the church should be involved in social action of any
kind. There is no evidence that this alienation led to a mass withdrawal
from membership (membership declines were almost exclusively due to
declining numbers of new members), but it did stimulate the self-
consciousness of evangelicals within the mainline denominations and
energized existing, or spawned new, oppositional special interest groups.

Confounding the institutional and theological controversies
surrounding social action within the mainline denominations during the

1960s was a growing ecumenism, especially as it manifested itself in an increasing number of proposals for denominational mergers and for modifications of denominational positions on matters of theology and church polity. Between 1958 and 1968 virtually every major mainline denomination either was involved in a merger, or involved in serious discussions about church union. Such involvements appear to have generated stronger reactions, and more opposition and alienation, than the social action controversies.

While there is little evidence to support suspicions that national bureaucracies grew in size during the 1960s and early 1970s, there is evidence that the grass-roots membership increasingly perceived the central agencies as taking on a life of their own. As the authors of a national study conducted among the members of 15 major mainline denominations in 1972 put it:

> Out of the inherited citizenry-versus-the-colossus mentality has grown a kind of schizoid image of the church, split between the intimate local congregation on the one side and the remote, impersonal denomination on the other. Sometimes, the implication has seemed to be that they are pitted against each other (Johnson and Cornell 1972: 14).

Mickey and Wilson's (1977) analysis of the national organizational restructuring that many mainline denominations undertook during the late 1960s and early 1970s suggests that the grass-roots' perception was not entirely misguided. Among their conclusions were: (1) that increased centralization was one of the major intended accomplishments of the restructuring; and (2) that "one unexpected result was a fracturing of the relationships between the bureaucracy and the regional and local churches" (1977: 148).

Still further confounding the theological and institutional trauma related to social action, ecumenism, re-organization and a growing gap between the bureaucracy and grass-roots constituencies was a growing sense that the dominant denominational currents had lost a sense of personal piety and spirituality. As a report of the American Association of Theological Schools (1972: 171) put it in regard to pastoral leadership:

> We would wish that seminaries today accept as their task the spiritual formation of people who will be more than able scholars, or vital human beings, or dedicated social change agents; of people also, whom--with considerable risk--we may speak of as sacramental.

As historian James Smylie (1979: 86) put it more directly, mainline Protestantism was unable to shape a holistic piety which would embrace both the "personal yearning for God-centeredness, and . . . the social order and destiny of human beings in their corporate existence."

During the 1960s and early 1970s the national denomination structures of mainline Protestantism gained a strong identity for universalizing notions of ecumenism and social justice, but at the cost of a weakened sense of personal spirituality, a weakened connection to the localism and voluntarism of their congregations, and significant decreases in membership.

The situation could not have been more opposite for evangelical Protestantism. Membership in its major denominations grew, its decentralized institutional infra-structure continued to expand, a number of adaptations enhanced the appeal of its personal spirituality, and it even developed a small, politically liberal, social activistic wing.

Institutional centralization has never been a major pre-occupation within the evangelical tradition in the United States, even within the vast majority of its denominations. To some extent this may be related to the relatively small memberships of all evangelical denominations except for the Southern Baptist Convention. But it is much more a reflection of the independent, separatist and entrepreneurial evangelical ethos that created and is more conducive to a diffuse, social movement/network-like institutional structure than to centralized bureaucracy. Within this structure local congregations, and particularly a vast array of "special purpose" groups and organizations, are more important than centralized, national denominational agencies. The growth and development of this network structure of "parallel institutions" during the 1950s straight through the 1970s is well documented by Hunter (1983) and Wuthnow (1988). Such non-denominational networks take on special importance for the evangelical movement because a significant number of evangelicals are dispersed throughout mainline denominations.

The expansion and coherence of this institutional infra-structure, coupled with substantial growth in evangelical scholarship--particularly apologetics--led Hunter (1983) to conclude that already by the end of the 1950s, evangelicals had successfully constructed a firm subcultural foundation. Not only had they established strong lines of "cognitive defense" against modernity, but they had also outgrown their insecurity at being a cognitive minority. And he further concludes that the trends established within conservative Protestantism in the 1950s continued through the 1960s.

The evangelical movement was born in the founding of the National Association of Evangelicals in 1943. It was a reaction against the negative and separatist anti-modernism of fundamentalism and set about to construct a more positive and engaged approach to modernism based on the standard tenets of Reformed Christian orthodoxy it shared with fundamentalism. Being "in but not of" the modern world necessarily required some accommodation to the latter, and the social respectability gained by the movement during the 1950s and the upward social mobility experienced by its membership added conciliatory pressures. One of the most critical aspects of the continued upward surge of evangelicalism during the 1960s is, therefore, how it managed this accommodation without losing its orthodox soul.

Hunter (1983) points to four inter-related developments in this adaptation, all of which originated or intensified during the 1960s. The first he calls the rationalization, codification and methodization of evangelical spirituality. By this he means the increasing tendency to approach the spiritual aspects of evangelical life by means of 'principals,' 'rules,' 'steps,' 'laws,' 'codes,' 'guidelines,' and so forth. The second development Hunter calls the rise of evangelical civility.

The third adaptation that Hunter points to is an accommodation to the subjectivism of modernity through: (1) adding a more explicit concern with the emotional and psychological dimensions of human experience, and (2) an intensified narcissism and hedonism. The former includes an increasing emphasis on achieving "psychological balance," "emotional maturity," and self-actualization; and an increasing emphasis on understanding and solving specific emotional problems such as depression and stress. The latter, especially in popular evangelical thought, contains a heavy dose of "enamoredness with self" and the related attitude that the world exists for the purpose of pampering the self with pleasure and enjoyment. But, as Hunter (1983: 97) notes, whereas the hedonism of the secular culture:

> reaches its apex in the phrase "If it feels good, do it," [t]he narcissism found among evangelicals is expressed not as self-infatuation or vanity or unseemly conceit with personal accomplishments. Rather, it finds expression in a fixation on the potentiality of the human being "under the lordship of Jesus Christ."

Fourth, and foundational for the others Hunter argues, is the shift in evangelical notions about God from God's transcendent nature to God's immanent and expressive nature. Gone is an emphasis on the wrath, the terror and the awesomeness of an infinitely powerful and untamable God. Gone also are the notions of benevolent, although impersonal and paternal, immanence that have traditionally served to mediate and mitigate a stern

and distant transcendence. Rather, Hunter argues, the transcendent God
of Righteousness whose immanence was felt as a Divine Protector has been
translated to "God, the Great Counselor" and "God, my best Friend." Not
only is a direct relation with God possible, but that relationship can be
personable and intimate.

One area, however, where there is no evidence for accommodation
is the entrenched evangelical affirmation of traditional personal morality.
In this regard, conservative Protestantism, even in the more moderate
evangelical movement, remained both at war with modernity and a
cognitive minority.

The latter presents a sharp contrast to the trajectory of U.S.
Catholicism during the 1960s, which was one of assimilation, convergence
and conformity into and with the mainstream of middle class culture and
life. Vatican II opened the floodgates for currents of change that had been
building for decades. The Council ushered in a new climate of openness
and freedom and inspired laity and priests alike to assume greater
autonomy in matters of faith, ethics and parish governance. Practices
unchanged for a millennium and a half were abandoned almost overnight;
and new liturgies and more democratized procedures of decision making
were introduced--although somewhat unevenly across dioceses and
parishes (see, for example, Hornsby-Smith 1989). The changes met with
broad approval from the majority of Catholics. But as Neal (1966) points
out it was a time of great uncertainty and restlessness. Among those
unsympathetic with the changes there was a reaction of "numbed
quietude" that only slowly energized in the formation of organized
movements such as the Catholic Charismatic Renewal. But even among
those most vocal in their approval of the changes, there was uncertainty
about the speed and direction of the implementation of the changes and
rising expectations that still further change may be possible.

As Hoge (1986) among others argues, the ecclesiastical reforms of
Vatican II fit well with the general assimilation of the Roman Catholic
population into the middle class that was occurring in the 1950s and 1960s,
including a convergence of Catholic and Protestant educational levels,
socio-economic status and birth rates; attitudes about family planning and
contraception; and political attitudes regarding racism, civil liberties, and
nuclear war. All of these, Hoge notes, are aspects of "convergence and
conformity." Continuing, he states:

> The ecclesiastical reforms after Vatican II can also be interpreted
> in this way--the introduction of English and hymn singing in the
> Mass, the changes in the confessional, the end of the Index of
> Forbidden books, the introduction of quasi-democratic

structures on all levels, and the greater autonomy and democracy in women's orders. Most of what the surrounding Protestant middle class culture would see as excesses or unintelligible curiosities were trimmed back or remodeled. New suburban middle class church buildings were built without kneelers, without confessional booths, and without all the statues. The new laity felt more at home in these churches (1986: 293).

Although mass attendance and devotional practice declined, especially among young adults, Roman Catholic membership growth continued to outpace population growth.

Greeley et al. (1976) argue, however, that Pope Paul VI's encyclical, *Humanae Vitae*, issued in 1968 and reaffirming traditional Catholic teachings against birth control, blunted much of young adult enthusiasm for the "new church," especially their respect for church authority. They in fact argue that the sharp declines in church participation among young Roman Catholics during the late 60s and early 70s are almost entirely attributable to the confrontation between the liberalizing changes in young adult sexual attitudes and the church's reaffirmation of tradition teachings. Interpreting this in a somewhat broader framework, Roof and McKinney (1987) argue that a crisis in authority was provoked by the sudden attempt of the Catholic hierarchy to place limits on personal choice at a time when the larger trends in this direction [freedom of choice] were gaining momentum.

Although as already indicated the visibility of the new religious movements was greatly disproportional to their numerical growth--being concentrated almost exclusively among young adults and even within this segment of society primarily among those related in some way to higher education, the movements' visibility nevertheless contributed an important symbolic dimension to the more general cultural upheaval of the 1960s. As Robbins et al. (1978) note, the new religious movements were of two general types: mystical-therapeutic and neofundamentalist. The former synthesized scientific, psychological and religious (particularly Eastern mystical) themes in a quest for personal meaning. The latter mixed strident theocentric dualism and traditional morality in a protest against the relativism and permissiveness of modern society. Of the two streams, Robbins et al., suggest that the mystical-therapeutic was numerically the largest. The symbolic significance of the two streams, according to Wuthnow (1988), was to broaden and redefine the outer limits of religious respectability: the mystical-therapeutic pushing to the left, the neofundamentalist pushing to the right.

1975-Present: Differentiation and Fluidity

Individual Involvement and Commitment

The cover of the February, 1987 *Washingtonian* magazine proclaimed: "God is Back." The declaration was a response to the growing awareness among Washington D.C. clergy that their churches suddenly seemed full of baby boomers, the oldest of who were just turning forty years of age. Research by Roozen, McKinney and Thompson (1990) showed that the situation was not unique to the nation's capital.

Comparing national survey data from the early 1970s to that from the early 1980s, Roozen, McKinney and Thompson found that regular church attendance among the older baby boomers (born 1945-1954) had increased from 33 to 42 percent over the 10 year period; that the magnitude of increase was relatively constant across all segments of U.S. denominationalism; and that two factors accounted for 90 percent of the increase. The two factors were the dramatic increase in the percentage of boomers who had school age children, and only somewhat more modest increase in the percentage of boomers identifying themselves as political conservatives.

The 1978 and 1988 Gallup surveys of the "Unchurched American" (despite the title, the surveys are representative cross-sectional surveys of the entire adult, U.S. population) show the same general pattern of change in worship attendance among the post-war cohort. Additionally the Gallup data show the same direction of change, but in more modest proportions, for a variety of traditional measures of religious belief, devotional practice and self-assessed importance of religion in one's life. It also shows that the increases in religious involvement and commitment over the 10 year period are greater for the post-war cohort than for all older cohorts.

A large study of the baby boom generation conducted by Roof (1993) adds nuance to the above findings. Focusing on the 96 percent of respondents who identified a religious tradition in which they were raised, this research shows that 33 percent have remained involved in religion throughout their teen and young adult years and continue to be involved. They may have switched congregations, even switched denominations or faiths, but they have maintained an institutional religious connection. Correspondingly, two-thirds of respondents had dropped out for a period of at least two years sometime during their teens or young adult years. Many of the people he and his research team interviewed have been in and out of churches and synagogues many times--their biographies read like searchers in serial quests. However, about a fourth of those who dropped out had returned to active involvement at the time of the study, although often returning to a denomination or faith tradition different from what they had left. Denominational loyalty is not very strong and returnees look for congregations with a variety of activities suited to their needs: family life, the religious training of children, and support groups are perhaps the most important reasons for their return.

The remainder of the "dropouts" remain outside of active church involvement. While many of them say they are not "religious," the majority say they are "spiritual"--a distinction of considerable importance to boomers. Many belong to 12-Step and other types of support groups catering to addictive and compulsive behaviors. There is a great deal of fluidity, or movement in and out of religious institutions and "switching" from one denomination or faith to another. In this switching mainline Protestant denominations, Roman Catholicism and Judaism are net losers, conservative Protestant denominations are gainers. But the biggest change has been to "no" religion which shows a net gain of nearly 300 percent, 13 percent of respondents identifying with no religious tradition at the time of the study. Conservative Protestantism has the highest retention rate--86 percent of those raised as conservative Protestants still involved in conservative Protestant congregations. Elaborating on the latter, Roof and Loeb (1990: 10) note that much of the appeal:

> has to do with experiential faith: conservatives make it possible to "feel" and to "express" your religion without being embarrassed about it. An authoritative stance toward moral and lifestyle issues also adds appeal: conservatives have answers for the most difficult and controversial issues, which is especially attractive to boomers who feel there is too much choice today.

But whether or not one goes to church is a choice. A common boomer refrain--among all faith groups--is that you go to church "if it helps you to grow." Such a response is typical of what Roof and McKinney (1987) call the "new voluntarism:" an ethos of greater freedom and choice in religious matters. Such a change in the religious ethos is consistent with what Wuthnow (1988) points to as a more general shift in the meaning of "freedom" in the United States. The nineteenth century legacy of the word ties it to notions of freedom of opportunity and, in even more specific terms, to upward social mobility. Today, Wuthnow notes, this traditional image has been replaced by a new connotation which equates freedom chiefly with "freedom of choice." And given a choice for participation within a religious institution, as Bibby's (1987) notion of "religion a la carte" implies, one retains the further choice of what within that institution to accept and what to reject, even as one participates. The latter, in fact, constitutes the main argument provided by Hout and Greeley (1987) for why church attendance among Roman Catholics stopped decreasing in 1975, despite continuing disagreement among a majority of Catholics with church teachings on marriage and sexuality. Catholics continued to participate, but exercised selectivity in terms of church teaching. "You do it if it helps you to grow" also reflects the widespread therapeutic culture in the United States today and a psychological approach to religion emphasizing how it can help people to overcome guilt, shame, abuse, and fear, all associated with feelings of victimization. Spirituality begins with personal experience and is a journey into the self. Both recovery theology and journey theology flourish today to help people with their inner needs and spiritual potential. Further characterizing themes of the post-war spirituality, Roof (1990: 22) states that:

> It celebrates experience rather than doctrine; the personal rather than the institutional; people's religion over official religion; soft, caring images of Deity over hard, impersonal images; the feminine and the androgenous over the masculine--all making for what Andrew Greeley (1990) has recently called "*imaginative*" religion over against "reflective" religion (emphasis added).

Bibby's (1987) phrase "religion ala carte" is an apt description of this generation's religious style. When asked if one should explore teachings of various religions or if one should stick to a particular faith, less than a third of the respondents in the Roof study said a person should stick to one. Sixty percent said you should explore the possibilities. More than half said they prefer meditating alone to worshipping with others. As one respondent put it, "religion locks you in." Whereas religion is seen as restrictive and binding, spirituality is liberating and expressive. Yet the two blend together in a variety of ways. "Multi-layered" meaning systems are commonplace, that is, beliefs and practices drawing off a variety of sources, both religious and quasi-religious--including Eastern meditation, Native American religion, psychotherapy, ecology, feminism, as well as more traditional Judeo-Christian elements.

Roof's book, *A Generation of Seekers* (1993), argues that the two most energized choices for the boomers are the evangelical and fundamentalist groups at one end of a theological continuum, and the various New Age spiritualities at the other end. These two streams are vastly different in terms of their religious content and modes of religious discourse, but as many scholars have recently noted (e.g., Albanese 1988; Luckmann 1990) both speak to popular concerns for healing, wholeness, unity, personal transformation and direct spiritual experience. Evangelicals and fundamentalists draw upon a dialectical imagination--the individual over against the world; New Agers draw upon a mystical imagination-the inner and the outer worlds are one.

In between these two extremes are two other boomer religious responses which Roof identifies: one, a sacramental outlook which finds the divine in everyday human relationships and serves as a balance to obsessive concern with one's own personal quests; and two, a highly privatized and vague type of religiosity. The first leads some returnees back to church or to get involved in small groups. It is engaging, deeply existential, and seeks coherence. The second is more common outside religious institutions, yet is found within them, of people who believe in God, occasionally pray, and hold to moral principles rooted in religion. It is a "low energy" response and weakly integrated as a belief system. The "sacramental boomer" may be a distinct new type. However, the privatized vague believer has striking similarities with what Berger (1961), Wilson (1966a) and numerous others took to be pervasive among middle class, mainline Protestantism during the 1950s. Clearly, there is no intrinsic connection within any of the types between spirituality and involvement in establishment religious institutions. Members of each type may or may not choose to nurture their spirituality within a church, synagogue, or mosque.

What is not yet known is neither the relative magnitude of those choosing these various types of response, nor some sense of which might be on the ascendence and which might be on the decline. The same is true with regard to how pervasive the new religious consciousness actually is within the post-war generation; or alternatively, what proportion of the cohort might still be characterized on the one hand by traditional "reflective" modes of religious consciousness, and on the other by the seeming total absence of any religious or spiritual imagery.

Religious Institutions: De-centralization of Organizational Vitality

Although made specifically in reference to the Presbyterian church, the following comment by John Mulder (cited by Long 1990: 2-3) fits the general situation of all mainline Protestant denominations in the 1980:

> It's not going to die. But a fascinating phenomenon is emerging. From the early 20th century through the 1960s, the denomination as an organization worked. Now it's no longer working.

"Beleaguered on every side" is how Wuthnow (1989) describes it, full of turmoil and struggle.

Although the steep membership declines of the mid-1960 to mid-1970 period have lessened (except for the Presbyterians) and a few mainline denominations have even experienced membership increases in a few scattered years since 1975, the membership of every mainline Protestant denomination has continued to decline relative to the overall United States population. Additionally, and unlike the 1965-75 period, declining memberships have been accompanied in the last 15 years by financial pressures at the national level. In the last several years, for example, most major mainline Protestant denominations have resorted to personnel cutbacks to balance budgets. The financial strain on the national bureaucracies, however, is not due to the decreasing giving of members or to the fact that there are less members to give. Rather it is due to less of what is given being passed "upward" from congregations to national agencies. Some of this decreased "upward" flow of financial support may be due to increased institutional maintenance costs at the local level; but there is clear evidence that much of it is due to local congregations opting to support alternative mission programs. As William McKinney (cited by Lyles 1990: 17) notes:

> The element of choice has come to affect not simply the way the individual relates to the congregation but increasingly the way congregations relate to their denominational bodies. Congregations pick and choose which missions to support. The selective participation in denominational life makes it difficult for denominational agencies to function, and raises profound questions about their future.

McKinney's analysis of the reasons for the national denominations' fiscal crisis is consistent with Wuthnow's (1988, 1989) recent argument about the radical re-structuring of the institutional character of mainline Protestant denominations. Wuthnow says:

> Denominations have not ceased to exist but have become to a greater extent diverse federations of special purpose groups rather than monolithic, homogeneous structures. They provide some continuing degree of identity and coordination, *but much of the concrete action in which religious people are engaged takes place in more specialized groups that may fall either within or across denominational lines* (1988: 125, emphasis added).

If "turmoil" accurately characterizes the liberal Protestant denominational establishment over the last 15 years, perhaps only slightly more muted terms like "tension and uncertainty" are appropriate for the U. S. Catholic church. The tension and uncertainty operate on a number of levels. At the parish level one finds, for example, an increasing organizational complexity related to expanded programming, which as Leege (1990) argues, is a direct consequence of Catholic assimilation into "American ways." More specifically Leege (1990: 10) notes:

> the contemporary complex parish with widespread participation in leadership by church professionals and educated laity is a measure of Catholic entry into the American mainstream. It is also testament to both the rational and voluntary nature of American religious organizations: time after time, parish leaders told us that, if the parish could not respond with a specialized ministry, it would lose the loyalties of parishioners to some other local church or voluntary organization.

Especially prominent among the "new" programs are what Leege calls "specialized life-cycle" ministries. Perhaps also indicative of the extent to which Roman Catholicism has been influenced by the trends noted in our discussion of the distinctive nature of religious expression of the post-war generation, Leege's data show that over 20 percent of Catholic parishes have an organized program of "charismatic renewal."

However, as Murnion (1990) argues, the movement from "a *traditional* to a *modern* spirituality and ecclesiology" has not been easy or entirely successful. By "spirituality" Murnion means both the experience of relationship with God and the means for expressing this experience in formally religious and broadly social programs. More specifically he says:

> attempts to make this shift in the past few decades in the United States (and probably many decades earlier in sections of Western Europe) did not adequately integrate important elements of traditional spirituality and ecclesiology into current patterns; changes in the spirituality have not been adequately reflected in changes in the ecclesiology; and on the one hand a kind of naive modernism and, on the other hand, a reactionary traditionalism, are working against the achievement of an adequate and authentic contemporary spirituality and ecclesiology (1990: 8).

At the national level a new element of tension was added to the unfolding of American Catholicism's engagement of modernity, which is, as Hoge (1986: 297) describes it:

> a change of mind in Rome. Whereas Pope John XXIII believed in opening the windows and Pope Paul VI generally agreed, Pope John Paul II wants them closed. The floodgates are closed again. John Paul has prohibited any discussion of institutional changes fervently desired by many Americans--on birth control, celibacy, women's roles and other topics. The pope and Cardinal

> Ratzinger think that most of the Council was a mistake, and the
> drift toward modernity in the Western nations is dangerous.
> They see no future for world Catholicism if it continues to move
> in this direction.

Hoge continues by demonstrating how serious the pope is and the practical
steps he has already taken to erect barriers between the church and the
modern culture. At the time Hoge wrote, the situation of the Dutch
Catholic church was the most dramatic example of this (see, for example,
the chapter on the Netherlands in this book, and Lechner 1989). However,
recent appointments of conservative bishops and the disciplining of
outspoken liberal theologians in the United States has made the "change of
mind in Rome" highly visible to American Catholics.

Hoge's conclusion about the implications of this are especially
insightful for our purposes:

> The most likely prospect is increased tension. Assimilation will
> not stop. American Catholics will not stop believing in citizens'
> participation and democratic processes. And yet the pope
> appears to be unbending. . .We will probably see new
> revitalization   movements   loosely   within   the   Catholic
> community which focus on the Bible or the Holy Spirit but not
> on the norms of church law or obedience to the hierarch. *The
> most vital stirrings today are indeed in lay movements and among lay
> ministries* (1986: 298-89, emphasis added).

The conservative Protestant movement in the United States, as
already noted, has never been highly centralized, and as Wuthnow (1988)
argues the independence of elements within the movement's structural
network was a crucial factor in the explosive growth in prominence of
evangelicalism in U.S. culture during the late 1970s and throughout the
1980s. Specifically he notes that the major institutional base for the
evangelical resurgence of this period was the television ministries of
several local, but nevertheless, "megachurches." They:

> provided a strong platform form which conservative preachers
> could launch a broad variety of programs. Acknowledging
> virtually no controls from the outside, in contrast with the
> situation that faced most ministerial entrepreneurs in the
> established denominations, these pastors were free to use their
> vast resources for virtually any activity the local market would
> bear (Wuthnow 1988: 197).

All national survey data suggest that the explosive growth in prominence was not quite matched by growth in numbers of members, although the numbers of evangelicals did continue to grow (Roozen and Hadaway 1993). Rather, the prominence was above all a dramatically increased public visibility related to conservative Protestantism's new found political activism. This new found political activism was both consequence of and contributor to a change in the issues within the political arena. Questions about public morality, abortion, and the relations between church and state all began to reappear as matters of public debate.

It is probably too early to tell how lasting an influence the merging of conservative Protestantism with a resurgence in the conservative political climate will have. But in the short term we have to agree with Wuthnow's (1988, 1989) contention that to the extent America may have a civil religion, it now consists of two alternatives: one closely connecting conservative political instincts to evangelical Protestant images; the second, a liberal view of America that focuses less on the nation as such and more on humanity in general, and which draws less on the distinctiveness of the Judeo-Christian tradition and more on basic human rights and common human problems. Over the long run such a duality may well undercut the legitimating power of both. But in the short term the prominence of the conservative alternative within the pair has served to further solidify the plausibility of the evangelical subculture, and to fan the flames of opposition to the liberal establishment among evangelicals within mainline Protestant denominations --and quite possibly within Roman Catholicism.

Interpreting 50 Years of Religious Change in the United States

We conclude by summarizing some of the major thrusts of our descriptive analysis and noting some directions for future research on religious change.

First, we believe our analysis points to a growing diversity in the ways that individuals give expression to their religious commitment, which is the result of a widening stream of subjective expressionism in matters religious. This has led to a differentiation of individual spirituality from the institutional structures of America's denominational establishment. Individual religious construction--"spirituality" in the preferred terminology of the post-war generation--is a matter of personal choice, including the choice of whether or not to relate to denominational religion. If one chooses to relate, there is a further choice of what in the denomination's official tradition to accept and what to reject. An adequate conceptual categorization of the diverse modalities has yet to emerge, but we have no doubt that of necessity it will be complex. It must at least encompass differing religious contents, modes of construction and discourse, and relationships to various institutionalized traditions. Each of these appears to vary somewhat independently in the experience of the post-war generation.

The reasons for the growing emphasis on individual choice in religious matters are complex. We believe, however, that they are largely a result of increasing affluence and the dramatic increase in college and university graduates following World War II. Both trends have helped to change the meaning of the highly salient U.S. values of freedom and self-fulfillment. Once tied primarily to more utilitarian concerns of economic security and upward mobility, freedom has been redefined as choice and self-fulfillment, or what Bellah and associates (1985) refer to as "expressive individualism."

While we agree that expressive individualism is a pervasive characteristic of the United States' post-war cohort, our analysis of the religious situation cautions against the tendency of many commentators to equate such individualism with anti-institutionalism and an erosion of community. We concur that the operative dynamic of individualism is autonomous choice, and that this certainly includes the possibility of choosing not to participate in, for example, religious institutions. Nevertheless, it also includes the possibility of choosing to participate. Indeed, the latter accounts for the fact that while religious individualism in the United States has increased in the past decade, religious participation has remained stable (Marler and Roozen 1993). Individualism does not so much erode a person's institutional commitments as clarify them (for an elaboration of this point and its implications for religious institutions see Marler and Roozen 1993; Roof 1991, 1993).

Second, the movement toward the centralization of denominational institutions that characterized the first 60 years of the twentieth century has reversed itself. In the last 15 years the highly centralized institutions of mainline Protestant denominationalism and Roman Catholicism have become internally differentiated. Such internal differentiation has been prompted in large part by competition among the diverse, multiple constituencies that these institutions seek to accommodate and serve. In some ways we believe this is a reassertion of historic religious localism or populism (e.g., Swatos 1981). Religion in the United States has always been characterized by a pragmatic willingness to accommodate or adapt to various life-worlds of present or new constituents. There is, however, a new twist in the present situation. Reflecting both the diversified patterns of individual religious expression and a growing array of disparate public issues dear to different groups of constituents, communities of special interest have been formed--e.g.

feminist groups, right to life groups, gay and lesbian caucuses, or a growing number of "twelve-step" self-help groups. In many cases, these have become as important as traditional social class and ethnic enclaves for the grounding of localistic religious expressions.

One consequence of this internal differentiation is a de-centralization of the centers of institutional religious vitality. Local congregations have increased in importance as centers of initiative. Additionally, an entirely new array of special purpose groups have evolved, institutionally situated between and/or along side congregations and denominations. Our impression is that those religious groups and organizations currently on the ascent are those that have strong identities and a clear affinity for either affective-particularistic religious expressions (e.g., evangelical or charismatic groups) or affective-universalistic expressions (e.g., various forms of New Age spirituality). Those groups and organizations that are currently stagnant are those that have weak identities and/or emphasize a universalizing, ethical rationalism.

As an overall assessment of the situation in the United States, as perceived through the experiences of the post-war generation, we therefore must agree with Wuthnow:

> In becoming more oriented to the self, in paying more explicit attention to symbolism, in developing a more flexible organizational style, and in nurturing specialized worship experiences, American religion has become more complex, more internally differentiated, and thus more adaptable to a complex, differentiated society (1988: 305).

Such a conclusion is consistent, of course, with any number of long standing analyses of the implications of America's denominational starting point which see denominationalism's formal tolerance of religious diversity conducive to religious innovation or adaptation both within and outside of establishment religion. Newly emerging social groups, either expressing or reacting to "modernistic" impulses, are free to use or reject religious legitimations. Nevertheless, as Martin (1978) has noted, cultural affinities and the political and economic context of American society seems to impart an advantage to those that opt for the use of religious legitimations. Also, as we have noted, quasi-pillarized religious subcultures have shown remarkable success in maintaining their plausibility in the United States, perhaps assisted by the Judeo-Christian content in America's vague "civil" religion(s).

In terms of broader interpretive theoretical approaches to "religious" change we view the situation in the United States as consistent with those evolutionary perspectives that emphasize increasing subjectivization of individual religion, and a differentiation of individual religious expression from traditional religious institutions. However, the situation in the United States also cautions that such broad evolutionary perspectives miss a considerable amount of variation and change. Secularization or modernization theories, for example, that offer little more insight than that religious institutions become differentiated from other social institutions and marginalized in relationship to them, are of little relevance to understanding the specifics of religious change in the United States. Such differentiation has always been present within this nation, but it has not precluded the influence of individual religious expressions or institutional religion on other social institutions. This influence has long been primarily mediated, with varying degrees of success, either through individuals acting on their consciences or by the collective action of religious organizations through special purpose groups that use similar tactics to secular organizations--for example, lobbying or manipulating public opinion. What is needed are frameworks to explain the varying degrees of success of these efforts. Here dialectic frameworks such as those proposed, for example, by Wentworth, Robertson, Walsh and Simpson (each in a separate chapter of Hadden and Shupe 1989) appear promising points of departure.

Likewise, since the institutional vitality of U.S. religious institutions reflects a complex pattern of decline and revitalization, theories attentive to the differential growth and development of movements are demanded. Resource mobilization approaches, for example, have begun to fill this void. Even these and other explanations of religious change, however, require more attention to the affinity between the "official" religion of institutions and the "popular" religion of the people--a topic almost totally neglected in the American literature, yet a critical dynamic in the "consumerism" of expressive, religious individualism (see, for example, Marler and Roozen 1993).

Finally and perhaps most important, if we are correct about the increasingly diverse and subjectivistic modes of individual religious construction and expression in the United States, then students of religious change need to give much more attention to the relationship between individual biography and the choice of religious expression. Attention must also be given to the social-psychological implications of privatization. Approaches to the former, often embedded in broad social class and secularization constructs (e.g., Martin 1978) seem inadequate for interpreting the contemporary situation in the United States. Privatization issues appear to hinge on whether or not it is true that increasing numbers of people hold what Roberts (1984: 258-60) refers to as a "multiple, narrow-range vector worldview" (viewing life as having many separate and distinct realms) rather than a single, integrated, "wide-vector worldview." For either type of world-view, we need to understand the role and function of religion. The assumption of most contemporary social theory appears to be that modernity pushes toward the former, and any religious construction--whether deductive fundamentalism or inductive New Age mysticism--toward the latter as a reaction against the psychological intolerance of psychic fragmentation. Yet it appears that at least a majority of the post-war cohort are neither collapsing from psychic fragmentation nor opting for either of the two polar extremes of contemporary American spirituality. If such is the case, then the vaguely privatized and weakly-integrated faith we have identified may in fact represent the dominant style of the post-war generation's religious construction and expression.

4

Tradition and Change
in the Nordic Countries

Susan Sundback

Introduction

Concentrating on "establishment" religion makes it easy to treat the five Nordic countries as a whole. Only there (besides the northern parts of Germany) did Martin Luther's sixteenth century separation from Roman Catholicism become a decisive and dominant social movement for centuries afterwards. The Nordic reformation was originally a matter of religious content more than of form. Protestantism was somewhat paradoxically made the state religion, imposed on the structure erected during the Catholic era.

The peoples of Denmark, Iceland, Finland, Norway and Sweden were separated religiously from the predominant Catholic culture of Europe. Internal similarities arising out of geography, history, the closely-related Scandinavian languages, and the ancient Nordic legal system were further enhanced by a distinctive, common faith.[1] At first through force, and later through tradition, Lutheranism became the only fully legitimate form of religious expression in the region.

The Nordic reformation ended the power conflicts between the church and the rulers. The nations that coalesced after the conversion to Lutheranism were governed by the secular power and the church in a symbiotic relationship, one in which the church was clearly subjected to the authority of the state (Allardt 1991:38). If the secular influence in the formation of the Nordic societies can be said to have affected social structures and forms, then the church's influence was long seen in the region's worldview and culture. Until the advent of modernization in the nineteenth century, the culture of the Nordic countries was extremely homogeneous.

There have been important religious expressions of the tremendous social change that has taken place since modernization started. The original Lutheran culture developed in an agrarian society which has disappeared due to urbanization and industrialization, thus the Lutheran churches have been steadily pushed to the margins of Nordic society. Fragmentation and secularization of the traditional worldview is far advanced, and is apparent in any comparison to other "Christian" nations.

Nonetheless, at the beginning of the 1990s, the rate of Lutheran church membership ranged between 88 percent (Finland) and 96 percent (Iceland), and all majority churches remained in a favored position compared to the other religious alternatives. Obviously, today's Lutheranism is very different from the Lutheranism of pre-industrial Nordic society. It is equally clear that the Lutheran churches are seen by the bulk of the Nordic peoples as the central bearers of tradition and cultural identity. Of course, there are those who view the church as hopelessly old-fashioned, while others respect the complex symbolic function the church serves for individuals and for Nordic society. However, most people seem not to think of the church at all, taking for granted that it is there and always will be there, just as it always has been.

This paper raises some questions regarding the future of the Lutheran church by looking at the religious change that has taken place during the lifetimes of the first generation to grow up after World War II. The large cohorts born in the 1940s could be described as the first generation without memory of the old, local society in which the church was insinuated into all aspects of social and everyday life (Bäckström 1989:13). This post-war generation grew up in an environment of material plenitude that had never existed before. During its youth, the Nordic welfare states gradually took over all the social functions that the church had fulfilled in earlier periods. The church was left with a narrowly defined religious and ceremonial task, totally separated from other aspects of everyday individual and social life. The 1968 youth protest was partly directed against the Lutheran church, not so much because of its religious principles as because of its perceived association with political and cultural conservatism.

The processes by which the Nordic Lutheran national churches have adjusted to modern, urban social life have shown tendencies to increased differences between the Scandinavian countries as far as the institutional arrangements between church and state are concerned (Gustafsson 1985:238-249). This fact, however, will not be a main concern of this paper since its emphasis is on a specific generational relation to the dominant religion, which is still the Lutheran church in all the Nordic countries. Indeed, it can be argued that general Scandinavian living conditions have actually become more similar during the twentieth century. The purpose of adopting a pan-Nordic perspective in this paper is not only motivated by the historical religious factor but also by the common institutional and structural traits of the modern Scandinavian countries (Allardt 1991:39-42).

Due to the insufficient supply of data on religion in Iceland, the smallest Nordic country, it will be mostly neglected. The fact that sociology of religion in the post-war period has achieved a more prominent position within higher education in Sweden and Finland than in Denmark and Norway also explains why some of the national comparisons in this paper will be limited to Sweden and Finland.

Finland is the most eastern Nordic country and a bridge between Scandinavia and Russia. This fact has always colored Finnish history. After its separation from Sweden in 1809, Finland was an autonomous region of Russia until it became independent in 1917. Although its political and social development was long marked by more conflict and drama than in the other Nordic countries, Finland's general social development since the 1960s has fit the Scandinavian pattern (Alestalo 1986; Alestalo and Kuhnle 1984). During the nineteenth-century Russian period, the Finns' Lutheran identity remained strong on a collective level, although Orthodox Christianity was made the second state church in Finland.

The Social and Religious Change

Increasing Pluralism

The Lutheran homogeneity of the Nordic peoples is not only an outcome of the lack of real religious alternatives or of the authoritarian political rule of preceding centuries. It was also the result of limited ethnic and social differentiation in a sparse population spread over a large territory. In 1900, the total population of all five countries was 12.5 million, half of today's population of 23 million (YNS 1988:35). The Lutheran religion in the old state/church system was not totally monolithic. From the beginning, there was space for differentiation within the church in the form of a high level of parish (local) autonomy. The tolerance for popular religious movements within the church increased, with some differences between the countries, in the nineteenth century (Ottosen 1986).

Religious freedom has existed since the middle of the nineteenth century in Denmark and Norway, since 1915 in Iceland, since 1923 in Finland and, officially, since 1951 in Sweden (although it existed in practice earlier). The right to renounce Lutheranism has led, to a very marginal extent, to religious pluralism in the Nordic countries. However, neither the free churches of the nineteenth century nor the new religions of the post-

TABLE 4.1: Foreign Citizens in the Nordic Countries in 1988

	Total population	Foreign citizenship No.	%
Sweden	8.4 million	421,000	5.0
Norway	4.2 million	136,000	3.2
Denmark	5.1 million	140,000	2.7
Iceland	252,000	5,000	2.0
Finland	5.0 million	19,000	0.4

(YNS 1989/1990:36,38)

war period have been able to recruit former members of the state churches to any large extent. Most of the disaffiliated have chosen to stay outside of all religious registration (Statistical Abstracts of Sweden 1990:402; SE 1991:13; SYF 1990:37; YNS 1990:103; Robbins 1988).

Immigration during the post-war period has proven to be the most important factor producing religious pluralism. Sweden, Norway and Denmark have been the major recipients of immigrants. In Denmark "only" 89 percent of its total population was Lutheran in 1990 compared to 91 percent of its official citizens. Less than 20 percent of the foreign citizens living in Denmark were members of the Danish Lutheran church and 70 percent had immigrated from countries outside of Scandinavia and the European Community (SE 1991:1-4).

In 1989, 93 percent of Swedish citizens were Lutherans compared to 89 percent of the total population (SCS 1989). Swedish data reveal a large increase in Roman Catholics and Orthodox/Eastern Christians from 1975 to 1989. Their religious impact, however, has been restricted since they are divided by their diverse ethnic backgrounds. Internal divisions are more pronounced among immigrants belonging to the Eastern Christian tradition than among those belonging to the Western Christian tradition. By 1989, the number of Muslims had reached 40,000 in Sweden, while there were 135,000 Roman Catholics. The Serbian Orthodox church constituted the largest Eastern church with 26,000 members (Skog 1989).

Although religious pluralism is increasing with immigration, this is a fact which probably will be of greater importance in the future than it has been during the lifetime of the post-war generation. The alternative churches and religions serve a cultural identity-focussing function among the ethnic immigrants similar to the traditional function served by the Lutheran church among native Scandinavians. This function is eroded primarily by the secularization process.

Secularization in the Post-War Period

The development of a more differentiated society was originally dependent on the industrialization of the economy. Secularism and the creation of a non-religious culture were important ingredients in the pre-war period, but they were processes occurring outside of the churches and mostly limited to small groups of intellectuals and political radicals. "Religion" was widely identified with the national church.

The emancipation of "religion" has clearly advanced in the post-war period at the same time as secular and "rational" values have gained legitimacy over the traditional religious values preached by the church. As a result, the function of national integration performed by the Lutheran churches is no longer rooted in the religious commitment of the people, but reflects the social function of state Lutheranism as a building block of the national identity.

The fission of the religious field into "real religion" and "cultural religion" is a process transforming the national churches. While "really religious" people can be found both inside the churches in revival movements as well as outside in free churches and new religions, the "culturally religious" are mainly the passive Lutheran members.

Cultural religiosity is strongly oriented towards the church and its civil religious and social function as the "national" church. However, an acceptance of the principle of religious freedom and secular values is integrated into this loyalty to tradition and the church. Strong religious commitment is not a necessary component.

In contrast, the "really religious" pay little attention to the church as an historic and social institution. The highly committed can be found both inside and outside of Lutheranism. Some dedicate themselves to seeking the "true Christianity" or "true Lutheranism" while others embrace renewal and syncretism. They are united by the effort to live according to a religious or spiritual worldview.

Although grossly simplified, the demise of the traditional religious homogeneity is sketched out in Figure 4.1. The economic stages represent gradual transformations of the economy. Industry was not fully developed in 1900 and the dominance of the service sector is more characteristic of the 1980s than the 1950s. Changes have been similarly gradual in the religious and cultural spheres.

Religious activity had already diminished by the turn of this century. Regular church-goers were by that time already a small minority. Nonetheless, changes in the religious field and in religion were significantly more dramatic after the World War II. This can be demonstrated by examining changes in belief patterns and the increase of disbelief. It has become relevant to question whether religion is still even a unifying element in Nordic culture. The Lutheran church obviously

FIGURE 4.1: The Breakdown of Lutheran Cultural Unity

Economic stage	Historic period	
Agrarian	Lutheran unity	Pre-1900
Industrial	Split between church and secular culture	1900 - 1950
Service	Split of concept of religion into "cultural" and "real" religion (Further emancipation of secular culture)	1950 -present

continues to be a widely supported institution, but its religious authority has seriously declined. One effect of secularization has been that the normative contents that used to be incorporated in the concept of "religion" are now absent for a great majority of people.

The collapse of religious dogmatism is seen in both the tendency towards religious syncretism among the "new" religions and in the tendency towards secularism in the civil religious functions of the Lutheran church (Gustafsson 1984:20). Of course, it is indisputable that the Nordic mentality has been shaped by church teachings even when the specific religious dogmas have lost authority. Ole Riis (1989:144) has suggested calling the general Nordic worldview after World War II, "Protestant Humanism."

Formal church membership is no indicator of individual religiosity measured as adherence to traditional Christian belief or behavior patterns. However, the argument is not that the Lutheran churches have lost all religious characteristics through a process of inner secularization. Rather, the point is that the national churches, in order to preserve their positions, have had to adjust to the conditions created by modernity. The secularization of society has primarily meant that the historic state-church system has been dismantled, although not completely dissolved. The close connections between the triad of the people, the church, and the state have survived in the "folk-church," that is, the state-supported church, which is open to *all* citizens and respects the secular ideal of religious freedom.

With increasing voluntarism on the individual level, the national churches have lost their authority in politics and over individual minds. They have had to accept growing heterogeneity among their members not only regarding lifestyles, but also regarding attitudes towards central Christian beliefs and religious behavior which have traditionally been defined by the churches.

There is no justification for assuming that members of the national churches will exhibit more religious tendencies than non-members. Indeed, it can be argued that the search for religious values has been regarded as a major motive for leaving the Lutheran church. Data from different studies, however, support the impression that church membership generally is connected with the ambition to live a respectable life and an adherence to moral values rooted in the religious tradition (Sihvo 1988:88; Pettersson 1991:283, 288).

In most comparative studies of religion in the Nordic countries, Sweden and Denmark appear as more secularized than Finland and Norway. This has been shown both in regards to the social position of the Lutheran church and in terms of religious attitudes (Gustafsson 1985; 1987). The full explanation for this cannot be given here, but it is plausible that the relationship between the church and the people during the eruption of democratic movements in the nineteenth century developed national idiosyncrasies in each of the five Nordic countries. How each national church adjusted to the breakdown of authoritarian society and the threat to the structural axis between the church and the king/aristocracy, as well as national variations in traditional popular support for church religion, are probably factors in explaining why the role of secular ideas within the political system has been different in each of the five Nordic countries during this century (Martin 1978:23, 33-36).

The continued relative importance of revival movements within the national churches is the clearest evidence of a democratic tradition within the Finnish and the Norwegian Lutheran churches. Such movements have played no comparable role within the Church of Sweden. In Denmark, their influence has been slight during the twentieth century (Ottosen 1986). Finland became a republic in 1917, more than 100 years after its separation from Sweden. Norway separated from Denmark in 1814, when a Norwegian constitutional monarchy was established together with a democratic constitution. The Norwegian revivalism of the nineteenth century was a democratic movement which successfully worked for increased religious liberalism within the church. Politically, it was an expression of the mobilization of the peasants (Ottosen 1986:59-69). Similar interpretations have been made concerning the Finnish revivalism of the last century (Suolinna 1975:36).

It is plausible that the relative religious traditionalism of Norway and Finland reflects a lesser degree of urbanization. In the early 1980s, the percentage of rural population was 29 percent in Norway and 24 percent in Finland (1985) compared with 16 percent in Denmark, 17 percent in Sweden and 10 percent in Iceland. The share of the working population living off the primary economy (agriculture/fishing/forestry) was 13 percent in Finland and Iceland, eight percent in Denmark and Norway and only five percent in Sweden. The population density was by far higher in Denmark than in the other four Nordic countries (YNS 1988:49; 1989/90:44, 48).

The Post-War Generation

Demographic Facts

The so-called baby boom cohorts that were born after the end of World War II were a visible phenomenon in the Nordic countries but not of the same demographic importance as in the United States. The temporary post-war increase in nativity was more distinct in Finland than in the other Scandinavian countries. In Sweden and Denmark, the baby boom started earlier in the 1940's. While the Swedish birthrate had declined considerably by the early 1950s, birthrates remained relatively high in Denmark and Finland during the first half of the 1950s. The main post-war hump in nativity occurred in Iceland in the 1950s and in Norway as late as the 1960s (Wiman 1978:85; YNS 1980:34).

In 1987, the largest five-year cohorts in the Nordic population as a whole were those born from 1943 to 1947 and those born from 1948 to 1952. The largest age category at that time was the 30 to 34 year-olds (7.7 percent of the total population) and the second largest category was the 35 to 39 year-olds (7.6 percent) together comprising 15.3 percent of the population. The 20 to 29 year-old age group comprised 14.9 percent and the 10 to 19 year-olds comprised 13.7 percent of the total Nordic population in 1987 (YNS 1988:36).

If we include in the post-war generation those who were born before World War II but who primarily grew up in the post-war period, then the older baby boomers who were born before 1948 had all passed 40 years of age by the beginning of the 1990s, while the younger baby boomers were approaching 40.

It could be argued that the political and cultural unrest associated with the youth of the Western post-war generation was to some extent a natural effect of their great numbers. The expansion of the educational system as well as increases in jobs and housing became important political goals by the 1960s since they addressed the basic needs of these large cohorts. The baby boomers themselves had to face hard competition for entrance to the kinds of education and jobs that were held in high regard. The competitive system necessarily emphasized the unique attributes of each individual. Success and failure tended to be seen as a consequence of the uneven distribution of personality traits. The majority of the post-war generation had to accept frustration with either the education or the job they got in the place that which they had dreamed of (Wiman 1978).

The impact of the large, post-war cohorts became obvious on a cultural and political level as they began to reach adulthood at the end of the 1960s. Generational conflicts wracked the whole Western world. Radical youth emerged in every Nordic country. A significant trend was a sudden rise in the amount of annual withdrawals from the national churches (Sundback 1991:76-83).

The Radicalism of the 1960s

The protests of Nordic youth in 1968 were a reflection of much more dramatic political events in Paris, London, Berlin and the United States, where university students and radical intellectuals rebelled against the "Establishment" and "bourgeois society." In a very European fashion, religion and religious values were given no place in these protests since the churches were viewed as hopelessly atavistic (Dobbelaere 1981:136). The notion of religion as "false consciousness" had been widely accepted in Europe, probably even outside Marxist groups, particular generations or even social classes. The quest was for political action and for personal fulfillment in the here and now, not for prayer or spiritual preparation for life after death.

Among those who believed in the potential of the individual and the power of political action, withdrawal from the church was a natural and not very dramatic step. Most of them, like their parents, had already come to see church membership as a mere formality. The Finnish church was the one Nordic church which had already experienced different waves of collective disaffiliation even before the protests of the late 1960s (Sundback 1986).

The international factors influencing the 1968 Nordic upheavals can explain the timing and the slogans of the radicalized, young, post-war generation. However, most of what actually happened is better explained with reference to the social and cultural context of the Nordic countries themselves. From this standpoint, factors can be identified that moderated and shaped the protests in ways distinctive to the national cultural settings.

A good example appears in the case of Finland. There the main protest was channeled through the political parties, particularly the sectarian, Stalinist manifestation of Communism. This trend was an outgrowth of the Finnish geopolitical situation, the political effects of the Cold War, the common fear of communism, the deep social cleavages present at the beginning of the century, bitter memories of the civil war in 1918, the lack of a leftist intelligentsia at a time when the universities experienced a larger influx of students than ever before, and other factors affecting the Finnish scene. The spectacular cultural influence of Communist dogma in Finland for a few years after 1968 had no parallel in other Nordic countries.

The increased rate of withdrawals from the Lutheran church was a phenomenon that occurred at the same time in all five Nordic countries. Statistical data indicates that anti-church opinions increased in all the countries although the particular motives for the disaffiliation behavior differed in each country. Norway seems to be the only country where the motives were explicitly related to religion, particularly Pietist Christianity, which has been a strong influence in Norwegian culture. Many young people were attracted to the "Human-Etisk forbund," an organization of free thinkers (Lundby 1985:185-186; Lundby 1988:64).

Withdrawals from the Lutheran churches occurred at a moderate rate, indicating that the trend did not generally concern others beyond the radicals of the post-war generation. Not even in Finland, where withdrawal behavior had been institutionalized within the leftist political culture, did the baby boomers ever leave the church at rates as high as those that occurred during the period of 1948 to 1959 (Sundback 1991:46). However, when the political protests were dissipated by the end of the 1970s, annual Nordic disaffiliation remained at a higher level than before 1968. This steady, though not very large, level of annual withdrawals has remained a constant trend, with one innovation--an increasing rate of re-entry into the church and an increasing participation in the baptism ceremony by teenagers and adults in conjunction with confirmations and church weddings. The rate of re-entries has varied between one-fourth and one-half of the annual number of disaffiliators. This is a general trend within Scandinavian Lutheranism[2] (Heino 1988a:27; Heino 1988b:46; Munck 1986:84; YNC; SCS).

The religious significance of membership in the Nordic Lutheran church has decreased during the post-war period. Movement in and out of the church is an indication that non-membership is no longer automatically judged as paganism. The trend towards returning to the church among the significantly secularized baby boomers and their children must, however, be explained. There seem to be two possible hypotheses, neither of which exclude the other. The first is the "life-cycle" hypothesis, which argues that religiosity increases with age. The second explanation focusses on "changes in the cultural climate" since the 1970s which have favored a return to conservative values. It should be noted that the obvious, though modest, trend in returns to church membership indicates only an external aspect of religion. Data on organizational registration do not illuminate aspects like belief or the nature of religious values. It should also be noted that thorough knowledge of the membership situation is possible due to the good availability of data.

Data on church rites of passage give a similar picture of the relative stability of Nordic religion. This is especially true of Christian baptism of children, confirmation and church burial. A tendency to

TABLE 4.2: The Church Rites of Passage in 1989 (Percent of the Total Population)

	Christening of newborns	Confirmation of 15-year olds	Wedding	Burials
Sweden	73	64	55	93
Denmark	80	83	55	94
Norway	79	78	59	94
Finland	90	93	79	over 90

(SCS 1990; SE 1991; YNC 1991; Statistics from the Evangelical-Lutheran Church in Finland 1990; SYF, 1990)

separate marriage from the religious sphere was already apparent before World War II, especially in Denmark. Only 64 percent of Danish weddings in 1938 took place in the church, a ratio which was much lower than in the other Nordic countries (Riis 1985:44-45; Sundback 1985:91-92; Lundby 1985:175-176).

The percentages in Table 4.2 would be higher if immigrants with non-Lutheran backgrounds were left out. The data therefore also reflect the relatively more restrictive Finnish immigration policy. The gradual loosening of the connection between rites of passage and the church can be seen either as a weakening of the whole folk church system (Vigestad 1981) or as an indicator of the continuing vitality of religious traditionalism in secularized society.

The picture of the ongoing religious change is totally different when the focus is placed on the inner aspects of religion--belief and values. The available data clearly illustrate the total dominance of secularization trends, and the post-war generation appears less bound by traditional church teachings than older generations. The two hypotheses presented above concerning returns to membership gain little support when we examine the worldview of the Nordic peoples. Valid conclusions as to what really is happening within overarching cultural meaning systems are difficult to draw because of a considerable lack of data and the privatization of all normative aspects related to worldview and lifestyle.

Secularization and Socialization

Data on religious belief reflect the position held by religion in the social context of individuals as well as the religious values, or lack thereof, that have been internalized during primary socialization. There is a dialectical relationship between society, culture and the individual under which individuals in a certain context express similar attitudes (Yinger 1970). In the international literature, the family has often been regarded as the central agent in religious socialization. However, due to the specific conditions created by the traditional union between state and church in the Nordic situation, the role of the official cultural institutions, especially the compulsory schools, has had an even more direct effect on the contents of religious socialization. What people should believe was formerly decided in an authoritarian way over which the Nordic family had little control. Consequently, the effects of secularization of societal institutions such as the schools have had a direct impact on individuals. Also, the privatization of religion has moved the responsibility for normative issues to an institution generally little prepared for it, the family.

The decline of state support for Lutheranism has favored the development of a liberal and individualistic interpretation of Christianity. The specific "Protestantism" of Lutheranism has until recently been a quality cherished mostly by theologians and pietist revival movements that never fully accepted the strong state-church system.

The increasing religious liberalism within the folk churches has underlined the need for individual decisions about personal religious identity. The setback in religious socialization within the family and society (particularly the schools) after World War II has created further insecurity regarding institutional religion and has undermined "religious knowledge." International as well as Nordic research supports the hypothesis that individuals who have been socialized in the traditional religious culture have tended to choose between conformity and non-religiosity, while those who have not been socialized in any kind of organized religion tend to be more open to religious alternatives and religious seeking. Although empirical data are scarce, it is obvious that alternative religiosity, especially within the New Age sector, has become more prevalent than the limited number of formal religious organizations reveals. The new religiosity is to a large extent concentrated in the more cosmopolitan, large cities.

The decline of religious content in the culture has been similar in all Nordic countries. Existing institutional variations should be explained historically and are important determinants of the distinct national patterns appearing among aggregate data on individual belief. The decline of Lutheran religious socialization through the school system has been greater in Denmark and Sweden than in Norway and Finland (Gustafsson 1985;

Riis 1984).   This trend can be illustrated through examining post-war developments in Sweden and Finland.

Case Study: Finland and Sweden
Institutional differences between the five Nordic countries already existed during the socialization of the pre-war cohorts. The use of Luther's little catechism in schools was resolved in Sweden by 1919, thus marking a transformation from dogmatics to Biblical material and a pedagogical view of religious education. This reform did not take place in Finland until the 1950s.   In both countries, the Lutheran church itself followed the development of the school subject.   The use of the catechism in the preparatory classes for confirmation lost its traditional compulsory status in Sweden during the 1960s and in Finland during the 1970s (Dahlgren 1985:221-223; Sundback 1985:97).

The socialization of the Swedish post-war generations took place while religion as a subject in the compulsory schools was changing. The confessional contents were phased out gradually from 1950 to 1980 and replaced with "objective religious education" which included study of other religions.   The most important changes took place in 1962 and 1969 (Dahlgren 1985:222-223). The younger Swedish cohorts have grown up in a period when the Lutheran element was absent from the schools. Developments in Finland have been different--religion as a subject in the compulsory schools is still supposed to reflect the institutional religious belonging of the attending children.   This means than nine out of ten Finnish children today are still to some extent socialized to the Lutheran heritage through the school system (Sundback 1985:74-75).   These differences in the religious context regarding the compulsory schools between, on the one hand, Finns and Swedes, and on the other hand, the older and younger Swedish post-war cohorts, are reflected in the next table. The data in Table 4.3 refer to the standardized questions of the 1990 European Values Study[3]. The comparability is somewhat diminished by the different national methods of collecting and processing the data. Interpretations must therefore be cautious and focus on the obvious trends in the comparisons between Finland and Sweden and between the generations.   (The central generation is the post-war generation represented by the cohorts that grew up during the first decades following World War II.)   A pervasive trend in the two national response patterns is that the Finns demonstrate more traditional religiosity than the Swedes. The detailed distribution of answers to the questions indicates that women in both countries exhibit personal religiosity more strongly than men. For example, 74 percent of Finnish women believe in God compared to 57 percent of Finnish men.   The gender differences, however, are less

TABLE 4.3: Religiosity in Finland (F) and Sweden (S) According to EVSSG 1990 (Percentage, F: N = 588;S: F = 1047).

	Generations*							
	All		Younger		Post-war		Older	
	F	S	F	S	F	S	F	S
1 Has received religious socialization in home	58	30	33	20	54	32	78	43
2 Is a religious person	54	28	36	22	54	30	66	40
3 Meaning of life is dependent on God	31	13	14	7	21	12	47	25
4 Believes in God	65	38	48	29	62	38	79	52
5 Believes in personal God	32	15	23	12	24	15	43	20
6 Believes in life after death	44	31	43	35	44	30	45	27
7 Believes in resurrection of the dead	37	19	35	15	34	20	31	25
8 Receives consolation and strength from religion	43	23	27	19	39	18	55	33
9 Praying is a habit	28	10	18	6	17	9	41	15
10 Denies personal importance of God	12	35	20	45	10	37	8	21
11 Never goes to church	14	48	25	57	11	41	9	40
12 Believes in spirit/"power"	46	44	45	43	54	45	40	41
13 Believes in reincarnation	24	17	20	20	30	14	23	12
14 Meditates/contemplates	25	33	16	28	14	34	39	42

* The age variable was originally divided into three categories in the Finnish data, with the youngest interviewed persons being 18 years old while it was divided into five categories in the Swedish data, with the lowest age being 16 years. The proper post-war generation was the 35-49 year-olds in the Finnish, and the 40-49 year-olds in the Swedish material. The younger generation is referred to as "younger," while the pre-war cohorts, those who were at least 50 years old in 1990, are referred to as "older."

important than the national patterns. Belief in God was reported by 43 percent of Swedish women and by 33 percent of Swedish men.

The age distribution indicates that traditional religious behavior increases with age more than does unconventional religiosity. The impact of age is debatable in items 6 and 7 concerning general belief in life after death and the more specifically Christian dogma of resurrection of the dead. Responses to item 13 show that the non-Christian belief in reincarnation is more widespread among the post- than the pre-war cohorts. All of these three items deal with death. An interpretation of the fact that age seems to matter less for attitudes towards death could rely on anthropological perspectives viewing religion as dealing with the "ultimate problems."

Table 4.3 illustrates a steady decline in traditional religiosity from the oldest to the youngest persons. The post-war generation, which in the Swedish material includes the 40 to 49 year-olds and in the Finnish material includes the 35 to 49 year-olds, exhibits a relative rather than an abrupt break with traditional religion. The post-war generation is in an intermediate position between the more religious, older, and the less religious, younger generation.

It cannot be determined, on the basis of these data, whether the post-war generation's religiosity has increased because of increasing age or because of the fact that it was socialized in a less secularized context than its children have been. As has been shown above, the socialization hypothesis cannot be discarded.

The national differences between Finns and Swedes are significant in 12 of the 14 items, pointing to the higher degree of secularization and de-Lutheranization of Swedish society. The two items that follow national patterns "not at all" (12) or "little" (13) concern beliefs in a non-personal spirit/"power" and in reincarnation, beliefs that do not follow church teachings. The impact of national origin on all generations is much more pronounced regarding church-related religion than other religious expressions.

The importance of socialization to the religious tradition within the school, or the church itself through confirmation classes, has grown as the level of religious socialization provided within the family has declined (1). This is apparent in both countries. No group has received as much religious education in the home as the Finnish pre-war cohorts. The effects of religious socialization within the home are probably reflected in all other variables, perhaps most visibly in church attendance (11). Interestingly, belief in God (4) seems to be more common than expected considering the level of religious socialization in the homes, while belief in a personal God (5) is less common.

Confirming the hypothesis that normative Lutheran religious socialization has declined in both countries, the belief in an undefined spirit or power is least common among the oldest generations. This belief is also a forceful indicator of the complexion of religious belief in very secularized societies. In Table 4.3, this belief is the strongest indicator of religiosity among the Swedes. Meditation/contemplation (14) not necessarily connected with Christianity is also more common among the Swedes in all age categories.

Variations in the national response patterns are great regarding the definition of one's self as a "religious person" (2). The relative prevalence of affirmative Finnish responses could either mean identification with the

TABLE 4.4: Religious Participation in Different Age Groups in 1951 and 1982 in Finland (percent 1951 (n=1235); 1982, (n=962))

Age	Attending church service within fortnight		Reading the Bible during previous week		Praying during previous week	
	1951	1982	1951	1982	1951	1982
18-24	10	3	9	9	36	30
25-34	10	12	11	8	42	36
35-49	15	11	20	9	53	45
50	24	19	30	14	69	61
Total	16	12	19	10	53	44

(Lotti 1983:6-9)

institutionalized religious culture or personal religious interest. Responses to items asking whether religion gives consolation/strength (8) and regarding praying (9) as well as concerning the personal importance of God (10) support the interpretation that religion among the Finns is not just a matter of social conformity and external behavior.

A Broader Cultural Change

In a plethora of Nordic research, conventional religiosity has been proven to correlate with sex and age. Women and the elderly indicate more religiosity than men and the young (Gustafsson 1983:29; Lotti 1983:10; Riis 1990:6-7). However, there is no doubt that Nordic religiosity has decreased during the twentieth century and that this reflects a deeper change in the status of the Christian worldview and of the Lutheran church as its chief proponent. The differentiation and expansion of mass communication is one of the most important influences undermining the traditional church monopoly over formulation of the central values of the common worldview. It has been shown that in all Nordic countries, especially after the 1960s, religious items have increasingly been treated by mass media independently of the church. Other religions, as well as critical opinions of religion and Lutheranism, have been discussed more openly during the post-war period than before it (Gustafsson 1985:255-257). During this fundamental shift, church religiosity has decreased among both sexes and all generations.

The double effect on religiosity of age and time period is illustrated in two Finnish surveys on religiosity conducted in 1951 and 1982 (Table 4.4). The decline of religiosity was sharpest among the youngest cohorts, those 18 to 24 years old, especially concerning church attendance and listening to religious broadcasts, while more stability was exhibited concerning Bible reading and praying. People over 50 exhibited a general decline during the 30 years that preceded 1982.

Eva Hamberg (1990, 1991) has used unique Swedish panel material in which the same 713 individuals were interviewed in 1955 and again in 1970 to prove that the 1960s were not only a time of political and cultural reorientation but also a decade in which religion as a worldview and as a lifestyle component lost considerable ground. The decline of religiosity, especially involving Christian belief, was not only obvious between age cohorts but also *within the cohorts*. The decline in Christian beliefs between 1955 and 1970 was most pronounced regarding the belief in Hell, but was also very marked regarding the beliefs in Heaven, in God as the ruler of the world, in God as a controlling factor in individual life, and in Christ (Hamberg 1990:17). The repeated interviews did not support the hypothesis that religiosity increases with age, but it could be concluded that stability in religious attitudes and behavior was more typical of the older cohorts, especially in the case of those born during the first decade of the twentieth century (Hamberg 1990:23).

A Norwegian study concerning "authoritarian," but not particular institutional, religious values in 1957 and 1988 stressed the effect of cohort membership and discarded the explanation that the change that took place in the 1960s and 1970s reflected a general cultural shift affecting all age categories. Authoritarian values regarding work, socialization and politics remained important for the older respondents (Jessen 1990:356). Jessen, however, ignores the fact that traditional Lutheran teaching was authoritarian by nature, emanating from a hierarchical worldview. The indirect cultural link between authoritarianism and religion brings us back to the impact of early religious socialization and the relative stability of the religiosity of the oldest population.

It is of course possible that the period effect has been more pervasive in the religious than in the secular culture. Such an interpretation would be logical with reference to the direct effects of secularization and the conscious politics of reducing the influence of church religion in the Nordic societies (Gustafsson 1983). Lifestyles determined by religion have gradually been overtaken by lifestyles centered around other values (Zetterberg 1983:14-20; Riis 1990:4-5).

The 1990 European Values Study (EVSSG)[4] showed that 45 percent of the Finns and only 27 percent of the Swedes responded positively to the question of whether religion was important in their personal lives. A third of the Swedes but less than a fifth of the Finns answered that religion did "not at all" concern them.

In both samples religion was a much more important issue to those over 50, the pre-war cohorts born before 1940 (with the Finns still more "religious" than the Swedes). The national difference was least pronounced between the youngest generations, those under 35 in the Finnish study and under 40 in the Swedish study. This fact supports the starting assumption of this paper--that World War II marked a qualitative change in the religious history of the Nordic countries.

The fact that the change in religious attitudes is an aspect of a wider cultural change in values has been proven by Thorleif Pettersson (1988) in a test of Ronald Ingelhart's theory (1977) of a "silent revolution." Pettersson used the 1980 Swedish EVSSG data. According to Ingelhart's theory, the Western climate of values is undergoing change from "materialism" to "post-materialism." The post-materialists comprise the young and well-educated cohorts. According to Ingelhart's theory, which stresses the effects of socialization, period effects affecting all generations tend to be temporary (Pettersson 1988:65). This point is debatable, at least from a historical point of view.

Religiously the post-materialists differ from the materialists by being less interested in a Christian commitment. They are more often non-believers, alienated from established religions. Paradoxically, their interest in existential questions is higher than among the materialists. The post-materialist values have been described as a turning away from the Judeo-Christian heritage of Western culture (Pettersson 1988:71).

Pettersson found that post-materialism existed in Sweden in conformity with the general European pattern. Thirteen percent of the Swedes in 1980 could be classified as post-materialists and 24 percent as materialists. Post-materialist values were characteristic of those under 35 years of age (those born after 1945) while materialism was clearly typical of those who had reached 45 years (born before World War II) (Pettersson 1988:121-123). Corresponding to this result, it was also demonstrated that religiosity increased with age and declined with education. The young, well-educated, post-materialists were the least religious people.

The impression given above that the first post-war generation was in fact more religious than the following generation can be explained by the fact that as middle-aged people, its members have received low or mid-level educations and that among them are both those with a "materialist" and those with a "post-materialist" bent. The oldest respondents had, of course, undergone the least education and were most clearly "materialists" (Pettersson 1988:131-132, 153).

Pervasive Cultural Values

Comparative studies as a rule show the Nordic population to be the most secularized in Western Europe (Listhaug 1990:229; Pettersson 1988:94-96; Harding et al. 1986:36-47). With this in mind, should the still very high formal adherence to the national churches be viewed as an epiphenomenon implying that most Scandinavians have a false consciousness? Or, if the predominating post-religious worldview in Scandinavia can be properly described as "Protestant Humanism" (Riis 1989:143-144), is there a hidden relationship between the values of the general morality and Christianity?

According to Riis' (1990:16-18) argument, the persistence of social norms, which originated within a particular religious culture which has since lost much of its legitimacy, and which were spread by the Lutheran church, which has since lost much of its authority, may explain why the Nordic countries have not experienced moral breakdown and social disorganization as a consequence of secularization. However, one effect of the lost sacrality of the Christian worldview, besides an increasing ignorance of religious tradition is a spreading insecurity about the foundation of the common moral values.

Such insecurity becomes more obvious as the Scandinavian peoples come into deeper contact with other peoples and other religions. This interaction increases through travel, immigration, European integration and the globalization process. The world's integration may lead to two different developments in Nordic religiosity--on the one hand, an increased cosmopolitization, and on the other hand, a renewed interest in the basis of national culture and religion.

The assumed relationship between religion and morality is not unproblematic. Case studies of specific religious cultures have proved the connection to be complicated and multidimensional, and sometimes even non-existent (Yinger 1957:28-34). The factors affecting individual attitudes towards religious and moral questions must be even more complicated in a secularized situation.

Pettersson (1988:93-98) has shown that the comparatively high degree of secularization in Sweden, measured by declining trends in religious belief and religious behavior, has not led to extreme moral permissiveness or decreased interest in existential and spiritual questions. Religio-moral differences between Scandanavia and Europe are clearly related to the split between Lutheranism and Catholicism--there are obvious differences between Catholic and Protestant countries regarding religious behaviour. The Lutheran national churches have little authority over individual perceptions of existential meaning, morality, and spirituality. There is a kind of Nordic inclination towards a rationalistic view of religion and a skepticism concerning the supernatural.

Compared with other Europeans, the Scandinavians maintain a relatively strict morality (little permissiveness) regarding morally dubious behavior that is connected with social life (i.e., lying, cheating, stealing) while they are relatively more liberal (permissive) regarding private morality (i.e., sexual preference, abortion, divorce). The conclusion that social morality has remained fairly strict among the Scandinavians compared to other Europeans has been reached by comparing Danish (Riis 1990:16-18) and Swedish (Pettersson 1988:85-92) response patterns to the 1980 European Values study (Harding et al. 1986).

This general conclusion is sustained by the 1990 EVSSG data, which show that less than 15 percent of Swedes and 20 percent of Finns agree that the church can give correct guidance in individual or family-related moral problems. Although even fewer think that the church has solutions for social problems, a majority in both countries think it is legitimate that the church take stands on questions such as disarmament, Third World problems, racial discrimination, euthanasia and environmental problems. The legitimacy of church opinions on abortion, extra-marital relations, unemployment and homosexuality was also widely admitted in Finland and broadly acknowledged in Sweden. Less than a third of both samples agreed, however, that the church had the right to take a stand on government politics. In conclusion, the national church is still widely accepted as an agent in the formation of social morality, but it is denied legitimacy in the fields of private morality and secular politics.

The Scandinavian value structure must be explained in reference to the relative secularization of the Nordic countries, but also in reference to the cultural implications of Lutheranism which developed long before the onset of modernization and secularization.

Although Lutheranism was imposed on a basically Catholic structure of organization, religiously it has been closer to the Anglo-American tradition of allowing for greater religious pluralism than Catholicism. David Martin (1978:23, 59) lists as foundations of the secularization process of the "Scandinavian pattern" the relatively harmonious co-existence of church and state premised on the clear authority of the state over the church, and, contrary to the history of many other European countries, the lack of totalitarian and collective religious (Catholic) or pseudo-religious (Marxist) opposition to the dominant churches, enhanced by the individualism and a stress on individual conscience which is typical of Protestantism as a whole.

Subjectivism, individualism and sectarianism never developed as strongly in the Scandinavian cultures as in other Protestant areas because Lutheranism was made the state religion and given a supportive function within a hierarchical and monolithic state. The basic organizing principle of Lutheran congregations has always been territory, not belief. Still, the religious message, at least as expressed by Luther, stressed personal commitment and devotion to a lifestyle which was premised on Christian ideals.

Through the effects of secularization, marginalizing the church in society and weakening the status of the Christian world-view, and as a result of social trends furthering individualism, privatization and subjectivism, the religious morality connected with the individual has eroded faster than the morality regulating the social relations between individuals.

The main Scandinavian religious culture is linked to the national symbolic presence of the Lutheran church. Although this link has existed since the Reformation, the abandonment of the traditional state-church association has changed the theological complexion of the church. The "folk church" was introduced in opposition to the strong state-church link over a century ago (Heikkilä 1982). This movement asserted that Lutheranism was the religion of the national collectivity, but no longer by threat of force. It was assumed that individuals would remain loyal in spite of increasing religious freedom due to the integration of nation and society and the tolerance and inclusiveness of the church.

The most visible empirical support for the idea of the "folk church" is the high level of Lutheran membership and the persistence of church rituals at important turning points in individual lives. However, this church ideology finds little other support today. Large segments of the Nordic population have been alienated from the religious activities of the church. Global integration has weakened the positions of all national institutions.

The far-reaching social and cultural changes of the twentieth century, especially those of the post-war period, have made the idea of the "folk church" less convincing. Today most Scandinavians seem to accept the church-related civil religion more than the traditional teachings of the church. Individuals tend to renounce formal church membership either because they do not hold religious beliefs or because they look for types of spirituality which are not found in the intellectual and diffuse religiosity of the national church.

Grace Davie (1990b:467), in her discussion of religiosity in modern Britain, coined the expression "believing without belonging," referring to the phenomenon revealed by Gallup data that religiosity is more common than church membership and participation. British studies show that approximately 10 to 15 percent of the total population are church members in the "meaningful sense" of active parishioners (Davie 1990a:397-403; 1990b:457-462). In recognition of the information presented earlier in this paper, the hypothesis regarding the Nordic countries might at first glance be inversely stated as "belonging without believing." However, there is a problem even with Davie's provocative British hypothesis. Namely, how should we explain the phenomenon of "residual," "latent" or "nominal" allegiance to churches, which also characterizes a large majority of the British population? Even in Britain more than 70 percent of the population can be classified with reference to the prevailing religious establishment, and more than 60 percent are clearly Christian.

Davie admits that membership is an indicator of less church alienation than non-membership and predicts that the more religious belief develops separately from the church's worldview, the more nominal membership will also decline. This conclusion is supported by British data showing that declining nominal membership among 18 to 24 year-olds can be interpreted less as a sign of increased religiosity and more as a step on the path to no belief at all.

The high level of Nordic church members makes it more difficult than in the British case to ignore the possible religio-ethical implications of "residual membership" although the regularly church-going population is a small minority, comprising fewer than five percent (Gustafsson 1985:260; Sundback 1987:344). The popularity of traditional church ceremonies like rites of passage which frame the life of the individual and church attendance even by alienated members on certain occasions can be explained as aspects of the historic civil religious/community-shaping function of the church (Sihvo 1991:22-23; Petursson 1987:369-373). However, can we *a priori* judge the religious contents which are central to these cultural events as irrelevant?

Without accepting a description of the Nordic situation as "belonging without believing," the "residual membership" could be interpreted negatively as a sign of the advancing disbelief which has been demonstrated above. However, the widespread church membership could also be positively interpreted as an affirmation of "Protestant Humanism" and as a factor which to some extent is curbing the trend towards disbelief as indicated by the popularity of at least temporary contact with the church. The Lutheran church (as well as the other established religious organizations) remains the central institution, which by its very existence reminds even the most secularized individuals of the "religious dimension" of human life. In all Nordic countries, religion is something that is visible. There are many religious buildings, and religion is present in the mass media, schools, hospitals and other social institutions (Gustafsson 1988:461).

The argument that Christianity remains a central element in Scandinavian culture in spite of secularization also relies on the methodological weakness of religious surveys. The validity of standardized questionnaires in the study of religion and in comparative studies is usually problematic. A more fundamental critique is that interviews are bad measures of the social processes by which culture and tradition are transmitted. Religiosity is not fully described with reference to the belief or disbelief of the individual. The religious culture is maintained by social interaction and communication, especially between members of the same family. Religion takes on many social forms. Ritual is one of them. "Residual allegiance" cannot be explained with reference to individual belief. The explanation must include the notion that the church still fills a symbolic function for individuals living in a social context because of its role in the history and identity formation of Western society.

Concluding Remarks

This paper has dealt with the tremendous change the established national church has undergone in the Nordic countries during the lifetime of the first generation to grow up after World War II. It has been argued that the marginalization of religion has been particularly significant in culture and values, the sphere in which the worldview of individuals is shaped. Traditional Christian dogmas have been relativized and have lost the taken-for-grantedness that was still widely exhibited before the 1960s. During the last decades, the acceptance of alternative religions and the open critique of the Lutheran faith have been recurring themes in Scandinavian culture. The weakened support for traditional religious beliefs has affected all individuals regardless of their ages.

The post-war generation is now mostly past the age of 40. These people were the radicals of the youth revolt of the late 1960s whose leftist leanings included rejection of religion and the Lutheran church. From today's perspective, the radicalism of this generation's youthful period seems to have been a temporary expression of its age and a general ongoing cultural change which made this generation the herald of certain tendencies inherent in the modern, more secularized way of thinking. This generation's tendency towards political radicalism clearly vanished during the 1970s. The baby boomers with their cohort-specific experiences and attitudes will remain in a central position for years, at least within the Swedish, Danish and Finnish populations. Their "fall from faith" has been farther than that of their elders, but it is probable that their children will change the religious culture even more. Today this generation is a stabilizing factor largely supporting the kind of cultural religiosity which includes a positive attitude towards the Lutheran church without implying religious belief. Although this study has found little verification for the hypothesis that religiosity increases with age, it is possible to see political adjustment as an effect of increasing age.

The low religious participation of the post-war generation is not remarkable in the Scandinavian context. Church attendance had already declined radically. The difference between the post-war generation and preceding generations lies more in its socialization, which has taken place in a clearly secularized context. Religion and the church have had much more marginal places in their upbringing and education than for their parents. The reasons are largely to be found within the political system, which already by the nineteenth century had wrested the power to formulate social rules from the church. The opinion that the church should have no political influence on society has become firmly entrenched in the post-war era.

Another important change affecting differences in cohort experiences is related to the urbanization process. The pre-war generations grew up in rural milieus in which local identity was strongly built on the concurrence of church and society. The post-war generation was the first to grow up in a predominantly urban setting in which church and secular society were clearly separated and in which local identity was hard to establish.

In this respect, the post-war generation is the first to have been forced to consider its relation to the church and religion in a conscious way, a task not expected of the traditional agrarian populace. The need for intellectually legitimate motives for church membership has grown during the whole post-war era, forcing the Lutheran churches to adjust to the changed conditions in order to stay on "speaking terms" with the large majority of church members and potential members. Insofar as the future of the church is dependent on its legitimacy among the population, the decisive development will be among the younger cohorts that followed the post-war generation. One can speculate what the effects of the ongoing social change will be on the worldview of today's youth, but certainly it will be affected by the end of the cold war, the dissolution of the atheist Soviet superpower, and the integration of Europe and of global society. It can be assumed that the taken-for-grantedness of Christianity itself as a building block for Western identity will be maintained. Such a development will clearly be reflected in Scandinavia, where Christianity has been institutionalized through the specific national churches.

This paper has argued that the role of Lutheranism in the modern Nordic countries cannot be judged on the basis of interview data relating to individual religiosity. Such data give a much too narrow view of the culture and its religious roots. Another argument for this opinion is the discrepancy between theory and practice on the individual level. Widespread church membership and the continued acceptance of church ceremonies related to certain events in secular society, the most sacred holidays, and the rites of passage centered on the individual indicate a vitality in religious traditionalism that cannot be explained with reference to the level of belief. It is suggested that the explanation must be found outside of the "pure" religious function of the church and within a conception of its role in civil religion as the "sacred" legitimation of national social identity. The social marginalization of the church as well as increasing individual alienation from church-related behavior and belief tend, however, to weaken the civil religious function of the church.

Secularization effects have proceeded with different speed in the Nordic countries as has been shown above in the comparison between Sweden and Finland. If, or when, the civil religious function of the church ceases to be meaningful within the national cultures, there will probably be a speedy decline in the formal church loyalty that today still characterizes most Scandinavians. Such a development is dependent on political decisions taken by the Nordic parliaments regarding the future of church-state relations in each country. These decisions may create different national patterns and reduce the cultural and religious similarities that have resulted from the common Lutheran heritage.

Notes

1. Finnish, which is spoken by a large majority of the Finns, is not a Scandinavian language. However, the Swedish influence was very important historically in Finland, and Swedish is one of Finland's official languages. There is also a Swedish-speaking minority comprising about 6.5 percent of the population. It is because of this overlapping historical and religious heritage that Finland is treated in this paper as part of Scandinavia.

2. Literature and sources regarding membership and re-entry are for Iceland (Petursson, 1985:129; Petursson, 1988:115), Finland (Heino, 1988b; Sundback, 1991; SYF, 1990:78), Denmark (SE, 1991; Sundback, 1989), Norway (Lundby, 1985; Lundby, 1988; Vigestad, 1981; YNC), and Sweden (Sundback, 1986; SCS, 1989).

3. The unpublished EVSSG material is used with the kind permission of Prof. Thorleif Pettersson of Sweden and Dr. Harri Heino, director of the Lutheran Research Institute in Finland. The author is aware of the fact that the two sets of interviews were not conducted in the same way, which may have affected the results. The Swedish interviews were conducted in a traditional fashion while the Finnish respondents answered with the help of computers. However, it is still maintained that the trend revealed in the table reflects real differences between the two national cultures. Furthermore, any bias produced by the different methods can be assumed to work counter to the dominating trend in the comparison.

4. See endnote three.

5

The Post-War Generations and Institutional Religion in Germany

Karl Gabriel[1]

The united Germany of today presents an encounter between two very different systems of religion. This sudden juxtaposition in itself invites comparison. The country's former separation, however has created an inequality in the amount of data available for studying nationwide religious trends. Thus, due to the unequal amounts of available data, comparisons are possible only to a limited degree. As a result, this paper focuses primarily on church-oriented religion in the area that was formerly West Germany. To the extent that there is relevant data available, this paper will also deal with the situation in the area comprising what used to be East Germany.

In this paper, I will first provide a rough sketch of institutional religion in Western and Eastern Germany. Then I will examine the data concerning the relationship between the various post-war generations and institutional religion in both Western and Eastern Germany. A third part of this paper will address the question of how to interpret the relationship of the post-war generations to institutional religion.

Institutional Religion in Germany

Since the Reformation, the subsequent wars of religion, and the emergence of confessional divisions, Germany has had first three (Roman Catholic, Lutheran, Calvinist) and then two (Roman Catholic, Protestant) established ecclesiastical systems (Schilling 1988; Gabriel and Kaufmann 1988). The development of the German national state in the second half of the nineteenth century, fostered by Prussia, resulted in Roman Catholics becoming a minority. As a minority, Roman Catholicism developed a different organizational form than the majority Protestantism. Roman Catholics created their own socio-cultural milieu, maintained by a network of Roman Catholic institutions (Gabriel and Kaufmann 1980).

The end of World War II marked a profound change in the position of religion in Germany. In the new Federal Republic of Germany (West Germany), Protestants and Roman Catholics were roughly equal in number. Throughout Germany the migration of refugees led to the disintegration of the confessionally homogeneous population areas which had existed since the time of the Reformation.

In the 1950s and early 1960s, the churches in the Federal Republic attained a very prominent position. Of all the institutions, they were considered the least tarnished by National Socialism (Naziism). Figures for worship attendance were at a high level and continued to rise slightly (Köcher 1987:175). The number of people leaving the churches was at an historically low level (Pittkowski and Volz 1989:96). Practically the entire population participated in the rites of passage offered by the churches. The privileged position of the churches found expression in the fact that church taxes were collected by the state, large segments of the state school system were denominational in character, church-controlled religious education was a compulsory subject in every school, and the social work carried out by the churches received financial support from the state. The social doctrine of the churches, especially that of the Roman Catholic church, exerted a powerful influence on the social policy of the state. The prevailing mood among the population of the Federal Republic was conservative and reflected a preference for traditional values (Klages 1985).

In the late 1960s, the society of the Federal Republic underwent a profound transformation. A period of value changes shifted people's priorities toward personal and societal development, while at the same time reducing the importance of traditional value patterns. The established religions were affected first and foremost by this revolutionary change. Within a period of only five years (1968-1973), the number of people who attended worship on a regular basis decreased by one-third (Köcher 1987:175). The number of people leaving the church increased severalfold. School reform abolished the denominational character of the state school system. In the political arena, church influence declined. Church members displayed a growing detachment from the teachings and ethical norms espoused by the churches. Both established ecclesiastical systems were affected equally by this change (Feige 1990; Gabriel 1990).

In the 1980s, the pace of religious change slowed markedly. The number of people leaving the church decreased, and the figures for worship attendance were declining at a slow rate. However, the process of differentiation with regard to forms of membership continued in both established ecclesiastical systems. The monopoly of the established religions with respect to rites of passage remained largely intact except for certain tendencies toward disintegration in the large urban centers (Daiber 1988). At the other end of the spectrum, a form of religiosity emerged that cultivated closer adherence to the practices of established church religion. In between these extremes were the majority of church members. In certain circumstances and on certain occasions, they fell back on established religion, but otherwise they borrowed from the established religions as sources of material to fashion patchwork quilts of personal religiousness.

Today, out of the 61 million people within the territory of the former Federal Republic, about 51 million are still members of either the Protestant or the Roman Catholic church and thus belong to one of the established ecclesiastical systems. However, among the post-war generations there has come to be accepted a new relationship to established religion--a relationship which is markedly different from the relationship the older generations had to the established churches. This change will be the topic of the following section.

First, however, let us examine the state of established religion in the former German Democratic Republic (East Germany). In 1950, the German Democratic Republic had a total population of 18.3 million, of which 14.8 million were Protestant and 1.37 million were Roman Catholic (Reitinger 1990: 3ff). The last statistical yearbook of the German Democratic Republic (1990) reported 5.1 million Protestants and 1.1 million Roman Catholics (Statistisches Jahrbuch der DDR 1990:451). Polls conducted since then have shown that these figures need to be corrected downward. In a representative survey conducted in 1990 by the Allensbach Institute for Public Opinion Research, 32 percent of the total population claimed membership in a denominational body (Köcher 1990:25). It seems realistic to assume figures of about 23 percent for Protestants and just under 5 percent for Roman Catholics (Hannemann and Franke 1990; Pollack 1991). The largest segment of the population by far does not belong to any denomination. The biggest drop in membership occurred among Protestants during the first two decades of the German Democratic Republic's history, a period marked by severe political pressure on the churches. Up until 1978, the number of church members decreased by more than six million according to official figures. From 1978 on, the relationship between the socialist state and the Protestant church improved. Since that time, the level of church membership stabilized to a certain degree (Reitinger 1990; Pollack 1991).

Within the Roman Catholic church the drop in membership was significantly less severe. From the beginning, Roman Catholics withdrew to a greater extent from the mainstream of society and exhibited a greater immunity to repression by the state. Roman Catholics paid a price for this immunity, however, as they were consigned to a very marginal role in society and had no external impact whatsoever (Zander 1988).

In discussing the former German Democratic Republic, it is difficult even to call the Christian churches "established" religions. Rather, it was the atheism promoted by the state that displayed all the traits of an established religion. According to the *Handbuch der Jugendweihe*, a manual for the atheistic civil youth initiation ceremony ("Jugendweihe"), approximately 97 percent of the eligible youth in any given year since 1976 participated in the ceremony (Reitinger 1990: 34). Through 1990, the government's changing attitude towards the churches had little impact on the atheistic stance of the majority of young people. In 1989, 85 percent of students in the German Democratic Republic still described themselves as atheists, and only 6 percent called themselves religious (Friedrich 1990:27).

In united Germany, members of the Protestant and Roman Catholic churches together comprise about 73 percent of the total population (37.6 percent are Protestants and 35.6 percent are Roman Catholics). All indications today are that over the next few years both established churches will attempt to preserve their positions in the West, while in Eastern Germany they will attempt to regain their influence. Whether this attempt will be successful remains an open question.

Post-War Generations and Institutional Religion in Germany

Before presenting recent data on the relationship of the German post-war generations to institutional religion, I would like to make two preliminary remarks.

First, I include in the post-war generations all people born after 1946, that is, those who are presently 45 or younger. The available data do not always permit one to separate age groups according to this definition. Therefore, in comparing generations, this age boundary is somewhat loose. In the case of Germany, it seems natural to draw the dividing line between the generations according to their conscious experience of National Socialism, the war, and the immediate post-war situation. The post-war generations accordingly include those whose experience took place in a world shaped by the existence of two German states, the continually expanding availability of consumer goods, the establishment of a functioning democratic welfare state within the territory of the Federal Republic, and the establishment of a socialist regime within the domain of the former German Democratic Republic. These are some of the factors taken into account in differentiating between different generations of Germans.

The second preliminary remark concerns the kind of data. They are for the most part taken from polls conducted within the last few years. The value of such data, especially when it comes to religion, is justifiably a matter of debate. The main problem, in my view, lies in the fact that it is currently not possible to reach a consensus about an adequate concept of religion that is suitable for the social sciences (Kaufmann 1989:53ff). Fortunately, I am not dealing with the various forms of religiosity among the post-war generations but with these generations' relationships to the institutional religions. This is precisely where the public opinion research concerning religion is most illuminating. Almost without exception, such research assumes a church-oriented concept of religion and then examines to what extent, measured against set standards, those questioned prove and understand themselves to be religious or involved with a church. This research orientation is inevitable since institutional religion is still a dominant focus of the public discourse on religion. Even though the data presented below indicate a clear detachment of the post-war generations from institutional religion in Germany, this does not necessarily mean that the post-war generations are less religious (Luckmann 1967; 1991). Such a conclusion would require a consensus concerning a particular definition of religion among the social sciences that does not exist. What can be discovered empirically by public opinion research is simply changes in the status of certain historically conditioned social forms of religion. The question as to what such changes mean in terms of the overall religiosity of the post-war generations is a different issue than is dealt with here.

Church Membership

In the former Federal Republic, the differences between the generations regarding church membership are at first glance not very significant. Table 5.1 indicates that in 1982 the differences between those born up until 1952 and those born after 1952 were between 1 and 1.5 percent. It should be noted, however, that among the younger generation those who did not belong to any religious community already made up nearly 10 percent, wheras among the older generation this group was only 7.3 percent of the total.

Other figures from the same study indicate that the share of those not belonging to any denomination was disproportionately high among those born between 1948 and 1957. It is apparently the youth of 1968 who in the late 1970s caused the figures for those leaving the churches to multiply severalfold.

TABLE 5.1: Church Membership According to Age (in Percent)

	Under 30 (n=604)	*30 or Older* (n=2385)	*All Repondents* (n=2991)
Protestant church (without free churches)	44.4	45.4	45.1
Roman Catholic church	41.1	42.6	42.3
Protestant free church and other Christian religious communities	5.0	4.6	4.7
Non-Christian religious community	-	-	-
No religious community	9.6	7.3	7.8
of these:			
formerly Protestant	5.3	4.2	4.4
formerly Roman Catholic	2.0	1.6	1.6
Total	100.1	99.9	99.9

Source: ALLBUS, 1982; Lukatis and Lukatis 1987:125

There were significant differences between the generations with regard to inclination towards leaving the churches. While in 1986, 25 percent of the Roman Catholics between 16 and 44 indicated that they had at least once considered leaving the church, only 6 percent of Roman Catholics 45 or older said they had done so. Among the Protestant respondents 30 percent of those who were 44 years of age or younger indicated that they had previously considered leaving the church, while only 20 percent of those 45 or older fell into this category (Institut für Demoskopie Allensbach 1986:Table 24a, 25a). The most substantial generational difference is thus to be found among Roman Catholics. Within the post-war generations, denominational differences dwindle. While differences between Roman Catholics and Protestants still amount to 14 percent within the older generation, they shrink to 5 percent within the younger generation.

A look at the former German Democratic Republic reveals a completely different picture. Table 5.3 lists the actual figures for 1990.

Although 20 percent of those between 16 and 44 currently still hold membership in a denominational body, the same is true of 47.5 percent of those 45 or older and of 61 percent of those 60 or older. Of the post-war generations, 60 percent have never been members of a denominational body and 20.5 percent have given up their memberships. The former East Germany is thus characterized by the fact that the

TABLE 5.2: Membership in Denominations by Age (in Percent)

Age-groups	Total	Protestant	Roman Catholic	No denomination
18 - 24	11	10	11	11
25 - 34	19	19	17	31
35 - 65	52	50	54	50
65 or older	18	21	18	8
Total	100	100	100	100
n =	2846	1350	1264	232

Source: ALLBUS 1982; Pittkowski and Volz 1989:103

generations differ very sharply in their respective percentages of church membership and that among church members there is a distinct overall increase in the percentage of older people. The Protestant church is currently no longer losing members due to people leaving the church but primarily because of the increase in the percentage of older members (Pollack 1991:3).

The issue of church membership as it relates to the relationship between the generations is a strong indicator of the fact that the united Germany consists of two societies whose characters are very different and whose adaptation to one another will take a considerable period of time.

Participation in Rituals

With regard to participation in church rituals, we have to distinguish between participation in the rites of passage offered by the church over the course of an individual's life and a more or less regular worship attendance. The data of ALLBUS (1982) for the Federal Republic, which have been evaluated by Lukatis and Lukatis (1987), show clear differences in attitudes toward baptism, church weddings, and funerals between those born before 1952 and those born after 1952, but these differences usually do not exceed a 10 percent limit. Significant differences of 11 percent (Protestant) and 10 percent (Roman Catholic) were found among those people already married in terms of their attitude toward church weddings. The high figure for younger people who currently "do not care" about a church funeral could be explained by their age-related distance from death and dying. The overall picture shows that about three-fourths (Protestant) to four-fifths (Roman Catholic) of younger people participate in the rites of passage offered by the churches. It is

TABLE 5.3: Church Membership in the New Federal States (in Percent)

	Population total	Age 16-29	Age 30-44	Age 45-59	Age 60 or older
Hold membership in a denominational body	32	20	19	34	61
Have left the church	28	9	32	44	30
Have never held membership	39	70	50	22	9

Source: Köcher, 1990:25

therefore primarily the rites of passage that insure both established ecclesiastical systems in the Federal Republic a relative measure of stability.

In contrast to attitudes toward rites of passage, there are significant differences between the generations when it comes to worship attendance. With impressive series of statistical data, Renate Köcher (1987) has demonstrated that in both denominations the "generations drift apart" with regard to regular worship attendance.

Table 5.5 illustrates that in the late 1960s and early 1970s, a large number of people in the first post-war generation stopped attending worship on a regular basis. This happened equally in both denominations. The trend which emerged then has continued. In 1982, 22.5 percent of Roman Catholics between the ages of 16 and 44 indicated that they attended worship regularly, while among those 60 and older the figure was 54 percent. Worship attendance among those born between 1923 and 1937 fell between these two groups at 29 percent. In the late 1980s, this decline gained further momentum. In 1988, just under 20 percent of Roman Catholics between 20 and 45 indicated that they attended worship every or nearly every Sunday, while 47.5 percent of those 45 or older fell into this category (Institut für Demoskopie Allensbach 1989a:33ff). All available data indicate that the situation is similar within the Protestant church, but here the drop was less drastic due to the fact that worship attendance among Protestants has traditionally been at a lower overall level. This is indicated by the data of two studies by the EKD (Protestant church of Germany) from 1974 and 1984 (Table 5.6). In 1984, 4.5 percent of those born in 1950 or later attended worship on a regular basis, while 15 percent of those born before 1950 indicated that they attended worship every or nearly every Sunday.

TABLE 5.4: Attitudes Toward Baptism, Church Weddings, and Funerals, and Toward Respondents' Own Past Church Weddings, and Baptisms of Their Own Children (In Percent)

	Protestant		Roman Catholic		No Denomination		All Respondents	
	Under 30	30+	Under 30	30+	Under 30	30+	Under 30	30+
If getting married: Church Wedding desired?								
Yes	77.7	85.6	86.4	90.9	4.4	12.1	74.9	82.5
No	22.3	14.4	13.6	9.1	95.6	87.9	25.1	17.5
If already married: Had Church wedding?								
Yes	76.1	87.0	82.9	92.6	33.3	40.1	75.1	86.3
No	23.9	13.0	17.1	7.4	66.7	59.9	24.9	13.7
If children in the future: Baptism desired?								
Yes	77.2	81.0	89.0	89.8	15.2	29.7	74.6	76.9
Do not know	14.3	14.8	6.7	8.0	39.1	34.3	13.8	14.8
No	8.5	4.2	4.3	2.1	45.7	35.9	11.6	8.4
If children already born: Baptized?								
Yes	91.9	96.8	96.3	99.1	***	62.6	90.8	95.7
Not all	-	0.2	1.2	0.2	***	4.7	0.6	0.8
No	8.1	3.0	2.4	0.6	***	32.7	8.7	3.5
Church funeral desired?								
Yes	64.0	86.7	79.7	91.2	**	**	71.9	88.7
Do not care	31.6	11.4	16.3	7.4	**	**	23.8	9.6
No	4.5	1.8	4.0	1.4	**	**	4.2	1.6

**Question was not asked
***Figure negligible

Source: ALLBUS 1982; Lukatis and Lukatis, 1987.

TABLE 5.5: Regular Worship Attendance Among Roman Catholics and Protestants (in Percent)

| | *Attended worship regularly* | | | | |
	1952	*1963*	*1967/1969*	*1973*	*1982*
Roman Catholics total	51	55	48	35	32
Roman Catholics age					
16 - 29	52	52	40	24	19
30 - 44	44	51	42	28	26
45 - 59	50	56	53	46	29
60 or older	63	64	62	57	54
Protestants total	13	15	10	7	6
Protestants age					
16 - 29	12	11	6	3	4
30 - 44	7	10	6	3	3
45 - 59	13	16	11	7	6
60 or older	23	24	22	12	12

Source: Köcher, 1987:175

Belief in God and Self-Assessment of Religiosity

The International Value Systems Study 1981-82 revealed remarkable differences between the generations with respect to their reported belief in God. Among those between 18 and 39, 56.5 percent indicated that they believed in God, while 80 percent of those 40 and older gave that response (Köcher 1987:172). A survey in 1989 produced similar results: 62.4 percent of 16-44 year-olds indicated a belief in God, while among those 45 or older 79 percent fell into this category (Institut für Demoskopie Allensbach 1989b:Table 1a). The data in ALLBUS (1982) also indicated that the generations differed most widely in their responses about their respective ideas about God when the questions used language that paralleled doctrinal statements of the institutional religions. Thus almost an equal number of respondents between 18 and 29 affirmed and rejected statements such as "There is a God who seeks to be God for us," or "There is a God who revealed himself in Jesus Christ." About three-quarters of those over age 30 gave an affirmative response to such statements.

FIGURE 5.1: Self-Assessment of Religiousness by Younger and Older Respondents (in Percent)

Under Age 30 (n=603)

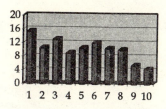

Religious --> Not Religious

Age 30 or Older (n=2383)

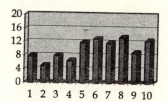

Religious --> Not Religious

However, the difference between the generations dwindled, with about three-fourths of all respondents agreeing with statements such as "Our life is ultimately governed by the laws of nature" (Lukatis and Lukatis 1987:137). The same trend applied to questions about the "meaning of life." Once again, there were only significant differences between the generations in responding to statements that reflected the religious formulations of the churches, such as "For me, life has a meaning only because God exists," or "Life has a purpose because there is still some kind of existence after death" (Lukatis and Lukatis 1987:139).

The International Value Systems Study 1981/82 revealed that the generations differed significantly in the concreteness of their notions of God. While in the Federal Republic 33.5 percent of those 40 or older affirmed the statement "God actually exists," the percentage among respondents between 18 and 39 amounted to a mere 17.5 percent (Köcher 1987:202).

When asked about the importance of God in their lives, the generations also responded quite differently. A survey in 1986 employing an 11-grade scale, ranging from completely unimportant (0) to very important (10), found that just under 14 percent of the 16-44 year-old respondents chose the 0 option, while only 5 percent of those 45 and older did so. At the opposite end of the spectrum, 31 percent of those 45 and older selected option 10, while only 14 percent of the younger age group did so (Institut für Demoskopie Allensbach 1986: Table 6a).

The next question concerns the trends that emerged when respondents were asked to assess their own religiousness. Lukatis and Lukatis also evaluated the ALLBUS (1982) data with respect to this question.

The two graphs representing the religious self-assessments of respondents under the age of 30 and those over the age of 30 reflect an inverse pattern as can be seen in Figure 5.1. The graph for the under-30 age group records a steady decline from the non-religious to the religious end of the chart and is the exact opposite of the graph representing those 30 and older.

Data collected in 1989 revealed the same trend. Among respondents between the ages of 16 and 29, 36 percent described themselves as religious, while 49 percent of the 30 to 44 year-olds did so. Within the 45 to 59 year-old group, the percentage increased to 58 percent and for those 60 and older it reached the 75 percent level (Institut für Demoskopie Allensbach 1989a:24). In this particular survey, respondents could choose between four response options: religious, not religious, decidedly atheist, and undecided. In surveys that have not included the alternatives "religious" and "not religious" among response options and instead only asked about personal attitudes and characteristics, far fewer respondents chose to identify themselves as a "religious person or a believer." Only 16 percent of those 16 to 44 did so compared to 28 percent of the 45 to 59 year-olds and 50 percent of those 60 and older (Institut für Demoskopie Allensbach 1989a:26). The data indicate that respondents in the former Federal Republic tend to avoid describing themselves as "not religious" given other alternatives.

A comparison between Eastern and Western Germany reveals differences of between 40 and 50 percent between comparable age groups regarding their beliefs in God. The differences between different generations are also more pronounced in Eastern Germany than in the West. While in Eastern Germany 68.5 percent of 16 to 44 year-old respondents said they did not believe in God, only 38.5 percent of those 45 and older fell into this category. The equivalent statistics are 17 percent versus 7.5 percent in Western Germany.

In Eastern Germany, only six percent of people who have left the church and two percent of those who never held membership describe themselves as religious. According to Renate Köcher,

> 38 percent of the total population in the German Democratic Republic, and 52 percent of the younger generation describe their attitude towards faith with statements such as: "Faith does not mean anything to me. I have no need for religion." In the former Federal Republic this group has a share of 12 percent among the total population, and 17 percent among the younger generation" (Köcher 1990:25).

Data gathered by the Zentralinstitut für Jugendfragen (ZIJ) (the Central Institute for Youth Issues) in Leipzig confirmed these results in principle.

TABLE 5.6: Belief in God: Comparison According to Age Groups Between the German Democratic Republic and the Federal Republic of Germany

	German Democratic Republic age groups				Federal Republic of Germany age groups			
	16-29	30-44	45-59	60 or older	16-29	30-44	45-59	60 or older
Yes	20	19	37	55	59	66	72	85
No	69	68	45	32	18	16	10	5
Undecided	11	13	18	13	23	18	18	10
	100	100	100	100	100	100	100	100

Source: Köcher, 1990

According to data from a survey conducted in 1988-89, 65 percent of apprentices described themselves as atheists and only 15 percent as religious. Among young blue-collar workers, the percentages were 64 percent atheist and 16 percent religious, and among students the figures were 85 percent and 6 percent respectively (Friedrich 1990:27). The difference between apprentices and blue collar workers on the one hand and students on the other is surprising when compared to Western Germany. There the percentage of those who describe themselves as religious is significantly higher among people who graduated from a secondary school than among those with lesser education (Institut für Demoskopie Allensbach 1986:40).

In contrast to Western Germany, the churches currently enjoy a high reputation in the new German federal states that were formerly East Germany. As many as three-fourths of the younger generation predict that the influence of the churches will grow over the next few years, and a majority foresee a revival of religion and faith (Köcher 1990:26). It is difficult to tell whether the churches are currently benefiting from a short-term boost derived from the role they played as part of the opposition during the revolution, or whether the churches will solidify a more prominent minority role in a society whose majority is secular and not explicitly religious.

Religious-Ethical Attitudes

Recent surveys in the Federal Republic that included respondent reactions to specific church values confirmed that the post-war generations are significantly more detached from church values than were preceding generations (Köcher 1987:233; Eichelberger, 1989:85; Institut für Demoskopie Allensbach, 1989a:42, 46). Especially interesting in this respect are the results of a 1984 study on "ethos and religion among executives" (Kaufmann et al. 1986). Examining about 400 variables, the study weighed the ethical convictions of 530 executives from southern Germany. A critical trend that emerged throughout the entire study was the difference between the post-war generation of executives born after 1945 and those who were older. Among the executives under age 40, for example, 55 percent were barely influenced by religion, 30 percent were nominal Christians, and only 15 percent were believers actively involved in a church. Among respondents 40 or older, 28 percent fell into the barely religious category, the nominal Christians were 40 percent, and the percentage of believers who were actively involved in the church was 31 percent (Kaufmann et al. 1986:259).

Differences between the generations were especially notable with regard to measures of ethical opportunism. The opportunism dimension gauged the predisposition to use any necessary means in the quest for material success, including dishonest ones, and to reject any ethical norms beyond "pure inclination." Figure 5.2 reflects that among those under age 40, 47 percent demonstrated a high degree of opportunism, 43 percent fell into the moderate category, and only 10 percent earned low ratings. In the 40 to 50 year-old age group, a significant shift in the ratio was already apparent, and for those 50 and older, the figures reveal 9.5 percent at the high end and 49 percent at the low end of the opportunism spectrum, a complete reversal of trends in the younger group.

The study also attempted to gauge elements of a non-religious ethos among respondents. Here too it was clear that as age decreased both religious and non-religious ethical predispositions decreased as well, while the ratings for opportunism correspondingly increased (Kaufmann et al. 1986: 272f). As Table 5.7 shows, the study developed a classification system of five different types of basic ethical predispositions. Again it was clear that the post-war generation of executives was the most religiously indifferent age group by far.

In summarizing the results so far, we see that all available data reveal significant differences between the generations regarding their relationships to the two established ecclesiastical systems. The post-war generations continued the traditions of the preceding generations only to a limited degree as far as religion is concerned. True, in the former Federal

FIGURE 5.2: Opportunism and Age

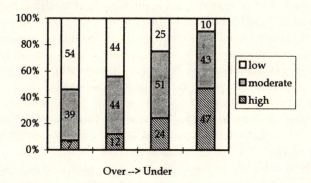

Over --> Under

Republic the post-war generation distinguishes itself only slightly from the older generation when it comes to church membership and participation in the rites of passage offered by the churches. However, with respect to their attitudes toward church membership and worship attendance, their reactions to statements of faith and values espoused by the churches, and their religious-ethical stances, they display marked differences from the preceding generations. The attitude of critical detachment from institutional religion increases sharply from the older to the younger generations.

In the context of the quite different social and ideological conditions in Eastern Germany, church membership has become a minority phenomenon. Here the churches have also lost the monopoly over providing rituals. However, similarities to tendencies in the West can be

TABLE 5.7: Religious Indifference and Age (in Percent)

C=.39			Age		
RELIGIOUS INDEX	*under 40*	*40- 50*	*50- 60*	*over 60*	*N=10 0%*
actively involved in church	12	20	50	19	100
connected with church	17	33	24	26	100
not connected to church, but Christian	21	31	33	15	100
not Christian, but ethical	26	39	23	12	100
neither Christian, nor ethical	47	34	14	5	100
all respondents	24	32	36	8	100

SOURCE: Kaufmann et al., 1986: 275.

observed, although in the East they are much more pronounced. It is now time to address the question of how to explain this rift between the generations with regard to church religion.

Interpreting the Post-War Generations'
Detachment from Institutional Religion

One interpretation which initially suggests itself can be discarded quickly as unsatisfactory, namely, that younger generations are naturally inclined to be less religious and involved in churches than are older ones. One need only look at the religious history of the Federal Republic to disprove this hypothesis. In the 1950s, younger people were by no means less involved in churches than the older generations. The prominent status that institutional religion enjoyed in the 1950s also undermines any claim that the change is part of a long-term process of secularization taking place in a more or less steady progression. What is needed is an explanatory model that fills the gap between the very general assumptions regarding the process of secularization in modern societies on the one hand and the actual characteristics of change on the other.

In my view, the patterns can be best explained by assuming a number of tracks, levels, and phases of different character throughout the process of modernization of Western societies (Beck 1986; 1991). The observed radical change in the relationship to institutional religion would then indicate the end of a particular pattern in the process of modernization and the appearance of a new phase in that process. My line of argument runs roughly as follows: in the Federal Republic, the 1960s and 1970s marked the end of a certain track of modernization which had its beginnings in the nineteenth century. This track was characterized by a complex mixture of traditionalism and modernity that in retrospect one can characterize as "semi-modern" society. In this "semi-modern" society, church-based Christian religion was able to achieve a surprisingly stable position in society in spite of the revolutionary changes that challenged its existence (Gabriel 1988). This was primarily due to two structural elements whose foundations were laid in the nineteenth century. One of these elements was that those segments of the population which continued to have a traditional character looked to church-based religion for protection. This resulted in a bond between traditionalism and attachment to the church. The second structural element was the formation of religious, church-oriented milieus on a denominational basis (Gabriel and Kaufmann 1980). A combination of these two elements influenced both denominations, the first being more significant in church-based Protestantism, and the second in Roman Catholicism. The churches were able to attract and retain those segments of the population that were less affected by the processes of modernization, and at the same time insulated these groups from the consequences of the uprooting processes of modernization. They thereby contributed to a social system that combined traditional and modern structural elements, one in which large-scale, ideologically-based groups played an important role. The change to a new level of functional differentiation was thus "cushioned" throughout by the existence of ideologically homogeneous segments within the social structure.

The post-war period in the Federal Republic produced, under special circumstances, a late flourishing of a "semi-modern" society with a traditional character in which institutional religion wielded an extraordinarily strong influence. This society was sustained by the generations who had lived during and between the world wars, and shaped by their experiences during the period of National Socialism. However, the extraordinary economic success that started in the late 1950s initiated a final phase in the structural pattern of this "semi-modern" society. The expansion of the industrial, market-oriented sector drew those segments of the population into the dynamic market process which had thus far not been involved in the market or the industrial environment. At the same time the milieus which had developed in the nineteenth century largely disintegrated due to widespread mobility processes (Mooser 1983; Kühr 1985).

A decline in traditionalism and the disintegration of milieus can thus be identified as the processes which led to the above-described rift between the generations regarding their relationships to institutional religion. The explanatory model of a new phase of modernization within a "semi-modern" society helps explain why the generations differ more in regard to institutional religion than in any other area. The unique occurrence of a late blooming of "semi-modern" society in the Federal Republic also explains why the difference between the generations is especially pronounced in the Federal Republic.

What the economic changes caused in the free society of Western Germany, namely the disintegration of the traditionalist and milieu-supported "semi-modern" society of influential churches, was accomplished even more thoroughly under the atheist political system of Eastern Germany. In fact, in spite of all the differences between both systems of religion in the East and West, one cannot fail to see certain structural analogies. However, in each case, such similarities were the products of entirely different factors.

Notes

1. Translated from the German by Reinhard Krauss.

6

The Case of the Netherlands

Leo Laeyendecker

Is the Netherlands still a Christian country? The answer is assuredly affirmative if one looks at the political influence of the Christian party, at the dominance of Christian schools and at the various Christian symbols that pervade the Dutch society and landscape. The answer is less clear, however, if one takes into account the decreasing formal membership of the Christian churches, the decreasing participation of church members in church life and the withering of the traditional Christian belief system (Schreuder 1990: 22).

The purpose of this paper is to provide a nuanced answer to our opening question, focusing particularly on the experience of the post-war generation. I first examine the aforementioned phenomena. I then discuss the concept of generations; the different time spans of social processes--long-term processes, conjunctures and historic events; and two important events which, in my view, had determinative influence on Dutch Catholics. Finally, I describe and analyze the religious differences between four generations during the post-war period.

Formal Church Membership[1]

A national census was conducted in the Netherlands every ten years from 1830 until 1971, with the exception of 1940. After 1971 protests against the census as an infringement of personal privacy grew in strength and an official decision was made to discontinue the censuses. Although the censuses only provide formal church membership figures, they are nevertheless important in establishing long-term trends as shown in Table 6.1.

TABLE 6.1: Church Affiliation as a Percentage of the Total Population

Year	Confessional Tradition			
	Roman Catholic	*Netherlands Reformed*	*Neo-Calvinist*	*None*
1849	38.2%	54.6		0.0
1859	37.1	54.9		0.1
1869	36.5	54.7		0.1
1879	35.9	54.5		0.3
1889	35.1	48.7	8.2	1.5
1899	35.1	48.4	8.2	2.3
1909	35.0	44.2	9.4	5.0
1920	35.6	41.2	9.1	7.8
1930	36.4	34.5	8.7	14.4
1947	38.5	31.1	8.6	17.1
1960	40.4	28.3	8.3	18.4
1971	40.4	23.5	8.7	23.6
1980	29.1	15.6	7.6	44.2

Source: 1849-1971 censuses; 1982 survey (Doorn and Bommelje 1983).

In terms of formal membership patterns the Netherlands represents an interesting exception to the rest of the West. The number of people who claim they are not affiliated with a denomination has steadily increased since 1859. In that year, dechurchment became visible for the first time, although the percentage of the non-affiliated amounted to only 0.1 percent of the population. This figure was the same in 1869 but started to increase in 1879 when it rose to 0.3 percent. Thirty years later the percentage had risen to five percent. Over the next decade, it rose to 7.8 percent and in another 10 years it had doubled. By 1947, 17.1 percent of the population claimed non-affiliation; in 1960, 18.4 percent and in 1971, 23.6 percent.

Since 1971 our only gauge of national church affiliation is survey data. The data show affiliation fluctuating somewhat, but a clear trend is visible: there is a steady and accelerating increase in non-affiliation to the church among the population in general and among the younger segment of the generation in particular. According to a large telephone poll of the Dutch population over 16 years-old (N = 20,000) conducted in 1982 (Doorn and Bommeljé 1983) the percentage of the non-affiliated was 44.5 percent. In 1986, the percentage of the non-affiliated in the overall population had risen to about 50 percent (*Sociaal en Cultureel Rapport* 1986: 418).

This situation was and is very exceptional. In the 1950s, for example, the percentage of non-affiliation amounted to 3.5 percent in West

Germany and that was comparable to the situation in Scandinavia, Switzerland and Ireland. Although percentages of non-affiliation are rising in the other Western countries at the moment, the differences are still remarkable. In the 1981 survey of the European Value Systems Study Group the percentage of non-affiliated in France was 16, in Belgium 15, and in Canada 13. In Great Britain, West Germany, Italy, Denmark, Spain, Ireland, Northern Ireland, Norway and the United States, the percentage remained below 10 percent (Halman 1991: 83).

Although J. P. Kruijt (1933) made a thorough and now classic study of the processes of dechurchment, there has been little work from a comparative perspective examining why these processes are so pronounced in the Netherlands. The only explanation given so far is that the tie between church membership and national identity is rather weak in the Netherlands compared with the situation in other countries (Staverman 1954: 41-49). It is rather strange, to say the least, that the search for more nuanced explanations has been neglected. Research has concentrated on church members, leaving the non-affiliated a relatively ignored group.

Recent decreases in membership are evident in each of the three largest denominations--the Roman Catholic church, the "Netherlands Reformed" church and the "Neo-Calvinist" church. The denominations' longer term trends, however, differ significantly. The Netherlands Reformed church has experienced a steady membership decline since 1859--from 54.9 percent of the Dutch population in 1859 to 15.5 percent in 1982 (with percentages of 44.2 in 1909, 31.1 in 1947, 28.3 in 1960 and 23.5 in 1971). It could be argued that, until recently, it was the Netherlands Reformed church which felt most of the impact of the general trend to non-affiliation, and that the long term processes affecting this denomination were not blocked by any specific factors such as was the case with Roman Catholicism and Neo-Calvinism.

The percentage of Roman Catholics was 37.1 in 1859, but fell to 35.0 in 1909. From 1909 until the early 1970s a slow but steady *increase* is perceptible (36.4 percent in 1930, 38.5 percent in 1947 and 40.4 percent in 1960 and 1971). The upward movement in this trend is due to the specific situation of Roman Catholicism in the Netherlands. Beginning in the sixteenth century when Calvinism gained a foothold in the Netherlands, Roman Catholics were in the position of a minority group. This status began to change in the middle of the nineteenth century through an emancipation process which expanded over the course of the twentieth century. Roman Catholics, however, continued to exhibit a kind of frontier mentality that manifested itself, as just one example, in a relatively high birth rate (van Heek 1954). They also formed a closed community with their own organizations based on Catholic convictions and practices. They became a so-called "pillar" inside of which social interaction and social control was relatively strong.

The Catholic figures, however, are somewhat deceptive. They show only net effects and hide the ominous fact that there was considerable defection by Catholics which was compensated for by their relatively high birth rate. Since the 1960s this situation has changed due to various coinciding factors. Their historically high birth rate began to approximate the average national birth rate, and defections continued to increase. The lowering of the Catholic birth rate resulted from the "completion" of the emancipation process after World War II. The Catholic community began to lose its cohesion and it became involved in a process of "de-pillarization" (Thurlings 1971).

In the decade 1971-1982, the percentage of Catholics fell dramatically from 40.4 percent to 29.1 percent, a decline that cannot be explained adequately by birth rate changes or de-pillarization. One must also examine the impact of, then, recent events in the Roman Catholic church in the Netherlands on its internal organization. I will return to this issue. For now suffice it to say that these events had a disastrous effect on Catholic membership and participation.

The Neo-Calvinists, like the Roman Catholics, present a unique situation. They too were a minority group, formed as the result of complicated processes in which different groups broke away from the Netherlands Reformed church during the nineteenth century.[2] Many of these groups came together in the denomination called *Gereformeerde Kerken in Nederland*,[3] which comprised 9.4 percent of the population in 1909 and remained above 8 percent until the 1980s. During the 1980s their membership dropped below 8 percent for the first time.

Table 6.1 shows a distinct turning point in Catholic church membership during the 1970s, as well as an acceleration in the trend to non-affiliation. A cautionary, methodological caveat is necessary, however. The censuses and the 1982 survey used somewhat different questions about church membership. In the censuses, a "one-step question" was used which read, "To what religious organization do you belong?" In the 1982 survey this question was preceded by the filtering question, "Do you belong to a religious organization?" This difference is important because the use of such a filtering question typically produces a higher percentage of non-church membership and a lower percentage of church membership. It has become customary to exploit this difference as a means of determining marginal church membership and identifying transitional phases (Doorn and Bommeljé 1983:14-15).

One could argue that the dechurchment process (evident in the trend for non-affiliates) was already accelerating in the 1960s, but that the "one-step question" used in the 1971 census muted its visibility. Similarly, one could argue that the significant turning point for Roman Catholicism came before 1971 and was less abrupt; but that in the 1971 census marginal Catholics still asserted affiliation with the Catholic church--i.e., their break was not yet complete.

It is interesting to speculate whether and to what extent these trends can be extrapolated. Of course, it is too simple to draw straight lines from 1971 to the future. It is possible to argue that at sometime in the future a kind of equilibrium will be reached between church entries and withdrawals. It has been suggested (Scheepens 1991: 27) that equilibrium will be reached at levels of 30 to 40 percent church membership and 60 to 70 percent non-affiliation, with a constant percentage of withdrawals. The ratio would be different if withdrawal percentages changed. When and if equilibrium will be reached, of course, remains an open question.

The process of declining church membership shows up more clearly when one looks at various age cohorts, a subject to which I will return when focussing on the post-war generation.

Declining Church Population

Formal church membership statistics such as those provided in the census data present only a partial picture. They tell us nothing about degrees of church participation, nor the beliefs and attitudes of church members. For this we must turn to survey data, in this instance, of those conducted in the last three decades. As is typically the case, there are difficulties in comparing results across time because survey questions differ somewhat. However, there can be little doubt about the trends.

Organizing responses to questions about church attendance into two categories-- "Going to church regularly or sometimes" and "rarely or never" attending--Table 6.2 presents the 1966-1988 trend for our three denominations.

As one can see participation declined for all three denominations. The decline was especially pronounced among Catholics; minimal among Neo-Calvinists; and the traditionally low degree of participation among the Netherlands Reformed became even lower.

Undoubtedly related to declining attendance is the fact that Dutch church members have relatively low confidence in their churches. The European Value Systems Study Group (EVSSG) survey conducted in 1981 gathered the following data: 13 percent had great confidence in the church; 28 percent had some confidence; 36 percent had little confidence; and 22 percent had no confidence at all (Halman 1991: 297). The category of little or no confidence amounted to 58 percent and was the highest percentage

TABLE 6.2: Participation In Church Services

	1966	1979	1982
Roman Catholic:			
Regularly or sometimes*	92%	71	62
Rarely or never	8	28	38
Netherlands Reformed:			
Regularly or sometimes*	66	57	53
Rarely or never	34	43	47
Neo-Calvinist:			
Regularly or sometimes*	95	93	92
Rarely or never	5	6	8

* For 1982, "Once a week or more."
Source: 1966 and 1979 (Goddijn et al. 1979: 132); 1982 (Doorn and Bommelje 1983: 85).

of the 13 Western countries. The Netherlands was trailed by Great Britain and Norway, both with 51 percent. Within the Netherlands it was the Catholics, of the three confessional groups, who indicated the least confidence (Halman et al. 1987: 39).

The Erosion of Traditional Beliefs

Orthodoxy, as indicated by beliefs in a personal God, in Jesus Christ as the Son of God, and in the hereafter, has decreased steadily in the Netherlands, at least since the 1960s. As can be seen in Table 6.3 it has declined for all three confessional groups. Declines for the Neo-Calvinists, however, have been minimal. Their faith appears relatively unshaken during a period when Catholics fell away from orthodoxy significantly.

For Catholics, and to a lesser extent for the Netherlands Reformed, the major change over time in regard to God is from belief in a personal God to belief in a higher power. This increasing ambiguity of definition is also evident in regard to belief in Christ and, to a lesser extent, belief in the hereafter. It could mark a transitional phase between belief and unbelief. But it could also reveal a reformulation of traditional beliefs--e.g., the recent interest in so-called process theology among Catholics.

It is apparent that the churches have been losing members rather rapidly over the last decades. This applies especially to the Roman Catholic church. For the Netherlands Reformed church it is no more than a

TABLE 6.3: Religious Beliefs, 1966 - 1979

Netherlands	Roman Catholic		Reformed		Neo-Calvinism	
	1966	1979	1966	1979	1966	1979
God:						
Belief in God	60%	36	65	56	95	91
In a Higher Power	36	53	27	37	5	8
None/Don't know	4	10	8	7	0	1
Christ:						
Son of God	70	47	73	63	93	93
Otherwise	30	53	27	37	7	7
Hereafter:						
Yes	71	46	73	62	98	90
No	20	33	17	18	2	2
Don't know	9	21	10	20	0	7

Source: Goddijn, et al., 1979: 120 sq.

continuation of a longstanding trend. The Neo-Calvinists "lag behind" in this respect. Participation in church life has also decreased, again with the Neo-Calvinists least affected. In the area of orthodoxy, the trend is similar. The Neo-Calvinists are the most orthodox group while the Roman Catholics and the Netherlands Reformed are on the less orthodox side of the spectrum.

With this general overview of the religious situation in the Netherlands, we now turn to differences between the generations and confront the original research question of whether these differences can be explained by taking into account the particular vicissitudes of the post-war generation. This is a complex question that cannot be answered without first grappling with several theoretical and conceptual questions. It is not sufficient to concentrate exclusively on statistical cohorts, as is done in the censuses and surveys. We first must clarify what we mean by the term "generation." Furthermore, we have to delineate the different kinds of historical factors and processes affecting change.

The Generational Concept

Following Karl Mannheim, a cohort is not yet a generation. A cohort consists of a number of people of about the same age. That, of course, is an important detail. Individuals "who share the same year of birth, are endowed, to that extent, with a common location in the historical dimension of the social process" (Mannheim 1952: 290). This common location limits the individuals who are part of a cohort "to a specific range of potential experience, predisposing them for a certain characteristic mode of thought and experience, and a characteristic type of historically relevant action. Any given location, then, excludes a large number of possible modes of thought, experience, feeling and action, and restricts the range of self-expression open to the individual to certain circumscribed possibilities." This is only a negative delimitation. Positively, one can say that a cohort exhibits a "tendency towards certain definite modes of behavior, feeling and thought" (Mannheim 1952: 290).

"Cohort" and "generation" in this sense are only "location phenomena"--they "fall . . . short of encompassing the generation phenomenon in its full actuality" (Mannheim 1952: 303). "Generation as an actuality, however, involves even more than mere co-presence in such an historical and social region. A further concrete nexus is needed to constitute generation as an actuality. This additional nexus may be described as participation in the common destiny of this historical and social unit" (Mannheim 1952: 303).

However, even this definition of the generation concept needs to be supplemented. The participation in a common destiny does not determine the kinds of actions and reactions people exhibit. That is, people of the same generation may react differently in the same social circumstances. Mannheim called those who react in roughly the same way to circumstances "generation units." A generation may consist of a plurality of generation units (Mannheim 1952: 305).

What produces a generation unit? In answer, Mannheim introduces the notion of "formative forces" or "formative tendencies." The effect of these forces or tendencies is that people develop a shared perspective and thus the possibility of shared reactions. Therefore, a generation unit is characterized by "an identity of responses, a certain affinity in the way in which all move with and are formed by their common experiences" (Mannheim 1952: 306).

Formative forces or tendencies play their role only during a specific period of life, the so-called formative years. It is supposed that this formative period lies between the ages of 10 and 25. During this period the individual is not only very sensitive to impressions and experiences but also develops attitudes and perceptions which exhibit lasting stability over the rest of his or her life. This is a result of the importance of the forces encountered during the early period of life when fundamental attitudes coalesce.

This theoretical view of "generations" and formative periods has been empirically confirmed by several authors (Inglehart 1981; Gadourek 1982). However, this theoretical perspective is not at issue here. We want to examine its relevance in relation to our research question.

The relevance is clear. Basing our conclusions on statistical cohorts is inadequate. We have to be wary of general statements about cohorts and delve into the formative factors affecting the post-war generations. It might also be necessary to look for the relationships between the different generations, at least as far as the socialization process is concerned. As empirical research has shown, the parental home is a highly influential factor in the religious socialization of young people (Stoffels and Dekker 1987; de Hart 1990). Religious disillusionment of elderly people may therefore have a negative effect on subsequent generations. That is only one aspect of the more general question--what kinds of developments and factors have to be taken into account?

Differing Time Spans of Social Process

Speaking of the post-war generation, we have a particular period of human history in mind. We suppose that the peculiarities of this period have had a decisive impact on the generation's religious attitudes and behavior. However, there are variations in the processes occurring in any period. Therefore, we must also examine the various time spans of these different processes.

According to Braudel (1969) one can, first, identify long-term processes such as structural differentiation, cultural pluralization, rationalization, increasing individualism and secularization. They occur over centuries and cannot therefore explain changes in individual behavior. Qualifications are necessary, at least, before it is possible to attribute changes in religious behavior, for example in the decade 1970-1980, to "the secularization process" or to "increasing individualism." Such qualifications could include, for example, changes in the tempo of these long-term processes. Beck (1983) has pointed to the fact that the process of individualization accelerated in the 1960s and deeply affected families. It is not difficult to postulate the consequences of this shift for religious socialization.

One can also identify shorter-term fluctuations (conjunctures), such as business cycles, including processes that last up to 50 years. A nice example of this perspective in the context of this paper is the process of de-pillarization. I have indicated that the process of de-pillarization started in the 1960s and that during it the Catholic community was fractured. Forces which had affected other population groups long before became operative within the Catholic community, and diminished the differences between Catholics and non-affiliated people.

Third, there is the category of so-called "events," such as World War II, the Second Vatican Council, and the Pastoral Council of the Dutch Catholics in the Netherlands. Such events undoubtedly have their effects, but mainly as influential catalysts.

A problem of historical sociology is the relationship between these three "layers of time." The ordinary life of individuals is lived in all three layers at the same time. One has to analyze different processes and look at their interrelationships in order to get an overall picture of the historical configuration in which individuals live.

These perspectives on the explanatory enterprise stress the difficulty of being certain about analyses of the post-war generation. I will nevertheless attempt an analysis of this generation in the Netherlands. However, since within the scope of this paper it is impossible to go into a detailed analysis of the vicissitudes of each of the three major denominations, to say nothing of the myriad other groups in Dutch society, it is necessary to limit the focus. There is no doubt that the Roman Catholics exhibit the most strikingly fundamental changes in religious attitudes and behavior. For no other denomination are the changes so abrupt. The Neo-Calvinists are relatively stable; and the Netherlands Reformed church exhibits only an acceleration of a long-term pattern. Therefore, I confine my analysis primarily to the Roman Catholics during the period between 1960 and 1980.

Elaborating on the preceding, it is evident that conjunctures and more discrete events were influential factors during the formative periods of the post-war generations. These had an impact directly and indirectly on the socialization processes that these generations underwent. This is not to say that long-term processes, such as increasing rationalization and differentiation or individualization, were not influential. However, their influence was blocked to a certain degree before World War II by social and economic isolation which continued after the war as part of the Catholic pillarization phenomenon. Catholics lived in a world of their own, insulated against the eroding effects that modernization generally had on religious convictions and behavior. On the other hand, the long-term processes did account for a number of defections. However, these defections were easily compensated for by a birth rate that was far above the average. When, under the influence of post-war economic growth and the increasing intermingling of population groups in Dutch society, the Catholic pillar began to crumble, the influence of "modernity" had a double impact: more defections and a decreasing birth rate. That this change happened so quickly is due to some specific events: the Second Vatican Council and the Pastoral Council. Perhaps it is more accurate to say that the developments which followed in the wake of these two events were decisive. Let us examine these two events.

Two Formative Catholic Events

The Second Vatican Council was announced by Pope John XXIII in January 1959 to address the traditional opposition between the church and the modern world. The church had not acknowledged the autonomy of secular society. Pope John XXIII was convinced that an attitude of openness to dialogue, and the renunciation of one-sided and authoritarian judgments were necessary. Moreover, he wanted to make the formulation of belief compatible with modern understandings and expressions. Pleading for dialogue implied striving for relevance. The Pope said the church needed "more clarity in her thinking."

Reactions were diverse. The bureaucracy was uneasy and not without reason. In the first place, the Curia saw its role as that of keeping control over church life. It was indeed difficult to see how it could continue to do so because doctrinal unity would certainly be affected by changing forms of expression. If formulations became mutable then orthodoxy would become more indefinite and the boundaries of Catholicism would blur.

The Pope also wanted to have greater "policy contact" with local bishops all over the world, and this certainly would have eroded the power of the Curia considerably. A third concern involved the Pope's intention of doing greater justice to the position of the laity, a traditionally neglected category within the church. This recognition of the laity's struggle for influence implied serious consequences for the church bureaucracy.

Though the Curia was generally opposed, other reactions were overwhelming positive because of the deeply felt need for change. As a matter of fact, the Pope could achieve his goals because he had allies outside the bureaucracy and among the bishops who were not generally allied with the Curia.

The Second Vatican Council exemplified a threshold effect. Throughout the church changes spread along with a growing enthusiasm for change. The Catholic laity discovered its potential as a molder of religious life.

Shortly after the Council began, Pope John died, and he was succeeded by a more hesitant pope, Paul VI. During the remaining sessions of the Council, the climate changed and a more conservative wind began to blow. It became even stronger after the final session when the bishops returned home and the Curia began rebuilding its position while curtailing the laity and the local bishops. A disappointing consequence was the publication in 1968 of the encyclical letter *Humanae vitae* which prohibited artificial birth control.

However, *Humanae vitae* came after Dutch Catholics had started, in the wake of the Vatican Council, to develop their own plan of church renewal. Immediately after the final session of the Vatican Council the Dutch bishops declared that "intensive deliberation on as broad a scale as possible should result in clear recommendations for policy decisions in view of the necessary innovations" (Pastoraal Concilie I 1968: 12). Catholics responded to this initiative "from above" with great enthusiasm. They participated in the project of renewal through writing letters, forming discussion groups (about 14,000), taking part on committees, writing reports and voting on proposals at official meetings. The degree and quality of mobilization were high.

The enterprise as a whole constituted an encompassing pastoral plan for the Catholic church in the Netherlands. The official reports addressed the issues of authority in the church, of missions and social and political witnessing, of Christian moral attitudes, of marriage and the family, of modern piety, of renewal of belief and practice, of the priesthood and the regular orders, of catechism and preaching, of ecumenism, of the relations between Christians and Jews, and of the struggle for peace. Not only were traditional formulations replaced with modern ones, but there was a fundamental shift in views of church and society. An important change was the stress laid on the emancipation of the Christian laity to shape religious life. The laity was willing to listen to the bishops, but only on condition that the church leaders were willing to listen in their turn.

It is not very difficult to understand that this enterprise aggravated suspicions already aroused in the Vatican. The autonomous organization of church renewal outside--at least from the Curia's perspective--the direct control of the church, often in opposition to its wishes, threatened the church's traditional system of control. The Vatican was unwilling to accept this and intervened harshly. The crackdown was also probably a symptom of the swift return to power of the traditional faction in Rome.

The reactionary response made itself felt dramatically. The Vatican prevented the Pastoral Council from continuing in its planned form. It appointed new, conservative bishops at the earliest opportunity, even directly opposing the wishes of the Dutch episcopacy. Since 1970 the Vatican has maneuvered to shift the balance at the bishops' conference towards traditional policy, with gradual success. It disqualified the bishops of the Pastoral Council on several occasions. Finally, in a special meeting with the Pope in Rome in 1980 the bishops were charged with the task of bringing the Dutch church back onto the "right track." This was understood to mean the assertion of clear authority relations, traditional policies on sexual matters, a sharp distinction between priests and laity regarding practice and liturgy, the regimentation of the priests, and extreme caution with respect to ecumenical interaction (Goddijn 1973).

It goes without saying that these measures provoked severe protests among those Catholics who had committed themselves to the church renewal movement. One manifestation was the formation of several protest groups (Laeyendecker 1989). An eloquent expression of the anger, captured by the mass media for the world, was the cool and distant reception of Pope John Paul II when he visited the Netherlands in 1980. However, some Catholics applauded the conservative resuscitation. The conflicting Catholic responses lead us back to the focus on the post-war generation.

Post-War Generations in the Netherlands

According to a study of cohorts and generations in the Netherlands (Becker 1990), it is possible to distinguish four generations in the Netherlands. They coexist in the post-war period. They have been labeled the pre-war generation, the silent generation, the protest generation and the lost generation. Ongoing research has more or less confirmed this classification of four generations, especially with regards to distinctions between the silent and the protest generations (Van Berkel-Van Schaik and Van Snippenburg 1991).

The pre-war generation was born between 1910 and 1930. Its formative period (1920-1955) was characterized by scarce opportunities for education. There was a dominant traditional value pattern (rigid sexual morals, "Protestant" work ethic, obedience to authority) and a tight labor market. Aspirations were relatively low. A rigidly controlled pillar circumscribed the social and religious life of Catholics. The pillarization process was interrupted by World War II but resumed between 1945 and 1955. Nevertheless, World War II had brought the Catholics into contact with other religious and non-religious worldviews and alternatives to their traditional way of life, as did the urbanization and industrialization processes stimulated by the Dutch government as means of recovery from the German occupation. These developments led to tensions within the pillar which began to surface in the early 1950s. By the end of the 1950s the announcement of the Second Vatican Council amplified these tensions, and they became especially pronounced during the Pastoral Council.

It should be noted that 58 percent of the participants in the Pastoral Council came from the pre-war generation (Goddijn et al. 1986: 80). They advocated changes in beliefs, morals, religious practices and authority relations. Democracy as a value, strongly asserted after World War II, was promoted within the church.

The silent generation was born between 1930 and 1940. Its formative period (1940-1965) was characterized by greater educational opportunities. This generation attained a higher level of (modern) education. However, the traditional value-pattern remained strong as this generation was socialized by the pre-war generation and its remaining predecessors. There was an expanded labor market and greater economic success. It is probable that this generation expected similar success in its struggle for religious innovation. This generation was more critical of pillarization, which in fact started to decrease by the end of the 1950s. Twenty-four percent of the participants in the Pastoral Council came from the silent generation (Goddijn et al. 1986: 80). In the 1970s, both the pre-war and silent generations were disappointed by the reactionary retrenchment of the Roman Catholic church.

Between 1940 and 1955, the so-called protest generation was born. Its formative period (1950-1980) was characterized by overcrowded educational institutions resulting from the post-war baby boom. This generation exhibited a high level of educational aspiration. Moreover, there was strong economic growth which fostered the illusion that desired innovations could be implemented at will. This generation grew up in the period of de-pillarization and the two Councils, therefore change and innovation were the main concepts in religious discourse. The protest generation aligned itself with the new value pattern that emerged during and after the cultural revolution that took place between 1965 and 1975. This included liberalized sexual morals, reduced respect for authority, and an increased regard for radical democracy (one man, one vote), political participation and emancipation. Immediately after its formative period, this generation was confronted with a labor market that became increasingly unfavorable and with the reactionary crackdown of the Catholic church. Both trends were immensely frustrating as rising expectations were quashed seemingly overnight.

The generation born between 1955 and 1970, referred to as the lost generation, had its formative years between 1965 and the present. The characteristics of this period included good educational opportunities but less freedom than the protest generation enjoyed. There was stagnation in the processes of change after 1975 that was accompanied by a redirection of value priorities towards personal growth and personal development. The labor market was very tight for this generation (hence the term "lost" generation) and was characterized by structural unemployment. The experience of Vatican policies made this generation skeptical of churches, but not necessarily of religion (Becker 1990: passim).

TABLE 6.4: Church Affiliation Of Four Generations Of Roman Catholics, Netherlands Reformed, Neo-Calvinists And Non-Affiliated As A Percentage Of The Total Population Of The, Respective, Generation.

	1960	1971	1982
Roman Catholic:			
Pre-war (born 1910-30)	38%	38	31
Silent (born 1930-40)	44	42	36
Protest (born 1940-55)	45	42	28
Lost (born 1955-70)	46	44	25
Netherlands Reformed:			
Pre-war generation	29	26	20
Silent generation	28	22	16
Protest generation	25	21	12
Lost generation	23	20	11
Neo-Calvinist:			
Pre-war generation	7	7	8
Silent generation	7	7	7
Protest generation	7	7	8
Lost generation	7	8	7
Non-Affiliated			
Pre-war generation	20	24	37
Silent generation	18	24	38
Protest generation	17	25	50
Lost generation	19	24	54

Sources: 1960 and 1971 censuses; 1982 survey (Doorn and Bommelje 1983: Table 17).

The Post-War Generations and Establishment Religion

The empirical data concerning the four generations, coexisting in the Netherlands after World War II are difficult to organize. I have already pointed out that after 1971 there are only survey data. The statistical cohorts examined in these surveys are not typically standardized according to the four generation classification presented in this paper. Therefore, data directly relevant to our analysis is limited. The quantification of the dechurchment process for each of the four generations is only possible for 1960, 1971 and 1982; and is shown in Table 6.4. As far as church participation, confidence in churches, and decreasing orthodoxy are concerned, no measurements are available by generation except for participation in 1982--the latter shown in Table 6.5.

As far as the Neo-Calvinists are concerned, it appears that the relative stability of this denomination extended to all four generations. That is not to say that there are no generational differences. Neo-Calvinists as a percentages of the pre-war and protest generations increased between 1960 and 1982, as did the percentage of the silent generation after 1971.[4] For all three of these generations this suggests a net Neo-Calvinist gain from denominational or non-affiliated switching. Neo-Calvinists as a percentage of the youngest generation (i.e., the lost generation), however, declined between 1971 and 1982. If this last trend continues, and subsequent data indicate that it has, it suggests that the Neo-Calvinists may not be immune to the general trend towards dechurchment.

The Netherlands Reformed church's historical pattern of declining membership is evident within each generation from oldest to youngest. Additionally, each succeeding generation has a lower group level of membership than its immediate predecessor; and the two youngest generations (i.e., the protest and lost generations) show the steepest declines. Future prospects are rather gloomy.

This can also be said for the Roman Catholics. Their decline has been dramatic. It is important to note the sharp turning point after 1971, which indicates an acceleration of the decline beginning at the end of the 1960s. We also see that even the church affiliation of the pre-war generation declined rather quickly after 1971, whereas that generation had held relatively steady between 1960 and 1971. The pattern of the silent generation is comparable to that of the pre-war generation. The most impressive decline occurred in the protest and lost generations after 1971. Their losses between 1971 and 1982 amounted to 35 percent and 42 percent, respectively. The lost generation's decline surpassed that of the protest generation in about 1973. It is difficult to be optimistic about the future of the Roman Catholic church in the Netherlands.

The non-affiliated category grew with the decline in Roman Catholics after 1971. Up until then, the non-affiliated primarily consisted of former Netherlands Reformed members.

Regarding participation in Sunday services, the data that corresponds to our four generation classification is weak. But Table 6.5 still shows distinct patterns between the different generations, although undoubtedly confounded somewhat by life cycle effects.

More severe limitations of data emerge in examining the degree to which church members have confidence in their churches. Referring to the EVSSG survey we can argue that the younger the generation, the less its confidence in the churches (Halman 1991: 68). However, we cannot draw comparisons between the three denominations. The same is generally true of the degrees of orthodoxy displayed (Halman et al. 1987: 39).

TABLE 6.5: 1982 Church Participation By Denomination By Generation:
Percent Church Participants Of All members In A Given Generation For A Given
Denomination.

Generation	Roman Catholic	Netherlands Reformed	Neo-Calvinism
Pre-war (born 1910-30)	50.3%	35.2	66.8
Silent (born 1930-40)	40.2	26.5	55.3
Protest (born 1940-55)	18.4	29.1	70.5
Lost (born 1955-70)	28.0	34.5	71.8
Total Denomination	34.5	31.2	66.3

Source: Doorn and Bommelje 1983: Table 17.

Concluding Discussion

It is a bit risky to draw conclusions about the tendencies of the
different generations. Nevertheless, some provisional statements can be
made. It is remarkable that in a climate of secularization and high rates of
dechurchment, the Neo-Calvinists have remained practically immune to
membership declines. They have not been as affected as other confessional
traditions by long-term processes, conjunctures, or specific events, though
they were active members of Dutch society. Their persistent stability is
difficult to explain. Of course, it is possible that in the future their
immunity will fail. As I have already noted, there are indications that
during the 1990s their fortress is going to show some cracks. However,
there is not currently enough data to make solid predictions.

The Netherlands Reformed, on the other hand, seems to have
adjusted themselves to a tradition of dechurchment. Table 6.1 emphasized
this characteristic. The Netherlands Reformed did not form a strong pillar
and from the beginning of the nineteenth century they exhibited a great
variety of beliefs and practices, from very orthodox to very liberal, as well
as conflict between various factions. The size of the orthodox wing has
grown in recent decades. It is evident that a higher percentage of liberals
have left the denomination. The youngest generations, influenced by the
cultural revolution, exhibit a somewhat faster decline. Nevertheless, all
these trends can be viewed as continuations of the traditional pattern.

As regards Roman Catholics, their rapid decline after 1970 can be
explained as the result of various factors: long-term trends, conjunctures,
and specific events within the church. No other denomination in the
Netherlands has had such a dramatic history since 1960.

In conclusion, I return briefly to an earlier discussion of the
Catholic situation. Long-term processes did not have much effect while the

Catholic pillar remained unshaken. Nonetheless, uneasiness grew within the pillar concerning the increasing discrepancy between Catholic life and modern society. After 1969, a rapid process of de-pillarization occurred which left the Catholics undefended against modern trends and attitudes. The cultural revolution found them "open to the world." Moreover, their leaders, the Pope and their bishops, took the lead in the process of change. The two Councils represent impressive efforts to reconcile the church with the modern world. They legitimated the changes, but then could not control them. Indeed, a reactionary re-assertion of traditional means of control after the Councils radicalized the dechurchment process.

The problem was that church leaders appeared eager to impose a new status quo under their supervision. However, a lot of Dutch Catholics, having tasted the fruits of liberty and free inquiry, did not want to give up their advances. Not without reason, they asserted lay responsibility. The Vatican disagreed and chose an authoritarian response. It reaped disillusionment and resistance. The aftershocks are visible in the data presented in this chapter. Of course, the four generations had different roles in these processes. The pre-war generation was educated in the unshaken pillar and consequently developed an attitude of obedience and loyalty to the church leaders. They were willing to follow their leaders towards innovation, especially those generation members who felt the rising tensions between traditional Catholic life and the modernizing society around them.

Nevertheless, many in this generation were hesitant about the innovations. They were accustomed to tradition and could not digest all the changes. They accepted the role of the Pope and the Vatican Council, but showed more doubts about the Pastoral Council, especially when their bishops were disqualified by the Vatican.

These hesitant members welcomed the Vatican's reaction and responded with loyalty to the new, conservative bishops. It is probable that this group is the oldest segment of the generation. The more liberal, younger segment of the generation has probably diminished its participation without formally leaving the church because that would have been too big a step given their strong Catholic education. Another segment of these pre-war generation Catholics remained in the Catholic church but took part in protest groups that clashed with the new bishops.

The silent generation experienced the beginning of de-pillarization and the break-up of the Catholic community during its formative period between 1940 and 1965. Therefore, it exhibited a more open attitude towards modern society, especially as far as authority relations and the attitude towards democracy was concerned. This generation had a more critical attitude towards the church. Social and economic prospects were favorable and nurtured an optimistic attitude about the possibilities for change. Moreover, there was a strong feeling that change could be achieved through rational argument. The heritage of the Enlightenment was obvious at the time. When the Vatican reaction occurred around 1970, this generation was between 30 and 40 years-old. Normally people of this age are less involved in church activities. As they age, however, their behavior reverts to traditional patterns, if no other factors intervene. In this case, there were many intervening factors. Developments in the church went contrary to their expectations and desires. A relatively high percentage of this group informally left the church. Another segment joined the protest groups. Few acquiesced to the conservative restoration.

The bigger part of the protest generation was brought up in a de-pillarized milieu as a wave of individualism spread over the society. What emerged in the silent generation proliferated in the protest generation. Only the older segment comprehended the ramifications of what happened during the Vatican and Pastoral Councils. However, the younger segment drew experience from their parents with a similar effect--a growing lack of trust in the church's capacity for change to accommodate modern society and its value patterns. It is no wonder that many from the protest generation left the church. The younger segment of the generation was not even interested in participating in the protest groups.

The transition to the lost generation is gradual. That is, the trends are continuing--the growing distance from the church develops into disinterestedness. Members of this generation do not expect much from the church and are going their own way. They sometimes look for religious alternatives outside the traditional church. The struggles over the Councils are less relevant to the members of this generation. They don't even know much about them. They are socialized by parents who have experienced frustrations in their church life and who have put distance between themselves and the church of their youth. They are growing up in a de-pillarized milieu that does not transmit church-oriented attitudes. As regards society-at-large, there is a strong individualism, which grew rapidly after the 1960s, and a decreasing relevance and influence for traditional religion.

This descriptive analysis is highly speculative. We have little systematic research concerning trends in the development of the generations, at least not as far as their religious attitudes are concerned. There is still some work to do.[5]

Notes

1. I concentrate on the dechurchment process, the decreasing participation in and the erosion of belief systems, and the developments pertaining to established religion as far as the three bigger denominations are concerned. I will not discuss the overall religious situation in the Netherlands and the changes in worldviews and value orientations. Much research has been done on these subjects in the last decade. (See, for example, Mady A. Thung, et al., *Exploring the New Religious Consciousness: An Investigation of Religious Change by a Dutch Working Group*, Amsterdam, 1985.) Two research programs deserve to be mentioned: SON (Secularization and De-Pillarization in The Netherlands) and SOCON (Sociocultural Research in the Netherlands). Both have been organized and implemented at the Catholic University of Nijmegen. Several reports have been published, most of them in Dutch and German. For a short bibliography of SON, see A. Felling, et al., *Geloven en Leven*, Zeist, 1986. For a general overview of the religious situation in the Netherlands until 1970 see L. Laeyendecker of the Netherlands in H. Mol (ed.), *Western Religion: A Country-By-Country Sociological Inquiry*, The Hague, 1972.

2. These processes resulted in a number of groups, some of which broke away and rejoined repeatedly. At the moment there are several "strictly reformed" groups. The Neo-Calvinists form the biggest such group. I do not take the other groups into account in this paper. For detailed information, see G. Dekker and J. Peters, *Gereformeerden in meervoud*, Kampen, 1989.

3. In Table 6.1, I give the first percentage for the Neo-Calvinists for 1889. That is because this denomination separated from the Netherlands Reformed church in 1882. Smaller groups split off earlier and later, but they are not taken into account in the tables and figures.

4. For each of these three generations of Neo-Calvinists the increase was small, for the silent generation not even reaching 1% across the 22 year period (and therefore not visible in Table 6.4).

5. It would be interesting to look at religious alternatives like the New Age Movement. Unfortunately, there is not yet quantitative data about the members of that movement though its numbers are probably substantial, as subscriptions to specific magazines indicate. We expect to get more information when the results of the SOCON survey (see note 1) are published. See C. Strijards and O. Schreuder, "Nieuwe spiritualiteit", in O. Schreuder and L. van Snippenburg (eds.), *Religie in de Nederlandse samenleving. De vergeten factor*, Baarn, 1990.

7

The Case of French Catholicism

Danièle Hervieu-Léger[1]

Rapid economic, social and cultural change in Western societies since World War II has not left religion untouched. The acceleration of secularization, the loss of influence of religious institutions in public life, the retrenchment of religious belief into the private sphere, the reconfiguration of the forms of religious sociability, and the transformation of religious groups into voluntary associations are the classic benchmarks for analyses which treat the relationship between modernization and religion. These general tendencies vary cross-nationally; they are neither uniform nor homogeneous. A nation's religious composition, its history of the relationship between religion and the state, its legal systems, cultural tendencies, and so forth, shape distinctive national forms of religious modernity. Therefore, a cross-national study, considering the religious trajectory of the population born after World War II (between 1945 and 1955),[2] will not only give insight into individual national cases, but it will also allow us to compare the trajectories and gain a sociological understanding of general tendencies.

The Post-War Generation in a Changing Society

Before turning to the changes in the attitudes and religious practices of the post-war generation in France, I will underline some major features of the "collective biography" of this population. These experiences place the post-war generation at the center of the transformations of French society during the last 40 years, as well as at the heart of the changes which affected the religious landscape.

A first feature concerns demographics: The post-war generation is a populous one. With the advent of the "baby boom," the process of the aging of the population that had characterized France between the world wars was interrupted. Birth rate declines, starting in the decade after 1910, were reinforced during the 1930s by a significant decline in the number of marriages. These trends, accentuated during World War II, reversed themselves in the mid-1940s. The birthrate went from 14.6 percent in 1939, to 16.2 percent in 1945. After 1946, 800,000 babies were born each year, compared to 600,000 in 1939.

This demographic increase favored, without completely determining, another significant development, namely, the remarkable increase in the number of students in the decade after World War II. Between 1945 and 1958, the secondary school population doubled and increased again by 65 percent between 1959 and 1964. In 1963-64, the total school population rose to 10,600,000 young people (out of a total of 54,700,000 inhabitants). Sixty-three percent of these students were in the elementary schools, 34 percent in the secondary schools, and three percent in the universities. From 1954 to 1962, the percentage of adolescents from 11 to 17 years-old who were in school rose from 35 percent to 49 percent. These figures are of interest because they indicate that the post-war generation was the first "youth" (*jeunesse*) generation constituted as an autonomous social grouping with its own unique behaviors. It not only was distinct from the adult society, but often in conflict with it. Adults, in turn, frequently viewed it with distrust and alarm.[3] The youth generation, segregated from the productive mainstream of society during its prolonged educational period, developed specific behaviors and values constituting an original "culture" that transcended (to a certain extent) social distinctions characteristic of the larger society. The post-war generation was the first generation reared in this unique cultural and social milieu. The consequences of this structural change were significant for the family, schools, and the entire range of institutions involved in the socialization of the younger generation.

The school system, more specifically the secondary schools and the universities, was the first area affected. An institution for the selection of the elite, the school system abruptly had to transform itself into an institution for the education of the masses. It had to develop the capacity for integrating a diverse student population of unequal cultural and social backgrounds and preparing it for entry into the labor market. The profound shock to the French secondary and university system was apparent in political terms. It could be seen in the succession of governmental plans for the reform of education that testified, even before the explosion of May 1968, to the destabilization of the traditional modes of transmission of knowledge and values in a France undergoing rapid modernization.

As the first youth generation educated *en masse*, the post-war generation lived its formative years in a society characterized simultaneously by the economic transformations of the 1960s and by the political and moral trauma that decolonization provoked. Its entry into adulthood at the beginning of the 1960s was effected under the triple influence of mass consumption, the institutional convulsions associated with the Algerian crisis, and the social and moral uncertainties generated by the destabilization of the main social units--family, schools, military, churches, for example--responsible for maintaining social continuity. One could argue that the tension between the level of material well-being achieved by French society, and the level of credibility of its institutions of collective identity, was at the root of the crises that smoldered throughout the 1960s and that exploded in May,1968. The post-war generation was 20 years-old and ignorant of the wars and deprivations that had affected its predecessors. On the other hand, it encountered new problems (economic as well as political and cultural) as its numerous members surged into the rigidly structured French society. France in 1968 was a society which was economically dynamic but institutionally petrified. The "monarchic republic," embodied in the figure of General de Gaulle, crystallized in a political sense the institutional inertia against which the youth movement of 1968 rebelled. Originating in the universities,[4] the anti-institutional wave of revolt spread throughout France. Its direct political impetus ended rather quickly. Its cultural and moral consequences have had an importance for French society that has yet to be fully assessed. For the generation born after World War II, which serves as our reference population, the revolt has led decisively to a new manner of thinking and of experiencing modernity. In effect, May 1968 marks France's entrance into the modern culture of the individual. If one looks beyond particular social differentiations that affect individual modes of entering into the culture, one can say without exaggeration that the post-war generation has been the historical subject of a true cultural revolution.

This generation also entered into politics with a utopian spirit in an era of apparently unlimited economic growth and with its faith in the virtues of technical progress still intact. It subsequently confronted the radical disenchantment produced throughout Western society by the shock of the first oil shortage and the economic and social crisis that this event generated. For the post-war generation in France, the crisis of the 1970s had a double effect: It provoked a critical reevaluation of the modern ideals of progress and development, at the same time that it called into question the utopian content of the cultural protest that had not been directed against these ideals, but against the institutional blockages supposedly impeding their social realization.

Those members of the post-war generation, currently 40 years of age, who now hold the reins of power, are also the ones who have had the most thoroughgoing experience of the secularization of politics. The Left, when it came to power in 1981, was still committed to a vision of social change directed "from on high" by a state charged with a "mission" entirely defined in reference to a political ideal. Since 1983, French socialists, confronted with the practical exigencies of the day-to-day management of public affairs, have embarked on a path of political realism and adjusted to the necessities of an economic rationality under which they no longer question market logic.

To a certain degree, this mutation of French political culture over the course of the 1980s signals the conclusion of a process of modernization which began at the time of the post-World War II reconstruction. First, there was economic modernization that dominated the 1950s and 1960s. This was followed by cultural and institutional modernization that marked the decade of the 1970s. Finally there was political modernization that has taken place over the past decade under the presidency of Francois Mitterand. From mass education to anti-institutional revolt, from political utopianism to reconciliation with capitalism and economic necessities, the post-war generation has been objectively and subjectively the central collective actor in the trajectory of French modernization.

Transformation of the French Catholic Landscape

One must keep the post-war generation's historical evolution in mind in examining its religious attitudes and behaviors. These attitudes and behaviors, however, have also evolved in the context of changes affecting the whole religious arena during the general process of modernization. It is impossible within the scope of this paper to analyze these changes fully. Therefore, I will limit myself to highlighting general trends while concentrating on the case of Roman Catholicism in its dominant position in French society.

The Decline of Religious Practice

Roman Catholicism is the faith to which 82 percent of the French claim to belong. Because of its numerical dominance, we have complete data and extensive sociological analyses of French religion, especially Catholicism. Large-scale investigations of French Catholicism have been conducted since the 1930s, initially instigated by the then Dean of the Faculty of Law in Paris, Gabriel le Bras, a specialist in the history of institutions. Originally focusing on rural French parishes and gradually extended to include all 40,000 French parishes (Isambert and Terrenoire 1980), and enriched by detailed regional inquiries (Boulard and Rémy

TABLE 7.1: Attendance at Mass

Regular Practitioners:	
Several times a week	1%
Every Sunday	6%
Occasional Practitioners:	
From time to time	19%
Non-practitioners:	
Only for ceremonies (Marriages, baptisms)	52%
Never	9%

Source: SOFRES, survey of 1986.

1968), these studies have made it possible to chart changes in the Catholic landscape. The studies obviously do not reveal a complete picture of the health of French Catholicism, but they clearly demonstrate general and long-standing problems in the rates of regular religious practice. In 1990, weekly attendance at Mass was calculated at below 10 percent (except in some very circumscribed regions).

According to a recent survey, the percentage of the Catholic population which practices regularly (attending Mass once or more a week) or semi-regularly (attending Mass once or twice a month) is 12 percent (compared to 20 percent in 1986). Regular practice is unequally distributed among different age groups. It is 2.5 percent for people under 25, but 22.5 percent for those over 60. It is less than 10 percent for those born after World War II (between the ages of 35 and 45).

Besides being more characteristic of older people, regular or semi-regular practice is also more prevalent among women, particularly those with no profession. Socio-professional status is also a determining factor: Religious practice is especially limited among laborers and self-employed workers (merchants). It is highest among farmers and management personnel.

Changes in the rate of participation in particular sacraments also attest to the decline in religious observance in contemporary France. The fall in the number of baptisms and religious marriages is significant in that those figures had remained extraordinarily stable until the middle of the 1970s.

TABLE 7.2: Religious Practice According to Age

Age Group	Regular or Semi-regular Practice
Under 35	2.5%
Between 25 and 40	6.2%
Between 40 and 50	10.3%
Between 50 and 60	19.0%
Over 60	22.5%

Source: CREDOC inquiry December 1989

The statistical evidence of declining religious practice in France is reinforced by the evidence of the dramatic decline in the recruitment of priests, monks and nuns since 1945. In 1948, there were 42,650 priests in France. In 1960, there were 41,600. By 1975, there were no more than 35,000 and their number had slumped further to 28,000 by 1987. The annual number of ordinations declined from about 1000 in 1959, to level off in 1975 at approximately 100. Annual ordinations have been less than the annual mortality rate of priests since 1959. The result has been the aging of the clerical population. Currently, one out of 10 priests is under 40 years-old and one out of three is over 65.

These figures underscore the gravity of the church's personnel crisis. The problem, however, is part of a wider problem concerning the position of priests in a laicized society. The "separated" status of the priest, traditionally associated by clergy and laity with the priesthood's "sacred" character, has suffered a decline, losing much of its traditional authority, prestige and local power. The social status of the clergy has eroded along with the church's ability to intervene in the social life of the nation. Devalued as a means of social advancement, the "clerical path" no longer even guarantees material well-being and security.[5] The problems associated with the aging (especially in rural areas) and marginalization of priests are complicated by the deepening uncertainties priests feel towards their mission. The lack of priestly personnel has led lay people of both sexes to take a greater part in the performance and even definition of the pastoral function through catechesis, the reception and preparation of those requesting the sacraments, liturgical arrangements, and so forth.[6] This questioning of the status and even the role of the clergy is one of the most crucial aspects of the disruption of the parish world which for centuries constituted the matrix of French religious life.

TABLE 7.3: Religious Participation According to Socio-Professional Categories

(Religious participation includes regular practice, attendance at ceremonies, and participation in Catholic organizations)

Socio-Prof. Cat.	Total	Men	Women
Retirees	14.6	9.3	20.2
Farm Workers	14.1	12.3	17.8
Management and upper level professions	14.0	12.5	17.8
Inactive	7.7	4.9	9.0
Employees	6.0	3.4	6.9
Intermediate professions	5.1	3.0	9.4
Artisans, merchants, small business owners	4.3	3.3	6.5
Laborers	3.9	4.2	2.8
Total	8.0	5.8	10.3

Source: INSEE, survey "Emplois du Temps" (Use of Time) 1985-1986

These declining trends, whether in religious practice or in the number of ordinations, are never more than indicators. Their real significance is in signalling the breakdown of the traditional religious structure. The questions of attendance at Mass and the number of priests are important to the sociological understanding of French Catholicism, not only because of their importance in Catholic tradition, but also because they are foundational aspects of the "parochial civilization" which dominated France for centuries. This parochial civilization, of which the bell tower--the chief focus of the rural French landscape--is the symbol, embodied an extensive system of territorial influence that placed each inhabitant within the jurisdiction of a parish (at least theoretically). It also enhanced the socio-religious power incarnated in the parish priest. The authority of the priest (for "whom the priesthood alone should suffice"[7]), reinforced by the priest's exclusive power to perform religious functions, supposedly extended to all domains of public and private life. In contrast to the traditional status of the priest was the typical status of the faithful believer, devoid of religious power and measured by the frequency of his or her participation in the various sacramental acts.

It would be absurd to imply that this paradigm of religious hegemony, imposed on the whole of Catholicism after the Council of Trent in reaction to rising religious individualism inspired by the Reformation,

TABLE 7.4: Catholic Baptisms and Marriages

	1977	1987
Live births	744,744	767,828
Baptisms	529,827	488,656
between 0 and 7 years old	525,797	477,654
over 7 years old	4,030	11,134
Civil Marriages	368,166	265,177
1 divorced partner	51,304	59,650
no divorced partner	316,862	205,527
Catholic marriages: as a percentage of civil marriages with no divorced partner	76.7%	70.4%
of which both partners Catholic	231,788	135,964
one non-Catholic	11,138	8,682

Source: Données Socialies (Social Data), INSEE, 1990

was only disrupted in the last 35 years. In fact, throughout the nineteenth century, it was challenged by the laicizing trends implicit in the formation of the Republic, as well as by the spread of industrialization, urbanization and social mobility. However, over the course of the last 50 years, the effects of modernization and individualism have completed the erosion of parochial civilization. This civilization, however imperfectly realized in particular towns and regions, epitomized the identity and ethos of French Catholicism for more than two centuries. Today, the churches are closing. The priests have rejoined the growing cohort of what Max Weber might have called "proletaroid intellectuals," a status which also includes teachers, social workers, and other cultural agents.

More profoundly, not only from the point of view of the church's social position, but also from the standpoint of Catholicism as a system of beliefs, these changes have toppled a whole worldview. A diffuse and private religiosity, oriented toward the immediate gratification of the psychological needs of the individual, has replaced, even among Catholicism's regular practitioners, the traditional orientation towards and pursuit of otherworldly salvation.[8]

TABLE 7.5: The age of the secular clergy as of January 1985

Under 30	122	0.4%
30 to 39	1181	4.2%
40 to 49	3281	11.5%
50 to 59	6810	23.6%
60 to 69	8532	29.8%
70 to 79	6781	23.6%
80 or over	1922	6.7%

Source: Julien Potel, 1988

The Recomposition of Beliefs

To explain this change one could obviously cite the modern advance of rationalism. In a world characterized both by a generalized dominance of rational mathematical thought and by the autonomy and increasing specialization of different sectors of human activity, the religious field itself has become no more than a specialized institutional realm. Functioning according to its own particular rules, religion cultivates the vision of a supernatural universe, a notion progressively discredited by the dominant scientific and technological sector. The marginalization of religion's vision of a unified world parallels religion's decline as a social force. This decline is most evident in the loss of influence suffered by the established historical religions.

While all modern societies have exhibited the same general religious trajectory, individual nations show unique variations. France is no exception, despite the evidence of empirical studies of Catholic participation which seem to confirm general hypotheses of the ineluctable effacement of religion in advanced societies.

For example, the decline in religious observances in France has not been accompanied by a general loss of belief. The decline in church participation has meant instead that religious belief tends to conform less and less to church-defined orthodoxy. A 1986 survey (IFOP-LaVie) showed that 31 percent of the French population still were certain of the existence of God; 35 percent considered it probable; 14 percent considered it improbable; and 12 percent denied it. (Eight percent did not respond.) In response to the question, "Do you consider Jesus Christ to be the son of

God?," 64 percent responded affirmatively, 17 percent negatively, and 19 percent had no opinion. These figures are not very different from those which were obtained in a survey of the same type conducted in 1958. What is evident, however, is a growing tendency toward syncretistic "tinkering" with beliefs that demonstrates the growing deregulation of the religious world. The same survey revealed, for example, that 20 percent of the French believed in reincarnation. A portion of these people were part of the 51 percent of the French who also said they believed in the resurrection of Christ.[9]

In fact, the spreading dissolution of Catholic beliefs and practices is only partly a manifestation of the growing dominance of a rationalism that accords with norms of science and technology. It also indicates the proliferation of beliefs and practices that had remained marginal during the time that the belief sphere was strictly controlled by Roman Catholicism. Thus, the market for horoscopes--not particularly congruent with the triumph of modern rationality, to say the least--has increased regularly since the 1960s, as well as the spread of astrology columns in daily newspapers and magazines. Guy Michelat and Daniel Bois have shown that belief in paranormal and occult sciences, far from characterizing only those branches of society which lag behind in measures of modernity, tends to increase with the social and cultural level of respondents (Bois and Michelat 1986). These facts suggest that the advance of rationalism under the aegis of science and technology has brought in its wake the reactionary development of beliefs and practices that challenge the dominant values and norms of modernity. While the social and cultural waning of Catholicism's institutional influence reflects the growing dominance of the modern worldview, it has also been a factor abetting the expansion of the "cloud of heterodoxies" that has developed in opposition to modernity (Maitre 1988).

Rather than reflexively attributing the disintegration of institutionally regulated observances and beliefs to the progress of secularization, one must recognize it as a complex symptom of the recomposition of the overall sphere of beliefs, whose makeup is determined by each society's particular evolution. In France's case, the principal factor in the process of recomposition is the fragmentation of the long-dominant Catholic tradition along with the marginalization of Christianity itself as a body of meaning. Christianity presents itself more and more as an "exploded Christianity" (de Certeau and Domenach 1974) as it ceases to define particular associations and practices or delineate specific groups and behaviors. Christianity as a cultural reality is not disappearing in France. It is present throughout the social matrix, well beyond the formal influence of the Catholic church. What has eroded is the link between France's Christian cultural roots (admitted and even asserted by the great majority of the French) and traditional Christian practices and associations. While the religious imagery of French Christianity is now appropriated by the wider culture that is outside the control of particular groups or associations, the decline of institutional religious influence has been accompanied by a disintegration of the link between objective conduct and personal beliefs.

The Post-War Generation of Believers:
A New Configuration of Institutional Religion in France

Along with the decline of parochial civilization, there has been a disintegration of the religion that pervades day-to-day personal and interpersonal life and that organizes experience through the repetition of cyclical rituals and liturgical feasts. Empirical studies examining these practices and beliefs confirm that the 1960s was the key decade of socio-religious change.

I have already discussed the economic, political and social circumstances peculiar to France that made these years a decisive turning point between two eras in the progress of modernization. It is also important to remember that these years were the time of the Second Vatican Council which opened a new phase in relationships between the church and the modern world. The transformations of the French Catholic landscape were shaped by these overlapping changes of society and church. The post-war generation was the first generation whose adult religious life was completely structured and organized under these changing conditions.

It is important to examine the new behaviors that are appearing in this transformed socio-religious world. One can identify five significant tendencies in the articulation of the new configuration of French Catholicism.

Festive Religion

The first tendency, linked to the demise of the traditional religiosity that pervaded everyday life, is the development of a festive religiosity that limits its expression to extraordinary and exceptional instances. This exceptional orientation, whether or not linked to conceptions of a sacred dimension, is an intrinsic part of the collective religious experience. The dwindling of institutionally administered religion produces a new situation that breaks the linkage of feasts and day-to-day piety. A new religious time--that of "peak moments"--replaces the cyclical time of the traditional liturgical life. A new religious geography--that of "high places"--imposes itself in place of the religious mapping of space that corresponded to the needs of locally-administered, pervasive religion. New behaviors appear, linked to this transformed vision of religious time and space. They are especially evident among youth but also appear among their parents. This became apparent in the 1970s, with regard to the routine of parish life: The new practitioners no longer attended Mass only in their own parishes but also sometimes traveled many kilometers to participate, for example, in the Easter Assembly at Taizé, or a youth encounter in a Benedictine Abbey, or the feast of Pentecost at Paray-le-Monial. Religion, more and more disentangled from the living memory of a locally-situated community, became associated with "places of memory" still invested with enough spiritual significance to serve as sites for the ephemeral celebrations and episodic rituals of a society shedding most such practices. Could it be that all religion (and Catholicism in particular, as far as France is concerned) functions as a "place of memory" in modernity? The analysis that Pierre Nora offers of the relationship between memory and history in contemporary society provides a fertile perspective for the study of modern religiosity (Nora 1984).

One could, however, also argue that the new phenomena of a separate sacred time and geography result from the development of a new religious sociability, based on voluntary association, temporary assembly and mobile participation. This sociability is transient, fluid, and "a la carte." It unfolds concurrently with the traditional forms of parochial sociability as well as the militant *Action Catholique* movement. Besides the "ordinary practitioner," who practices regular observances and the "militant" who seeks religious transformation of the society, there emerges the figure of the "festive adherent," who combines without inner conflict a social and personal life that is completely secularized and a religious life that is intensive but episodic, organized around exceptional observances.

A New Picture of the Regular Practitioner

As opposed to the "festive adherent" who exhibits the turmoil of the world of Catholic practice, the regular practitioner--the one who conforms to the ecclesiastical requirement of weekly attendance at Mass-- seems to be a vestigial figure participating in a world of observances that are in the process of disappearing. In fact, changes are perceptible even in the remaining "ordinary parishioners." A study done in December, 1989 by CREDOC (*Centre de Recherch pour l'Etude et l'Observation des Conditions de Vie*), produced new data that suggested the emergence of a modified version of the regular practitioner.

For the 25 to 39 year-old group, the percentage of those who regularly attended Sunday Mass was small (6.2 percent). However, this small group revealed some interesting characteristics in comparison with the population of regular practitioners in preceding generations. There used to be a consistent link between a high level of education and a weak degree of religious involvement. "New practitioners," on the contrary, are more educated than the average member of their age group (27 percent hold university degrees compared to 14 percent for the group as a whole). In contrast to older regular practitioners, those from the young generation express great confidence in science and technology and a lively optimism with respect to future economic and social changes. This rapport with scientific and technological modernity manifests itself in patterns of consumption. A large number of younger regular practitioners are owners of personal home computers, cellular phones and microwave ovens, and they favor all the innovations that allow them to modernize everyday life. These data may seem anecdotal, but they reveal a change of mentality that is perceptible in comparison to the attitudes and behaviors of preceding generations of practitioners who exhibited pessimism with regard to science and a marked distrust of technological modernity. These younger practitioners, while identifying themselves with the middle and upper middle bourgeoisie, are more traditional regarding marital and sexual matters,[10] but at the same time are more intense in their social and cultural involvements than the average members of their age group--for example they make more frequent use of libraries and they participate more in local, associational life.

These fragmentary data obviously do not permit us to draw a comprehensive profile of the "new practitioner," but they do tend to invalidate the hypothesis (which certain observers of the end of parochial civilization have tended to develop) that regular observance in advanced society can only be the practice of individuals who are inadequately adapted to modernity. Qualitative studies reveal, however, that regular practice has changed in significance for those concerned. For one, the idea of obligation has been rejected and regular practice is maintained, not because the institution demands it, but because it provides personal spiritual benefit. Religious practice is characterized, not as "constrained" time (the use of which is ordered by the institutions to which the individual belongs), but as "free" time (that the individual can dispose of according to his own choice and personal preference). This concept of optional practice is not unlike the irregular, "a la carte" involvement of the "festive" adherents. It is interesting to observe these modern orientations even among those who, in opting for regular Sunday observance, appear to be the most in conformity with traditional religious standards.

Subjectivization of Religious Experience and Institutional Deregulation

The changed relationship to religious practice has taken place within the more general phenomenon of subjectivization and individualization of religiosity that pervades all aspects of the religious life of Catholic believers in this generation and that has also led us to remarkable levels of institutional deregulation.

This is most visible in the domain of morals: Only seven percent of the already limited group of regular practitioners between the ages of 25 and 39 claim to take papal directives into account when it comes to the use of contraception. Although the question of the freedom of choice of Christian couples in procreation has not given rise in France to an organized protest movement among the faithful, it is clear that people (particularly those who belong to the age group most directly concerned with the issue) generally ignore institutional norms in this matter. When ethical questions that directly concern the individual's conscience are involved, the regulating capacity of the church appears to be conclusively weakened.

This loss of normative authority even extends to the domain of religious doctrine. In the area of beliefs, one observes (especially among those less than 40 years-old but also among older believers) a phenomenon of increasing formulation of "small narratives of belief" only loosely related to the institutionally promulgated "Great Narrative" of Catholic tradition. In this trend, personal experiences and the individual's spiritual search are valued to the point of becoming the primary criteria of verification. The "authenticity" of the personal approach is emphasized over conformity to dogma: "That which counts is not what the church says; it's my experience; it's my inner reality." This insistence on the primacy of the individual's religious path, the value of inner experience, and the importance of the individual's emotional experience are particularly characteristic of the new charismatic Christian movements.[11]

Loss of normative authority is also apparent in the parishes, movements, seminaries, and schools of theology. In them, communitarian intimacy--warm and intense interaction among a small core of believers--is sought as the basis for achieving personal illumination. The shaken Catholic world is pervaded by this "religion of emotional communities" which is above all a religion of voluntary groups.[12] It implies, on the part of each person involved, a personal engagement (if not a conversion in the revivalist sense of the term) of which one must render an account before the group. This dimension of voluntary commitment creates a strong link between the community and its members, a link that assumes the most intensely emotional form in the case of communities of disciples assembled around a charismatic personality.

In each case, however, the repetitive expression of each member's experience tends to become the principal manifestation of community solidarity. This intense expressive dimension of community life is very often associated with a recognition of the importance of sensuality and the body in the spiritual life. It leads some groups to extreme forms of collective enthusiam, including singing, dancing, the practice of glossolalia or other "gifts of the Spirit." In most cases, however, emotional religiosity manifests itself in more moderate forms as a mild communal euphoria, often accompanied by an explicit distrust of formal theological doctrines that are seen as obstacles to the spontaneous expression of faith.

The studies that examine the new forms of religiosity (like the current religious groups of the "esoteric mystical nebula" (Champion 1989)) find the greatest involvement among the generation born after World War II--those who most directly experienced the passage through the "psychological culture" that coalesced after the 1960s as the dominant modern culture of the individual. The effects of this new culture also altered the Catholic world in subtle ways.

Cultural Availability of Christian Symbolism and Reaffirmations of Identity

One will observe that the tendency towards emotionalism and subjectivism in religious expression is only one of the characteristics of the institutional deregulation, noted above. Deregulation also manifests itself in the progressive replacement of the officially sanctioned expressions of Christianity with informal constructions that incorporate elements from the available stock of Christian symbols. In the emotional communities, one can see this process at work in the choice of those elements from the church's tradition (texts, rites, images, etc.) that are the most relevant for intensifying the group's expressive and affective life and the personal fulfillment of individual members. Using the tradition as a "symbolic toolbox," without the mediation of a regulating institution, has also produced a proliferation of identity-affirming variations of the tradition unrelated to any experience of belief. Beyond the control of ecclesiastic institutions, Christian symbols are employed in diverse political, aesthetic and cultural applications, from the invocation of Joan of Arc by the leader of the extreme right, Jean-Marie le Pen, to the utilization of religious figures by the film and advertising industries. These symbols are also used by ideological political operatives concerned with demarcating the dimensions of the national community in the face of the advancing multiculturalism that widespread immigration has brought to all of Europe. The notion of the "Christian (and Catholic) roots" of France thus occupies a central place, for example, in the current debate over the position that Islam should occupy in the French national identity. Currently there are more than three million Muslims in France.[13]

The Catholic church, confronted with the double challenge of preserving the credibility of its cultural position in an increasingly multicultural France and of attracting believers in a society grown indifferent, is hampered by the unregulated appropriation by individuals and groups of the resources of the nation's religious inheritance.

Ethical Homogenization and
Integralist Renewals of Catholic France

Finally, one must point out that, while religious and non-religious appropriations of the Christian tradition are proliferating, there is a growing tendency towards accommodating these "traditions within the tradition" on the basis of similarities with earlier periods in the religious development of France. Contrary to popular notions, France has never constituted a homogeneous "Catholic bloc." Historical and sociological research has long emphasized the diversity of the different regional religious cultures that made up the face of French Catholicism.

Paradoxically, the diffusion of Christianity and the empowerment of the laity have increased the homogenization of French Christianity. As institutional Catholic culture was dissolving, French Catholicism emerged as a more diffuse, but also more homogeneous, ethico-affective milieu. It exhibited a minimal unity based on certain shared values: tolerance, concern for the excluded, attention to interpersonal relations, etc.

Against the notion that the Catholic contribution to society should be limited to this minimal ethical position, and also against the atomization of the Christian heritage that makes it available for the most varied social and cultural appropriations, there has emerged, both within and outside the Catholic church, the assertion of a religious integralism. Integralism rejects the modern differentiation of social spheres and the privatization of religious choice to which this leads.

The crudest and most regressive form of this integralism is that advanced by the factions supporting Monseigneur Lefebvre. (Lefebvre died in 1991, and has been replaced as head of the Saint Pius X Fraternity by a German abbot.) Committed to reconstructing a Christianity identified with the anti-modernist structures of the last century, this faction has come into direct, sometimes violent, conflict with the "modern perversions" of freedom of conscience, freedom of expression, democracy, moral permissiveness, and so forth.[14]

The integralism that the Archbishop of Paris, Mgr. Lustiger, promotes is more subtle in that it does not confront modernity head on. It does not challenge the ideals of modernity. On the contrary it validates them, though it argues that the weakness of modernity is its inability to achieve its own ideals.[15] This form of integralism points out the modern values that modernity fails to preserve: solidarity, the rights of persons, and justice, for example. It asserts that modernity's inadequacies reveal the delusional nature of the modern stress on liberty, and it affirms instead the virtue of subordination to God as the means to liberation (under the auspices of the church as the legitimate bearer of religious power and knowledge).

In a cultural context where there is the spread of improvised belief systems, the church strives to present itself as an institution of refuge. It offers itself as a bulwark against the uncertainties of the modern world. This strategy of Catholic reconstruction may attract certain segments of French Catholicism, particularly among those of the post-war generation most affected by the political disillusionment that followed the utopian dreams of the 1960s. It is not very likely, however, to halt the massive phenomenon of fragmentation and trivialization of Catholic culture that characterizes the contemporary French religious landscape.

One can argue, therefore, that the post-war generation is the one that experienced most directly a major cultural transformation in France. At the moment when it was reaching maturity, it encountered, not the end of Christianity in France, but the disappearance of the traditional social affirmation of Catholic identity that the triumph of cultural modernity brought about.

Notes

1. Translated from the French by Elizabeth Miel.

2. For ease of presentation, we will call this population the "post-war generation" without giving a more technical definition of the word "generation".

3. On the emergence of youth in post-war French society, see Galland (1991).

4. The works of Bourdieu (1964, 1970) constitute the cornerstones of the sociological analysis of the mutation of the French educational world. Among the numerous books which have been published in this area, see Morin (1968) and de Certeau (1968).

5. Several sociological studies have analyzed this crisis in the French clergy. For example, see Rogé (1965), Potel (1977 and 1988). There are also an impressive number of personal accounts, some of which are very illuminating (Duclos, 1983; Bessière et al., 1985; Charles, 1986; etc.).

6. The catechesis of children is now almost entirely conducted by a corps of lay catechists (200,000 in 1984, constituting 87 percent of the total number of catechists). Of these 200,000 catechists, 84 percent are women. The responsibility for the liturgy in those parishes not regularly served by priests tends more and more to be assumed by lay people who organize ADAP (Dominical Assemblies in the Absence of a Priest). This intensification of the participation of the laity in parish life can also be seen in the extremely rapid increase in theological training sessions for the laity (350 centers were counted in 1990 with several thousand students). Also important is the spread of diocesan synods which gather, often over the course of several months, those church members concerned about the ecclesiastical life to discuss and draft pastoral guidelines for their dioceses. More than 30 dioceses have already held or are in the process of holding synods (Hébrard, 1989).

7. According to the philosophy of seminaries inspired by the French school of spirituality (exemplified by Cardinal de Bérulle, 1575-1629, founder of the Oratory of France, and by J-J Olier, 1608-1657, founder of the Company of Priests of Saint Sulpice). These seminaries multiplied at the beginning of the nineteenth century and for the next 150 years trained the bulk of the French clergy. The majority of them are closed today due to the lack of seminarians.

8. Yves Lambert (1985) has made an excellent study of the toppling of the parochial civilization based on the case of a Breton village.

9. On these transformations of and "tinkerings" with beliefs, see surveys presented in the work of Maitre, et al. (1991).

10. While 14 percent of the members of this age group live with a partner without being married, no regular practitioner between 25 and 39 has opted, according to the data of the study cited, for sexual cohabitation.

11. On the charismatic renewal in France see Hébrard (1987); Cohen (1986, 1986b, 1986c); Hervieu-Léger (1987).

12. On the analysis of the religion of emotional communities in relation to cultural modernity, see Hervieu-Léger (1986, 1989).

13. As opposed to 600,000 Jews and about 700,000 Protestants, Islam is now the second largest religious group in France. One of the aspects of the debate concerns the opening of religious centers and mosques (11 in 1970, 1500 in 1990), the minarets of which might someday rival the bell towers, those symbols par excellence of Catholic (and rural) France.

14. On the recent history of the integralist faction and the schism of Monseigneur Lefebvre, see Perrin (1989).

15. This position is particularly well expressed in the book of interviews which Dominique Wolton and Jean-Louis Missika (1987) held with Cardinal Lustiger (*Le Choix de Dieu*).

8

The Surviving
Dominant Catholic Church in Belgium:
A Consequence of
Its Popular Religious Practices?

Karel Dobbelaere

Before discussing certain trends in church involvement and religiosity in Belgium, there are certain particular characteristics of the Belgian religious scene which should be taken into account.

On the societal level, the Catholic church is very visible in Belgium. Although more than one religion is financially supported by the Belgian state, the overwhelming amount of tax money goes to the Catholic church. Catholic churches make up the skylines of the cities, and in the villages they line up alongside the town halls on the main squares. On public holidays--the King's birthday, the national holiday, armistice day--the Catholic church performs the civil-religious rituals. Moreover, the fact that Catholic voluntary organizations--schools, hospitals, trade unions, banks, insurance companies, cultural associations, youth movements, mass media--attend Belgians from the cradle to the grave means that the omnipresence of the so-called Catholic world is palpable. In the political world, the Christian parties -- the so-called political channel (Rokkan 1977) of the Catholic pillar--have governed the Belgian state (with the help of various coalition partners) every year since World War II except for four years. This has consolidated the presence of Catholicism on the institutional level. However, as we will see, due to religious changes on the individual level, the "Catholic" pillar during this time has had to adjust and become a "Christian" pillar (see also Dobbelaere and Voyé 1991: 213-214). On the level of the individual, nearly 65 percent of all Belgians call themselves Catholic: 70 percent of the Flemings, 63 percent of the Walloons and 50 percent of those living in the Brussels region (European Value Study 1990). There are, of course, people living in Belgium who are members of other religions: 2 percent are Islamic, 1 percent are Protestant, 0.5 percent are Jewish, and there are Orthodox, Anglicans, sectarians and members of cults. However, members of these religions add up to only 5 percent of the population at the most, and the material density of these groups is so low, that--except for the Jews in Antwerp, the Muslims in Brussels and some other cities, and the Protestants in a few communities--they are almost invisible. In fact, the "Secular Humanists" are the second largest ideological community, representing about 10 percent of the population (the remaining 20 percent are religiously indifferent). Modern Belgian political history might even be written in terms of the conflict--starting in the mid-nineteenth century--between Catholics and Radical Liberals and, later on, Socialists, since the core of the Secular Humanists which make up these party machines was actively anti-Catholic and later even anti-religious. Consequently, if in the Belgian collective consciousness there is a kind of pluralism, it is to be characterized less as pluralism per se than as a dichotomy of Catholicism and secularism--with the latter ceasing to be anti-Catholic so much as manifesting indifference to Catholicism and interest in the magical (Elchardus et al. 1990: 115-117).

Let us now turn to the dominant Catholic population and discuss recent changes in their religious involvement.

Involvement in the Catholic Church: Descriptive Data

The most extensive study of the opinions, beliefs, values and practices of Belgians was undertaken by the European Value Systems Study Group (EVSSG) in 1981 (Kerkhofs and Rezsohazy 1984; Harding et al. 1986). Table 8.1 gives a comprehensive overview of the mean Belgian results and the social factors explaining significant differences in the religious field (Dobbelaere 1984: 71, 105). In 1990, the study was repeated. All the data of this new survey will be available in 1993. If data from the 1990 survey which are already available disconfirm the 1981 findings, this will be made clear.

The table clearly indicates that church involvement, beliefs and ethical views vary according to age differences (and gender when combined with occupational status). Indeed, the existing so-called gender differences are solely attributable to women not in paid employment; women who are employed display an outlook in religious and moral matters close to those of men (Dobbelaere 1984: 111). In the 1990 Belgian survey, differences only appeared concerning beliefs, praying and general

TABLE 8.1: Comprehensive table of significant differences in religious commitment and church involvement according to gender, age and economic involvement in Belgium (EVSSG-unpublished data, 1981)

Gender, age & employment	Believe in a "personal" God (%)	Do not believe in God (%)	Accept that the First Commandment is totally applicable to them (%)	Regular church attendance on weekends (%)	Permissiveness in sexual morals and bioethics (mean score)	Pray, meditate and contemplate (%)
Employed women and men according to age						
18-34 yrs (289)	26	19	34	22	3.5	49
35-54 yrs (275)	37	12	48	25	3.0	49
55+ (175)	38	13	48	31	2.3	49
Women without occupation according to age						
18-34 yrs (109)	37	10	41	28	3.2	55
35-54 yrs (102)	43	5	55	42	2.3	70
55+ (189)	57	5	65	43	2.1	74

religiosity. The differences in external behavior--church membership and church practice--had almost disappeared. All other traditional social variables--such as level of education, income, social class, home ownership and urbanization--had no impact or only an incidental impact. No stable trends could be detected relative to these variables, which is a change since the 1950s and 1960s (e.g., Dobbelaere 1966 and Voyé 1973). These results are confirmed by other European studies and EVSSG studies undertaken in other European countries (Dobbelaere 1984: 102-105; and Dobbelaere, 1992).

The big question about age variations is, do they indicate a cohort change or are they life-cycle variations? Data on Flanders adapted by J. Billiet allow us to answer this question (see Figure 8.1). First of all, when comparing cohort trends over a 15-year period (1975-1990), the figures suggest a decline in church practice within cohorts, the more so in the younger than the older cohorts. Comparing age categories over a 15-year period of time, we find a lower percentage of people practicing on Sundays, and this is more pronounced in the younger than in the older age categories. This suggests that we are witnessing period effects having a differential impact on the cohorts. The fact that the J-curve became more pronounced over the last 15 years corroborates this conclusion. Figure 8.2, registering the number of people declaring that they are not Catholic, indicates a rise in all cohorts. Comparing age categories we see a rising number of self-declared non-Catholics, and this is higher the younger people are. In this figure we see a more accentuated reversed J-curve. This reinforces our interpretation of a differential impact of period effects on the cohorts. In the long run, even in Flanders, the eventual result might be nearly 40 percent non-Catholics and only 10 percent practicing Catholics, and this is a consequence of cohort changes.

In a recent study we conducted with parents whose children were confirmed at the age of 11-12 years in the Catholic church in 1987 and 1988 in area of Leuven, the cohort differences were still more clearly marked (Table 8.2). I should warn, however, that these figures on church attendance are slightly distorted: a high percentage of parents not involved in the church are not represented in the data since, first of all, their non-response rate was much higher than that of parents involved in the church, and, secondly, the parents whose children do not take classes in Catholic religion in primary schools--estimated at 8 to 10 percent--and whose children are, consequently, excluded from confirmation, were not included in the study.

It is clear that the younger cohorts are less and less involved in the church, and this is true even among those parents who want their children to be confirmed in the church. Those born in 1952 were 16 years old in 1968; in their young adulthood, they experienced an enormous decline in

FIGURE 8.1: Regularly practicing Catholics in Flanders comparison 1975 and 1990 (GLOPO and IAO)

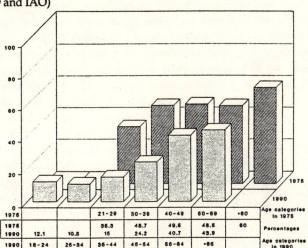

			21-29	30-39	40-49	50-59	+60	Age categories in 1975
1975			35.3	48.7	49.6	48.6	60	Percentages
1990	12.1	10.8	15	24.2	40.7	43.9		
1990	18-24	26-34	36-44	45-54	55-64	+65		Age categories in 1990

Source: J. Billet and J. Vanhoutvinck, 1991: 53

attendance on weekends monitored by the Catholic church (see Figure 8.3), especially in Flanders (1968-73). Those born later were, in the large majority of cases, raised by parents who had already stopped attending church on weekends.

Some people might, of course, object that my analysis is based only on church attendance, and that beliefs and ethical practices are more important in evaluating the religiosity and church involvement of individuals. However, the EVSSG study undertaken in Belgium has clearly shown that the beliefs people hold are strongly related to their church attendance, and that the most important belief tenet is their conception of God. The belief in a "personal God" correlates well with traditional beliefs in life after death, a soul, Hell, Heaven and sin. Furthermore, the majority of those believing in a "personal God" attend a church service weekly. Those conceiving of God as a "spirit" or "life force" and those who "do not really know how to 'conceive' Him" attend less frequently. Finally, people who doubt His existence or do not believe in Him overwhelmingly are not involved in church. This relationship was also confirmed in other EVSSG studies. Moreover, in our recent study on parents and children who were confirmed, this relationship between the conceptions of God and church attendance, studied with more complex indicators, was confirmed. In the Belgian EVSSG study, the predictability of a person's affiliation to and involvement in the church based on his

FIGURE 8.2: Self-declared Non-Catholics in Flanders

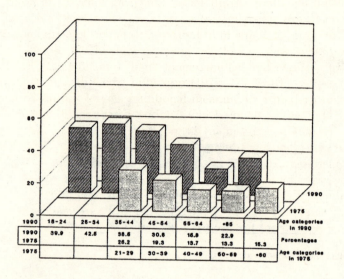

Source: J. Billet and J. Vanhoutvinck, 1991: 54

conception of God was statistically higher than the reverse (Dobbelaere 1984: 82-84).

    According to the EVSSG studies, the divergence of expressed beliefs concerning God also has implications for the ethical points of view which people adopt: the belief in a "personal God" tends to promote the acceptance of absolute moral guidelines as opposed to the notion that good and evil depend entirely upon the circumstances at the time. In contrast, a "relativistic" position, which takes into account the status of the person, his motives and his circumstances, is more likely to be endorsed by those who believe in a "spirit" or "life force" as well as by those who either do not believe in God or are uncertain of their beliefs (Harding et al. 1986: 49). And again, just as for affiliation, involvement and beliefs, moral attitudes--attitudes towards the Ten Commandments, permissiveness in the area of sex and bio-ethics, etc.--vary with age, not only in Belgium, but, in all nations studied by EVSSG. The younger cohorts, whether affiliated to a church or not, are less orthodox and less traditional, than the older generations (Dobbelaere 1992).

    We may then conclude our descriptive section by stating that beliefs, church attendance and ethical views are strongly connected and

TABLE 8.2: Data on church attendance in percentages of parents whose children were confirmed in the Catholic Church in parts of the conglomeration of Leuven in 1987 and 1988.

Gender & age	Nearly every week to every week	On important religious holidays to once a month	On special occasions or never
Women born			
Before 1946 (57)	54	28	18
1946-51 (119)	39	42	19
1952 and later (84)	18	47	35
Men born			
Before 1946 (91)	44	33	23
1945-51 (112)	32	30	38
1952 and later (45)	5	33	62

that these dimensions reveal a clear difference between generations. Let me also stress the importance that the conception of God has on these dimensions.

Changes Explained: Secularization and the "Conception of God"

To explain the decline in church religiosity, references have been made to secularization, the process of functional differentiation, and the accompanying processes of rationalization, mechanization, societalization and bureaucratization. However, as all these processes occur on the societal or macro-level, a link has to be made between these societal processes and changes on the individual level. Durkheim's sociology of religion and knowledge gives us a clue.

It is my contention--in keeping with Durkheim (1912), Swanson (1960), and other sociologists and anthropologists--that people develop a concept of personified supernatural beings directly from the model which their society provides. But, as Swanson added, any satisfactory explanation should not only account for faith, it should explain disbelief as well. He suggests:

> any of the following to produce disbelief:
> a) Lack of contact with primordial and constitutional structures of society.
> b) Alienation from those structures.
> c) The assumption that all, or the most significant features of those structures are knowable and controllable by human effort.

To assume that humans can know and control all, or the most
important, aspects of such structures, is to destroy, in principle,
many of the features which give certain social organizations a
supernatural aura--their properties of invisibility, immortality,
pervasiveness, inescapability, and their control over conduct
through what seems to be direct induction of purpose (Swanson
1960: 188-189).

Consequently, I suggest the following hypothesis. Changes in
social structure have produced two major changes in the belief structure of
contemporary people: control over societal substructures--e.g., the
economy, illness, procreation--has destroyed for more and more people the
belief in God; and the growing impersonality of the societal relationships
has undermined the belief in a "personal God" even for those who still
believe in God. However, since the increased differentiation of society (if I
may take Toennies work about the decline of the *Gemeinschaft* as a
landmark) was already developing at the end of last century, we may
expect the recession of the belief in a "personal God" to be more advanced
than the disbelief in God.

It seems to me that this prediction proves to be correct according to
the data in Table 8.1. These categories of people are differentially involved
in a secularized world: the younger cohort more than the older cohorts
and, except in recent times, those employed more than the non-employed.
Therefore, fewer of those who were or are more involved in a secularized
world believe in a "personal God," and a smaller percentage, however
along the same lines, no longer believe in God. This latter percentage is
still rising in the younger age categories since the number of non-Catholics
in Belgium is rising (see Figure 8.2), a fact which in Belgium is associated,
as I indicated, with doubt and non-belief.

Let me make the argument clearer. Young adult men and young
adult employed women have always lived and worked in a world that is
considered controllable and calculable. The world of young adults is a
world of the "here and now" in which interaction is based on role
relationships that are planned and coordinated. A more and more
rigorously applied functional differentiation, specialization, and
rationalization of labor which mechanizes and fragments jobs results in
work that seems less and less "meaningful" and in task relationships in
which "humane" contact diminishes more and more. Relations are
superficial, functional, hierarchical. Everyone is replaceable in his or her
role. Communications are shallow and utilitarian: people relate to one
another in a "segmented" way: as workers, clerks, employees, merchants,
buyers, vendors, neighbors, functionaries. Personal, lasting relationships
are very much reduced in our society, even outside the work sphere, and
remain typical only in the family and friendship relations.

Middle-aged and older men and employed women have also become progressively caught in the industrial and commercial world. But are young adult unemployed women not somewhat screened from this economic world? Important changes have also taken place in the family sphere during the last decades. Since the 1960s, the mechanization of domestic tasks has advanced much further, and even the most intimate, sexual relationships and their "consequences" are considered to be calculable and controllable. Not only can one better control the consequences but the sexual act itself is also presented in most modern "handbooks" as "technically improvable." In these books, love is almost reduced to an obligatory orgasm which at best--due to its inherently fleeting nature--is of no "consequence."

The most "traditionalist" group comprises middle age and older housewives. They have known a different world where other values predominated: tradition, love, devotion, loyalty, humility, and service. The world in which personal, lasting relationships were still possible (a family undisturbed by the mass media), in which the total person was implicated, and where attachment and reciprocity rather than competition dominated, offered a favorable substratum for monotheistic religions. Religions that offered total and personal salvation and could develop in a *Gemeinschaft* belong to the past, and today have become alien to more and more people (Wilson 1976: 273; Wilson 1982: 27-32; and Martin 1978: 160-161).

For many, a *jenseitige* God who controls a *diesseitige* world is, if conceivable, more and more unacceptable: human beings are thought to be capable of commanding and solving their own problems, "*they* have the whole world in *their* hands" is an altered version of a well-known Afro-American spiritual. And if individuals themselves cannot solve their problems, there are many specialists available to help them: medical doctors, psychiatrists, psychologists, social workers, family therapists, and so on. These days, people consult them rather than priests. In cases of long-lasting infertility, Belgian people formerly went on pilgrimages praying to a lovely, noble, and merciful lady in white with a rosary in her hands; now people resort to a serene, noble, and competent man or woman in white with a stethoscope around his or her neck. What an older generation still saw as "grace from the One above" now receives a natural explanation. What was thought to be under the control of a "creative God" is now commanded by human beings within the domain of the medical profession.

For many people life no longer comes from God. Humans control it, command it in test-tubes, even experiment with it, while television cameras track the process and bring it into the living room. Couples are invited to "play doctor *and* God" through gender choice kits. Hence, life has lost its sacredness and people have taken control of it: suicide and euthanasia are more and more accepted and propagated, and abortion is increasingly regarded not as a "sin" but as a "solution" for genetic failure, for physical, psychological and social threats to the well-being of the mother and the family, and for contraceptive failure. Generally, the Christian notion of sin has disappeared from moral discourse or, if it is still used, has lost its Christian meaning. Sin has become synonymous with guilt feelings or shame. It no longer implies repentance, penance, and reconciliation with God. Luhmann (1977: 227-228) has stressed that the notion of sin has lost its traditional meaning in a modern society. In a functionally differentiated society, which involves the individual only segmentally and where religion as a meaning-system has lost its overarching position relative to the different functional subsystems, only "partial" failures and technical defects can occur. Human beings in their "totality" are never involved in a functional subsystem. Consequently, a situational ethic is adapted to such a system. This ethic takes into account the particularity of the functional subsystem, the circumstances, those involved, and their motivation. The majority of the Belgian interviewees rejected objective ethical norms and adhered to a situational ethic, which confirms the secularization of ethics.

When people take command of their world, God is more and more removed from it. However, if for some people the notion of God lingers on, He is more and more conceived of as a general power, a spirit, "something" vague and general, a "higher power" and not as a "personal God." How could He be thought of as a "personal God" if people experience fewer and fewer "personal relationships" in their social lives? In a society where control, calculation, and planning are the basis for success, where results are of utmost importance, where competition -- even in families -- is legion, where people do not have time for one another, but where role players have superficial encounters, there the belief in a "personal God," and consequently the celebration of the Eucharist, seems for many an atavism (see Table 8.1). In the Eucharist, one celebrates one's relationship with a caring, forgiving, and comforting Father, who is the Lord, Creator, King, and Savior, the Protector and Comforter of the oppressed.

My basic argument is that many people can no longer believe in God because not only the physical but also the psychological and social worlds are now seen as controllable and calculable. Consequently, human beings can manipulate these worlds: their actions become calculated, systematic, regulated, and routinized; they also become disconnected from religion and God. This not only has had an impact on church attendance and the desacralization of ethics but it has also desacralized for people the meaning of life, suffering, and death. Indeed, recent sociological studies in the Netherlands have documented the impact of the secularization of the social system on the meaning people give to life, suffering, and death. "An idea like Kluckhohn's that there are 'sets of existential premises almost inextricably blended with values in the overall picture of experience' cannot be postulated any more" (Thung et al. 1985: 147). Value orientations seem to vary independently of beliefs and interpretations of life, suffering, and death; nor is a relationship established between such interpretations and people's beliefs (Thung et al., 1985: 112-113, 157-159, and 194-195; Felling et al. 1982: 26-53; Felling et al. 1983: 144-147). These studies suggest that the organizing principles of life have been detached from religious interpretations: they document a process of "secularization" on the level of the individual (Felling et al. 1986: 76; and de Moor 1987: 47). The differentiation of the personal life-world, which we can aptly describe as *compartmentalization*, results in the marginalization of religion in the personal life of the individual. This desacralization on the individual level often results either in the rejection of God or in His depersonalization. Indeed, if for some the notion of God lingers on, it is no longer conceived as a personal God but as something vague, a "higher power." And as Durkheim (1960: 144 and 272-276) suggested, the more general and vague God becomes, the more removed He is from this world and the more ineffective He is. At the same time such a belief is very shaky. It is a belief in an abstract notion without real impact on people's lives, and can easily be disposed of.

Church Attendance: A Historical Process

The data collected in 1981 by EVSSG and those presented in Table 8.2 and Figures 8.1 and 8.2 were a cross-section: they are the consequence of a still-developing historical current. This development can easily be seen in Figure 8.3, which gives the proportion of people regularly going to church on weekends (related to the total number of inhabitants 5-69 years old) in Belgium and the three Belgian regions. The mean yearly percentage point decline per region by historical period is also shown.

It is clear from this figure that the decline accelerated in the period 1967-1973: before then it was -0.7 percentage points per year in Belgium; then for six years it increased to -1.8, i.e., more than 2.5 times the previous rate. How can we explain this drastic acceleration of the decline in church attendance? First, it cannot be explained solely within the Belgian context: it happened in the Catholic church all over the world. Second, as it was not limited to the Catholic church (Van Hemert 1980: 10-11), it cannot be explained as an exclusively Catholic phenomenon. Consequently, Greeley's explanation that the decline was caused by the papal encyclical on birth control in 1968 (*Humanae Vitae*) is too simple; in the Netherlands, the decline started even before the publication of the encyclical

(Dobbelaere 1988a: 88-89).   Others suggested that the decline was a consequence of Vatican II. However, this other *institutional* factor does not explain why it started in the early 1960s in France, and especially why in Belgium, as in Canada, the attendance drop-off starting after Vatican II was far from uniform within countries (Bibby 1987: 19-22; see Figure 8.3 for Belgium: twice as high a rate of decline in Flanders than in Wallonia and the Brussels region). An analysis of the available data points to *contextual* circumstances to explain what happened: i.e., the industrialization and modernization processes producing secularization. Their acceleration in Flanders and Quebec in the 1960s explains the belated and more dramatic declines that occurred there. How is this related to the explanation developed in the previous section?

Several studies have established that social behavior is dependent on social control, and consequently this behavior lingers on much longer than beliefs and opinions. In the Netherlands, for example, pillarized behavior was still very prominent when people's mentality was already de-pillarized (Thurlings 1978: 210-218). In my research on the Catholic character of the Catholic University of Leuven in the early 1970s, I observed that many professors were still going to church every Sunday, although their beliefs and moral attitudes no longer conformed to the church's theological and moral teachings (Dobbelaere et al. 1976: 880). Consequently, one might surmise that under the growing impact of people's capabilities, belief in a "personal God" and in other articles of faith had already been strongly undermined in the 1960s when Western civilization was in its "golden age," but that overt traditional behavior simply continued under the impact of social control. Sunday Mass became for many a duty--a tradition--not supported by belief in a "personal God."

When, by the mid-1960s, a religious discussion started--very explicitly in Flanders regarding Robinson's *Honest to God*, in Belgium with regard to the publication of *Humanae Vitae* (1968), and also, but more explicitly, in Flanders, after the refusal in 1966 of the Belgian bishops to divide the Universitas Catholica Lovaniensis according to the particularistic language situation of the country--it could be acknowledged for the first time in public discourse and the mass media that the religious understanding of beliefs, church ethics and church authority were very much undermined. Public discussion about the implementation of the conciliar resolutions of Vatican II also made this apparent, and had an impact on the clergy, who, in the same period, left the church in massive numbers (Dobbelaere 1988b: 104), a fact which had repercussions for the beliefs, attitudes and behavior of lay people.

The sharp decline in Sunday Mass attendance at the end of the 1960s and in the early 1970s may, consequently, be seen as the collapse of a traditional behavior that was no longer supported by the belief in a

FIGURE 8.3: Proportion of People Regularly Attending Church

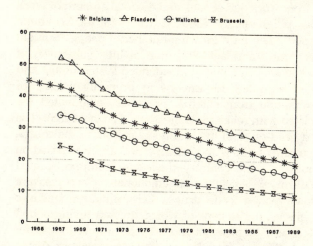

Mean Percentage Point Drop Per Year: Per Period and Per Region

1964-1966	*1967-1972*	*1973-1979*	*1980-1989*	
-.7	-1.8	-.8	-.9	Belgium
-	-2.3	-.9	-1.1	Flanders
-	-1.2	-.8	-.7	Wallonia
-	-1.6	-.6	-.4	Brussels

Source: Office of Church Statistics, 1992

"personal God" and the traditional values that the church proclaimed. It was a downwards convergence of public behavior and the personal general disbelief in the doctrines and values of the church. Since then, social control has increasingly had a completely different impact: it has begun to keep people out of church, whereas before it had induced them to attend. Compared to France, where the sharp decline in regular church attendance started in the early 1960s--between 1961 and 1966 it dropped from 38 to 20 percent (Donegami 1984: 56)--it seems that in Belgium--like in the Netherlands and Germany--Catholic organizations, i.e., the Catholic pillar, held people in the fold of the church much longer. However, when the dikes finally gave way, the flood was heavy: in six years time, 10.6 percent of the Belgian and 13.5 percent of the Flemish populations stopped attending church regularly on weekends.

This behavior was also occasioned by a structural change: leisure time increased and the development of leisure activities led to a "leisure culture." In the 1960s and 1970s, an increasing number of people were granted more and more leisure time: not only more vacation time but also granted more and more leisure time: not only more vacation time but also Saturdays were freed from work and school, and the total amount of work time each week was progressively reduced from 48 to 38 hours. Consequently, in a period when for a growing number of people "Sunday mass" became a "sheer duty" and an "obligation of little substance," it became more and more located in a period of extended leisure time. And the pleasure associated with leisure time--being primarily a time of "freedom" and of "exemption from external pressures"--aggravated the feeling of "duty" associated with religious "obligations" (Yonnet 1985). The leisure culture collided head-on with the traditional culture of the church which legitimated a "culture of duties and self-restraint" and was based on the notion of "community." On the contrary, the leisure culture celebrated freedom and individualism, massification and emotionalism, and pleasure and ecstasy--which some looked for in drugs. Leisure culture was also promoted in advertisements, the slogans of which stressed "living it up," enjoyment, and indulgence. The pleasure and excitement to be looked for were fashionable--new looks, new trends, new fashions, new products-- whereas the church in its teachings and rituals "repeated"--it stressed tradition and continuity.

It seems then that after World War II parents introduced their children to a religion of "sheer duty," of "obligations without substance" which came to conflict with the societal culture. An empty tradition revealed parental doubts but these could not be discussed due to lack of time, as increasingly *both parents* were working. As a result, more and more children rejected behavior that they considered hypocritical. A new generation had come of age that was openly less attached to the church (Rezsohazy 1985: 278-279), and the vanishing church-going elderly were no longer replaced by the young. Consequently, the relative number of people attending church on weekends still declined (see Figure 8.3). The slowing down of this decline in the Brussels region might indicate that a rock bottom is being reached, a hypothesis which the survey data for Flanders presented in Figure 8.2 also suggests. An estimate of fewer than 10 percent practicing Catholics in Belgium might easily be realized in less than two decades.

I have been arguing that people now think and act more and more in terms of knowledge, control, and planning, and less and less in terms of the random, or in terms of beliefs and magic. The application of science to technology has reduced the relevance of the supernatural and of God. This emerged very clearly in a recent study of Flemish farmers who were born in the 1930s (Van Trier 1986: 195-211). In the 1970s, about 35 percent of this sample had stopped putting "sacred palms" (distributed in the churches on Palm Sunday) in their fields. Some stopped because they no longer grew corn, but the vast majority stopped because this custom had become, in their own words, nothing more than "an outdated usage," a "tradition." Several added that it had become "useless": "artificial fertilizers are now much better than before" and "it doesn't bring rain." In other words "there is no need for it any more"; in the farmers' opinion the practice had lost its "instrumentality" and no longer had an "expressive" function.

The exodus from the church was also well documented in that study: the higher the farmers scored on a modernization index, the less they believed in a "personal God" or used "sacred palms." Does this not indicate that the more people think in terms of control and planning, the more difficult it is for them to believe in a "personal God"? And might we not hypothesize that in the long run a belief in God as a "vague, general power" could end up in unbelief, after a period in which the individual was a "seasonal Catholic"?

We need to be careful with such predictions. In Belgium, according to the European Value Study, people believing in a "vague, general power" which they still call God have not severed all relationships with the church: they still participate to some extent in rituals, at least in "rites of passage." Such people represent a middle position: to the right are those who believe in a "personal God" and who normally go to church on weekends; to the left are those who no longer believe in God and who have mostly quit the church altogether. This middle category now represents the average commitment to the church. In the 1950s, most Belgians were practicing Catholics. Now nearly 60 percent are affiliated with the church only for the sacralization of some religious holidays (Christmas, Easter, the Assumption, All Saints Day) or of certain role transitions: births or parenthood, adolescence, marriage, and death (the "rites of passage"). How do we explain such ritualization?

Religion as Celebration and Incantation

Figure 8.4 clearly indicates that a high percentage of Belgians are brought to church at death. This percentage has been quite stable over the last 20 years: there has been a drop of only two percentage points (84 to 82 percent). This stability is in striking contrast with Mass attendance: since 1967 the difference between both percentages (church burial and church attendance) grew from 40 to 60 percentage points. There was however also a clear change in seasonal ritual behavior among those young adults marrying and having children. Fewer and fewer marriages were celebrated in the church: during the last 22 years a decline of 26 percentage points has been registered. Regional differences in Belgium--a greater decline for example in the Brussels region, an area that is religiously very pluralistic with a heavy Muslim population, than in Flanders--suggest the differential impact of immigration but also the growing number of remarrying divorcees. There are more and more divorced people who, even though they can now remarry in the church, are declining to do so. This number has tripled since the mid-1960s, and continued to grow rapidly in the 1980s. The decline of the proportion of children brought to church for baptism was a little less : 18 percentage points. Here again, immigration does not explain the complete picture. A detailed study confirmed the average decline of baptism as twice the average decline of Belgian live births in 1968-1979 (0.8 versus 0.4 percentage points per year) (Dobbelaere 1988a: 49-51). Consequently, we may conclude that more and more young adults disaffiliate from the church, which is another indicator of the cohort changes in Belgium, and confirms the survey results presented in Figures 8.1 and 8.2.

However, the graph also reveals that during the last 22 years, the number of non-practicing Catholics brought to church at birth or at death, or going to church for marriage, grew 1.1 to 1.5 times, depending upon the criteria used. The same is true when comparing the number of practicing Catholics with those calling themselves Catholic. After Vatican II, the church officially adapted to the modern world. It did so in a number of ways: by recognizing the specificity of the secular world; by reducing its formalism and by rationalizing not only its conception of Heaven, but also its rituals and practices by eliminating magical and festive elements; by small steps in the direction of democracy; and by requiring an explicit and voluntary adherence. It frowned on "cultural" Catholics, sometimes even, until the early 1970s, refusing them or their children rites of passage. Yet in this period the proportion of "cultural" Catholics grew. For lack of alternative religions, people wanting to sacralize changes in status asked the Catholic church to perform the rites. And for lack of pluralism in Belgium, the church could not, as in the United States, refer "lax" Catholics to Protestant denominations for sacred rituals. Consequently, the church became less demanding and recognized "lax" Catholics. In France, the change of name from "cultural" to "festive" Catholics (Bonnet 1973; Pannet 1974), was a clear indication of a change in attitude towards them and of the recognition that they manifested an important aspect of the culture.

Indeed, the tension between the "rational" and the "festive" is very clear in the recent history of the church. Over a few decades, the church changed "Solemn Communion" into a "Confession of Faith" or "Confirmation," seeking to stress the sacramental dimension and the intellectual aspect of the commitment of the young person or adolescent to the "community of believers." However, our studies point out that for a large number of parents, what counts is not only the churchly and community aspect of the rite, but also the festive and familial aspect of it as the occasion helps reunite close kin and friends around an abundant table. For many Belgian children, since confirmation is a "rite of passage" marking the transition from childhood to adulthood, it is nearly a rite of "*au revoir"* to the church rather than a rite of "commitment" as adulthood means the abandonment of church attendance on weekends for most Belgians (Dobbelaere and Voyé 1991: 104-105).

This example makes it clear that rites are polysemic; people attribute meaning to them which differs from that of the church (Voyé 1973: 225-238). It reveals that people assemble a "bricolage" of religious elements to make their own religion. Religion becomes a personal "collage" rather than a "received" one, a "subjective" rather than an "objective" religion. This is of course related to the individuation of decisions, which is a structural consequence of functional differentiation and the inclusion requirement (Luhmann 1977: 232-248). It is also related to the cultural adage "cogito ergo sum" which may be understood as *I* think and *I* choose *my* practices to express *my* religious feelings and *my* beliefs and norms, only now emphasized to a greater degree. Indeed, even practicing Catholics "pick and choose" the beliefs they can accept, not only rejecting some of the traditional tenets of the Catholic belief-system, but even adding elements drawn from alien religions. In Belgium for example, the EVSSG research established that 20 percent of practicing Catholics believe in reincarnation and only one-third of them believe in Hell and the devil (Dobbelaere 1984: 72-73).

These structural changes had an exceptional impact on the upper classes, especially on intellectuals. Their professional concern with intellectual scrutiny, and their disposition to doubt and to offer hypotheses rather than theses, were finally extended to religion. Since the church had lost credibility as a consequence of scientific discoveries, and since the process of secularization had divested the church of its capacity to legitimate the status of the upper classes, intellectuals and members of the upper-middle and upper classes dissociated from it. This explains why the well-established relationship between the upper-middle and upper classes and church involvement which persisted until the late 1960s (Dobbelaere 1966: 361-394; Voyé 1973) has, in the period since then, gradually dissolved. This development, according to the EVSSG studies, is not limited to Belgium. Now all social classes practice equally little.

Not only "modernity," but also "post-modernity" had an impact on individuation, the latter underscoring even more the process of individualization. Modernity still stressed collective identities--the proletariat, the bourgeoisie, women, consumers, militants--who had a historic role to play: their actions would build a new society, a new world (Touraine 1984). However, the militant vanished and with him *"les visions totalisantes"* (Balandier 1985: 138-140), and "the grand narratives" (Lyotard 1984: 37). Now, more than ever, the person is thrown back on himself in his confrontation with daily problems, creating his own solutions to them (Voyé 1985: 269-2; 1988a: 129-130).

FIGURE 8.4: Frequency of Catholic Baptisms (related to live births), Catholic Marriages (related to total number of weddings), Catholic Burials (related to the total number of funerals) and Regular Church Attendance (related to total number of inhabitants 5-69 years old) in Belgium (percent).

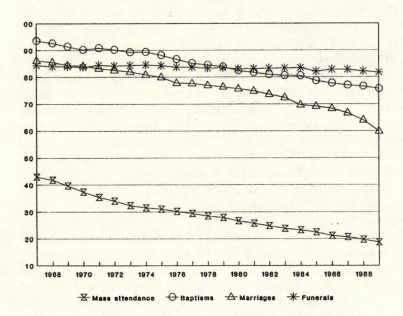

Source: Office of Church Statistics, 1992

Here again, Catholicism offers some relief: popular religion--pilgrimages, candlelight blessings, charms, novenas, etc.--helps ritualize petitions, not only to God, for help, but especially to the Holy Mother and particularly the saints (Voyé 1988a). These forms of popular religion allow the individual not only to respond directly to his own problems of everyday life but also to those of his kin and friends, with whom he lives in close networks, these "*niches individuelles*." According to a recent study on pilgrimages, it is especially (although not exclusively) those Catholics practicing irregularly who are motivated to go on pilgrimages to the Holy Mother in Scherpenheuvel (Flanders) to address their "actual needs." The subjective image of the Holy Mother is very much related to "needs," most of all among non-practicing and irregularly practicing

Catholics. For practicing Catholics, on the contrary, going on pilgrimage is more a devotional practice (Robbrecht 1986: 64).

Do the preceding data indicate the decline of religion in general and the vanishing of the spiritual or the disappearance of the sacred? I do not think so. One aspect of post-modernity is the emergence of post-materialism. Defined by R. Inglehart (1990: 87) as the stressing of ideas over fighting rising prices, participation over law and order, freedom of speech over a stable economy, ecology over economic growth, and "Gemeinschaftlichkeit" over societalization, research indicates that in the Western world post-materialist values are rising and reflect "intergenerational value change." However, studies also indicate that "Post-materialists are significantly less likely to say they believe in God, and less likely to describe themselves as religious, than those with Materialist or mixed values" (Inglehart 1990: 192). In Belgium, according to my analysis of the EVSSG data of 1981, Post-materialists exhibit less church practice than Materialists or those with mixed values. This is most pronounced within the older population--aged 55 years and older. Despite their seemingly relative rejection of traditional religion, in each of the Western societies studied, "the Post-materialists are *more* apt than the Materialists to spend time thinking about the meaning and purpose of life." These data then suggest that since the traditional answers of the churches do not respond to their quests, Post-materialists have to look for the satisfaction of their spiritual needs elsewhere.

Conclusion

The church largely lost its social functions during the secularization process which also compartmentalized the individual's *Lebenswelt* and resulted in the marginalization of religion in private life. The decline of the church was also a consequence of the way in which it distanced itself from everyday life as it attempted to adjust to modernity through rationalization and functional differentiation. The continual use by the church of its "global vision," its theoretical, universal, and deductive approach to the problems of everyday life -- e.g., matters of abortion, in vitro fertilization, birth control and divorce -- also alienated many people. However, its surviving popular practices with their possibilities for celebration and for incantations still kept a lot of people more or less in its grip. Today, the church seems to survive in Belgium largely because of the polysemic nature of its rituals and practices, and, to a lesser extent, as a consequence of the survival in the collective memory of the old opposition between the Catholic and the secularist world. However, this opposition is receding, and cohort comparisons (see Figure 8.2) and cohort value changes indicate also that in the near future the church might more and more lose its ascendancy over the younger generations, especially as the second generation of unchurched becomes more numerous.

The changes in behavior and attitudes of Catholics were clearly influenced by the Catholic pillar. At first, the pillar kept people in the church, at least as far as external behavior was concerned. However, when personal criticisms of and questions about church doctrine, ethics and policies were made public, the pillar could no longer prevent the disengagement of its flock as we have seen. Consequently, the Catholic pillar was forced to adapt to the conceptions of its members and clients. As we have described in previous publications, the "Catholic" pillar became a "Christian" pillar: it no longer referred first of all to Catholic doctrine. Instead, it stressed more and more the so-called Christian values of solidarity, social justice, a human approach to its clients, "Gemeinschaftlichkeit," etc. This new "sacred canopy" is symbolized by a "C," referring more and more to *Christian* (i.e., the Gospel) rather than Catholic (i.e., church) doctrines. The former is considered more universalistic, the latter more confining and particularistic (Dobbelaere and Voyé 1991 : 213-214).

Nevertheless, the religious changes on the individual level not only influenced the pillar; the "new" pillar also helped people to adjust to modernity. In the Christian adult and youth movements, educational programs were set up to counsel the lower and middle classes in the professional and economic sphere, the religious domain and family life (Van Molle 1990; Laermans 1992; Peeters 1990). On the other hand, the new pillar also constituted for parts of the upper-middle class and the lower-upper class a way of affirming their social status. However, this was only true for a fraction of these strata. Others had to create their own networks to adapt to the contextual changes. L. Voyé's chapter in this collection makes clear how some have done this in Belgium.

9

From Institutional Catholicism to "Christian Inspiration": Another Look at Belgium

Liliane Voyé

In the preceding chapter, Karel Dobbelaere has described various changes in Belgian religious life. Despite these changes, Belgium remains a mono-religious, Catholic country. Although it is not officially established, the Catholic church is still called upon to provide ritual markers for all the official events of the nation. Remarkably, too, the vast majority of Belgians still unhesitatingly call themselves "Catholics" (Voyé 1988b: 135-167). Religious practice, however, continues to decline; knowledge and respect for Catholic doctrine and morals concern only a very small minority; and there are many, especially youth, who have absolutely no contact of any sort either with the church or its representatives. They never cross the threshold of a parish church except "accidentally" to join their relatives for one of the rites of passage such as a baptism, wedding or funeral. All of this takes place without open hostility to the church; rather, it reflects ignorance and indifference. Only occasionally is there a fleeting burst of curiosity about the church, usually occasioned by a media report of some church controversy--for example, the excommunication of a priest who celebrated a Mass in Latin or, more recently, a highly-contested appointment of a bishop.

This situation upsets some, particularly Catholic priests, as it raises questions about the meaning of their work and of their lives in general. Still more so it upsets the church hierarchy who sees the churches emptying, seminaries deserted, and its words seemingly unheeded. Yet the hierarchy sometimes seeks to reassure itself by pointing to the formation of numerous voluntary groups that, in one way or another, call themselves Christian. The hierarchy views these groups as a sign of renewal and hope.

What are these voluntary "Christian" groups like? Who participates? What do they involve? Is their existence as positive for the institutional church as the hierarchy believes? In this chapter, I attempt some answers to these questions.

The research considers the history, goals, composition and activities of some 30 groups in Brabant Wallonia (a province situated in the French-speaking region south of Brussels). Each group in one way or another considered itself Christian. While I do not pretend to have carried out an exhaustive inquiry of such groups, I have met with a sufficient number of them, often dissimilar at first glance, to be able to formulate plausible hypotheses about their formation and character.

In what follows, I describe the groups, how they were selected, their composition and characteristics, and I draw inferences about them. Especially important is the question of their relationship to the institutional Catholic church. Thus, as I consider their dominant characteristics, their origin and evolution, I do so with an eye to how they approach the established church. Following this, I reflect on how these groups relate to other available cultural models, especially those that might be called post-modern.

Selection of the Groups for Study

First, how were the groups selected for the research? Their identification was done progressively, beginning with two or three of them already known to the author through professional relationships. Members of these known groups identified other groups which, like their own, openly declared themselves to be "of Christian inspiration." By "Christian inspiration" I mean that all the members of the group are baptized as Catholics; they received a Catholic education; and their identification is with Catholicism, even if they distance themselves from the church as an institution. Data were collected through interviews with two or three members of each group. The interviews consisted of a list of topics to be talked about in a free and open discussion. If the group permitted, I also participated in some of their meetings.

The way in which the identification of the groups occurred provides an interesting initial piece of information: There exists no official census of these groups. In contrast to what is the case (or was the case) for traditional Christian groups, such movements are not automatically listed as related to a local church, since they no longer draw their life from it, meet in its buildings, or have an officially appointed chaplain. Arising mostly during the 1960s, these groups have no such ties. They are born of a lay initiative (to adopt the designated vocabulary which, we shall see, is hardly adequate to describe their formation); their places and times of meeting are exceedingly varied; and few of them count a priest among their members. When there is a priest, it is because he has a voluntary relationship with the group. He does not hold any official relationship with it or represent any ecclesiastical authority. Moreover, these groups unanimously claim radical autonomy from the Catholic church. Indeed, the difficulty one has in contacting them and taking censuses of them quite often is due to their fear of being co-opted by the church. Thus, these groups prove to be quite different from previous small groups (some of which still exist) studied by Dobbelaere and Billiet (1976).

Composition of the Groups

Except for the particular circumstances surrounding the formation of individual groups, these groups do not differ significantly from each other. Members' socio-cultural characteristics and their views on religion are quite similar across the groups. Nonetheless, several comments about the groups' composition are necessary.

First, although these groups are relatively numerous, their membership is small, ranging between eight and fifteen members. At times one or more of the groups may sponsor "conferences" that may bring together dozens of people, but these are exceptional circumstances and do not affect the size of the sponsoring group. Expanding the group's size is something that members consider undesirable and which, in any case, would be difficult given the nature of these groups, as we shall see.

Also, groups always include members of both sexes (contrary to the practice in typical church-sponsored groups). The majority of members participate as couples, sometimes with their children. (In some cases, however, their children are not involved.) The familial dimension is thus underlined from the outset.

Furthermore, these groups consist essentially of people from middle and upper social classes. Of course one might argue that the region that was studied is largely made up of these classes. Also, since these groups were brought to my attention by one another, the risk of a biased account exists. Such objections are not really pertinent. On the one hand, while it is true that the sample was drawn from recommendations of the initial groups known to the author, the information that they had about other groups was quite sparse. The groups have little contact and lack precise information about each other. On the other hand, it seems reasonable to assume that these groups recruit mostly from within the middle and upper classes because, in Belgium, Catholicism is traditionally associated with these classes. The lower classes, particularly workers, are much more estranged from the church, since the church has long been associated with the employers. In some cases the church was itself the "boss" (as owner of large agricultural tracts). In other cases, it most often took the side of the employers in underlining the sacred character of social status, thus upholding hierarchy and inherent inequality. Also, what is known from other sources about similar groups in other regions confirms the relatively elevated social status of the members of these groups. In what follows we shall see that their origins and their projects also largely explain this selectivity.

Finally, these groups, small in size and with middle or upper class members, consist essentially of persons who are between 35 and 45 years of age. Thus the majority were born approximately between 1945 and 1955, and were 18 to 20 years old between 1963-65 and 1973-75. These references to the ages of members are important for two reasons. They show that the groups are made up mostly of the post-war or "baby boom" generation who were part of the counter-culture of the 1960s and early 1970s--the generation of primary interest in this volume. At the same time, especially important for understanding these groups, their members' typical age indicates that they have known, more or less personally, the pre-conciliar church and have lived through the changes introduced, promised or expected from Vatican II (Dobbelaere and Voyé 1991: 215-25). Thus from early in their lives they have had a vision of the church marked by this transition, even if it has come primarily from their parents' recollections of the contrasts between the pre- and post-Council church.

Also regarding the age structure of the groups, almost no one younger than age 30 participates. Why is this the case? Several reasons can be suggested that are not mutually exclusive. It may be that these younger persons have lost all explicit Christian reference. Thus, the groups which they join--even those with similar objectives to the ones under consideration in this chapter--have no sort of "Christian inspiration." Or it may be that these younger persons (and this certainly appears to be the case for a small number of them) yearn to find more affirmative, institutional forms; therefore they do not appear in the kind of groups under consideration here, but rather they seek out places more specifically marked and shaped by the church. Or perhaps the young have simply not yet encountered the questions which lead to the formation of such groups to arise and account for their existence. While these are untested hypotheses, each seems plausible. In the case of those born prior to the Second World War, such persons are more often members of groups related to the institutional church.

In sum, with reference to age, the informal groups that we are considering are to a large extent made up of persons whose formative years spanned the Second Vatican Council and who experienced the counter-culture of the late 1960s and early 1970s. In addition, group membership is small; members are not segregated by gender; and they come primarily from the middle and upper classes.

Characteristics of the Groups

Having discussed the selection of the groups and some of the characteristics of their members, we turn to how the various groups characterize themselves and how they situate themselves vis-a-vis the Catholic church. Recall that all have been selected on the basis of their avowal "of (Catholic) Christian inspiration." Beyond the diversity of their goals, all of these groups have four major traits in common: (a) all affirm their emergence from a specific life experience; (b) all say that they are "on the way," "searching," "learning," "in initiation"; (c) all employ diverse means and gestures; and, (d) all distance themselves from the institutional church in a manner that is unequivocal without being strident.

The Importance of Specific Experiences

All members of these groups begin telling their stories either by reference to an event in their personal lives--for example, the death of a child, the choice of a lifestyle as a young couple, the existence of a group of friends, an exceptional meeting--or to a confrontation with the church which, either overtly or subtlely, has provoked dissatisfaction. Some members cite "official" pastoral teachings on marriage as an example of such dissatisfaction. They experience them as theoretical, general, imperative and dogmatic. Similarly, others complain about the cold, bureaucratic character of the church. In contrast, they cite the warmth and affectivity of relationships in their small communities, relationships that are voluntary and not imposed.

Besides these direct or indirect criticisms of the institutional church, many group members insist that, for them, God can only be found in a concrete, lived experience, that is, in a privileged relationship to another person or persons. Particularly revealing in this connection is what members who have experienced the loss of a child say: "We don't need advice, prayers, celebrations; God only takes on a face through our dead children made present by a photo or an object belonging to them. Without that, it's impossible to be united with God. It's utter darkness."

The importance of concrete, lived experience is perhaps much more prominent since, as we have noted, these groups are essentially composed of couples.[1] Participating as couples no doubt contributes to bringing to the fore what is at the heart of family life, especially that which one might otherwise brush aside for fear of appearing too emotional or perhaps too trivial. Whether this is the case or not, the emphasis on lived experience throws into relief the more general dual character of these groups, namely: the rediscovery of the individual as one who is *not* the impotent product of impersonal social structures; and, complementing this, the recognition of the importance of various forms of association with an intersubjective basis. Such associations encourage cooperation and mutual assistance in sharp contrast to large bureaucratic institutions. These groups, however, are not the same as the "communities" of traditional society that issued from "the substances of blood and earth" (Petitat 1987: 109).

The Importance of Personal Progress

Along with this first characteristic, all of these groups insist that they are "searching," that they are "on the way." Without a doubt it is here that the critique addressed to the church is most direct and explicit. This critique is structured around three axes.

First, the personal approach that the group encourages is opposed to the magisterial teaching of the church and to the regimentation that accompanies it. In the groups, it was common to hear such statements as the following: "You must be able to make your way by yourself; you must not be obliged to pray, or attend the Eucharist, or have to affirm certain things, or teach certain things." "The priest was the one who knew (best); then we told him that he didn't suit us. Now we have chosen a new one (who hasn't come by way of the hierarchy), and we feel the difference. He dares to speak about himself. It's richer for the group than if he acted as the one who knows and who dictates."

Second, the rejection of a ready-made discourse, of imposed knowledge or messages, is accompanied by an emphasis on the emotions, on "what is felt." Here are typical comments: "This group, I don't know, it was formed all by itself, little by little, without any definite project, with people who felt the same thing." "At the beginning, we had the same need for contacts, the same intuitions." "That (the group's formation) came spontaneously; some got into it; that can't be forced." "It's not a question of intelligence, but indeed of a spiritual family."

Third, opposed to the dogmatic pronouncements of the church is a sense of welcome, of listening, of exchange. This, group members say, permits a degree of pluralism, even if those who remain in the group are only those who feel themselves to be in accord with the group's direction and what is expressed in it. Some leave and may found another group: "People come and go, according to the evolution of their project, of their needs, as a function of their life." Such coming and going of group members, while highlighting the unstable composition of the groups, does not bother their members. To them it seems the best way to realize their concern "not to abandon themselves to what happens but to use events to develop oneself."

The Diversity of Means and Gestures

Another aspect of these groups deserves attention: While all of them, as we have pointed out, claim a "Christian inspiration" (a self-definition that was the basis of their inclusion in this study), they are far from being homogeneous in terms of "practices." Indeed, the means and gestures they employ belong only partially to the repertoire of Catholic means and gestures. Such groups mingle Catholic elements with borrowings from other sources. Some mix readings from the Bible with selections from texts of oriental religions and from scientific texts, subsequently exchanging comments and impressions regarding the readings. Others refer to a sort of "guru" who is supposed to initiate them in his or her own life experience. One group proposes for its members a weekly "retreat" of a half-day spent in a sort of hermitage they have constructed on land they have acquired together. The idea is to "make an uninterrupted chain of prayers in a deserted place in order to find oneself alone, face to face with God." Still another group insists on "animation techniques" which are designed to allow each one to discover his or her potential and thus, "to feel happy." For others, the feast--the communal meal--is seen as the heart of their spirituality. Yet others wish to experience the familial dimension of daily life and the "prophetic value" of living together in neighboring houses on a communally-owned farm. Assuredly, these groups make recourse to very different means, but all say they do so with the same objective: "to allow things to happen as life goes by, without definite goals, in order to discover by oneself the footsteps of Christ."

When they do make recourse to specifically religious actions, these groups often do not retain the institutional forms, rhythms, or modalities of the actions. Such is the case, for example, with prayer: instead of a set formula, prayer becomes a spontaneous and timely expression. Occurring at diverse times and places, it manifests the sentiments of the moment in ordinary terms. In addition, some groups have communal prayer: "every one of our gatherings is prayer." The Eucharist is not generally the center of their religiosity: "The danger," they say, "is that this becomes too far from reality, that it takes off." "We've tried all sorts of celebrations, but it's difficult because it's artificial. It would've been much better if we could've done it during dinner, but the priests are used to a certain rhythm, and that spoils the atmosphere."

Certain groups, consequently, never celebrate the Eucharist, and others only do so "when the urge strikes them." Some members say they "can't miss it," while others "are reticent." It is worth noting that all of this is said without the slightest expression of guilt, without any manifest concern to defend oneself, or with any intent to educate others or serve as a model. Rather members emphasize the importance of freedom of expression and their desire to find in group life "a place where they can breathe; can be themselves."

Distancing from the Institutional Church

This desire of group members to be themselves is accompanied by another characteristic that all groups generally share with a certain vehemence: the fear of being co-opted by the church. While some groups rarely mention this fear, those who count a priest among their members vigorously stress that he is there only on a personal basis, without any institutional mandate. And when a group has someone "in charge," each member must take care, they say "lest the leader become clerical."

This distancing from the institutional church is quite evident. Although one or two of these groups may show concern to remain "at the fringe of the church," the majority seem to position themselves outside of all reference to it. The "Christian inspiration" which they claim does not come by way of the church. It is nourished by the Bible, the life of Christ and the emotion brought about by experiences like those of the Taizé Community.[2]   In addition to reflecting the groups' preoccupation with autonomy, this distancing from the institutional church is explained by some as a reaction to the disappointment of hopes placed in Vatican II: "Then one had the impression that it would be possible to work in the real world, on human problems, going beyond the dogmatic, . . .but since then, the church is backing up, is restoring the rules. It is again too far from life. So you cannot agree with what is done and what is said within the church." Thus you have "to be outside in order to be yourself, to be in touch with life. . . ." "God reveals Himself in history; the truth is not given once and for all." This conviction, shared by all the groups studied, is supported by members' experiences of similar groups in other regions and countries or about which they have at least heard.   The knowledge that others far away think and act more or less as they do serves to convince them that their criticisms of the institutional church are well-founded, and that the confidence which they put in group life that allows them to be themselves and develop themselves spiritually is legitimate.

But do they need this external support for their group life and practice? After all, they have above all else insisted on the uncertainty of the way, the imprecision of the goal, the progressive discovery of the self, the priority of the present and the permanence of change! These are the things that voluntary groups hold in opposition to fixed certainties, ready-made answers for everything, the avoidance of diversity and conflict, and what some feel are nothing more than attempts to engender guilt and infantile behavior.

The Religious in Post-Modernity

The various characteristics which mark these voluntary groups that are of "Christian inspiration" suggest the appropriateness of describing them as "post-modern." I will not debate here whether this term is justified. I simply wish to show that these groups, whose major characteristics I have sketched, are one expression among others of a new phase of social and cultural development. In the religious domain, the post-modern phase goes beyond secularization, which, in the sense that I use the term, corresponds essentially to "modernity." Before developing this point, however, let us see in what respects these groups participate in a logic of post-modernity.

The End of Great Narratives

One of the major characteristics of post-modernity is, as Lyotard designated it, "the end of Great Narratives" (Lyotard 1979: 7). One way of conceptualizing this end is to consider the incredulity with which the Great Narratives are greeted, with the consequence that their efficacy and their power to impose themselves as explanations are diminished. Lyotard specifically calls into question the two great modes of representation of society which, he says, have largely dominated thought and action during modernity (Lyotard 1979: 24-25): (1) that proposed by functionalist language (from the French school to Talcott Parsons), which sees society as a self-regulating organic whole; and (2) that of Marxist language, which is based upon the idea of class struggle and alienation (Lyotard 1979: 24). Both cases for Lyotard represent discourse which pretends to monopolize "a [sphere of] knowledge" in order to endow its recognized enunciators with the capacity not only to proffer the good denotative news, but also "the good prescriptive news and the good evaluative news" (Lyotard 1979: 37). Such "knowledge" is thus the basis of power which seeks to impose itself upon all whom it defines as "not knowing."

Lyotard's analysis can also be applied to certain elements brought to light in the interviews of members of the voluntary groups studied. In fact, we have seen that the distance established by them from the church is explicable in terms of what they see as "the theoretical dogmatic character of [the church's] language, the ready-made responses that it imposes on everything." We have also seen how group members dread "clerical discourse" which pretends to know from the outset and to impose its teaching on "lay persons." Against the systematic, universal answers given by the priests, members of voluntary groups point to the uncertainties of life, its tenuousness, to events which upset its course, and to the diversity of personal history. Thus, in the religious field, as elsewhere, one might expect to find the incredulity with which great narratives are now greeted, especially to the extent that their content appears far from confirmed by life and daily existence. To the extent also that the Great Narratives are perceived as not having kept their promises, whether this be the achievement of social progress, human equality, the mastery of the world, or even that of the accomplishment of the beatitudes ("Blessed are the poor," "Blessed are those who mourn," and so forth), growing disbelief can be expected.

At the same time, the bearers of these "narratives" see themselves devalued and their capacity to proclaim the good, the just, the sane contested. Just as in politics or economics, religious functionaries lose their power and only gain back a certain credence when they talk about themselves and their lives. "He dares to speak about himself. It's richer for the group than if he acted as the one who knows and dictates," one person said about a priest who participates in the group.

The Mixing of Codes

Besides "the end of Great Narratives," the "mixing of codes" is another characteristic of post-modernity. One finds it, for example, in architecture, where styles from the most diverse epochs and places are juxtaposed. Again one finds it in literature and music where the popular and even the trivial are blended with the most "noble" of languages and melodies. Such a phenomenon also seems to emerge in the interviews conducted with the voluntary groups. Indeed, all the groups readily claim "Christian inspiration," but they only retain certain Christian elements which they choose and interpret themselves. For example, nobody referred in any explicit way to the teachings of the church. Moreover, some of these groups combine elements borrowed from other religions or philosophies (the guru, for example). Still others adopt practices from what may be called popular religion--candle burning and prayer chains, for example. Many groups also use scientific methods--for example, animation, psychosomatic therapies--and read scientific texts as part of their gatherings. We are thus witnessing the "erosion of the boundary" between the institutional and the popular, and "the collapse of hierarchical distinction" (Featherstone 1988: 203) between what emanates from ecclesiastic authority and what arises from the people. Everything can be placed on the same level of validity if the individual "believes" in it, and as long as she or he finds meaning therein.

What is particularly remarkable is that religion and science are not seen as mutually exclusive: the former cannot deny the contributions of the latter or neglect to take them into account; and science cannot pretend to extend its grasp except by encroaching on religion. For those interviewed, science and religion support one another, since neither one embraces all their concerns in all dimensions. Also, although members define themselves as Christians, they draw also on oriental religions--their writings and practices--to provide additional elements that aid in "discovering their potential" and thus "bring them face-to-face with God." They no longer share the long-held vision of the supremacy of Christianity or even of Catholicism over other religions, a view which corresponded to the economic, political and cultural hegemony of Europe in the world (Featherstone 1988: 213).

Thus the mixing of codes introduced by post-modernity is reflected in the religious field in a threefold manner: references and practices blending the institutional and the popular; occasional borrowings from scientific discourses as well as from religious ones; and inspiration sought in diverse religions, notably, oriental religions. Accordingly, three of the traditional hierarchal relationships are disrupted: that of the clergy over the laity, that of religion over science (or the inverse!), and that of Catholicism--that is to say of the West--over the rest of the world.

The Voluntary and Civil Character of the Social Bond

There is also a third element of post-modernity that these groups exhibit: the voluntary and civil character of the social bond.

The social bond, or basis of group participation, is "voluntary" and thus is opposed to the ascriptive bases for belonging characteristic of traditional society: the extended family (clan), the local group (neighborhood), or religion (the church). The social bond is "civil," because it is differs from those bonds which, during modernity, located individuals in great, overwhelming and anonymous organizations (business corporations, governmental structures, large unions, and so forth) which were to resolve all problems through the self-regulating, depersonalized mechanisms of the welfare state. It is "civil" in so far as it is structured on the basis of the spontaneous association of individuals who gather together because of affinities, needs, interests (material or not), and preoccupations which are their own and which arise without any external juridical or administrative constraint.

It is in fact striking that these "groups" emerge as a result of events which have marked the lives of their members--for example, the death of a child or of a spouse--or because of shared sensibilities--for example, the search for contacts, dissent with some church doctrine. Moreover, two things which have been and remain important for the organization of the church's pastorate are absent in the formation of these small communities, namely, spatial proximity--the basis of the territorial pastorate--and professional leadership, which was emphasized (especially during the 1960s) as the foundation of pastoral activity. In contrast, these groups appear instead as "networks," often temporary and multiple, of persons who choose to associate with one another for specific purposes in an affective environment. Rarely do they live in the same immediate geographical area. For these groups, or rather for these "networks," the affective ambience is of major importance. Practically speaking, the groups last only as long as this dimension, this "feeling good together" which engenders confidence and a sentiment of an unconditional solidarity, remains present.

In these various ways we witness, even within the solidly Catholic Belgian society, a multiplication of religious expressions legitimized by a concern for the diversity of life, its uncertainties and its paradoxes. What goes on in the religious domain thus links up with other phenomena studied by Lyotard in other areas of life. Post-modernity fosters a critique of all forms of universal knowledge which it considers impossible (Lyotard 1979). Thus since "there is no one reason but rather only reasons," it seems obvious to participants in these groups that there is not one, but rather many, ways of expressing their religiosity--a religiosity that, furthermore, is one of sentiment rather than reason.

It is not only the universal claims of particular religions that find themselves placed in question. The same is true for every pretension to any sort of universal validity. As a result we are radically removed from typical bases of alliances formed during the 1960s--for example, political engagement, social militancy or social change projects. In such alliances, the Marxist utopia of the classless and stateless society was often merged with the Christian vision of paradise brought to earth. Such an epic vision appears now as a romantic quest. Instead, today one simply asks the other to be there with the spontaneity of his or her own life. The certainty of the righteousness of one's cause, with which the militants of yesteryear fought, is exchanged for uncertainty. This, in turn, gives over to a pluralism of religious expressions that refer primarily to one's private life and its interwoven relationships. Thus, the church's capacity for imposition of its teachings increasingly falls to pieces as its usefulness for supporting the political and the economic world is lost.

A Certain Re-Enchantment of the World

The fact that the institutional church has thus lost its relevance and can no longer pretend to be the "sacred canopy" of which Berger speaks, no doubt helps us to understand why the church's efforts at internal rationalization have contributed to the strained relationships with just those groups we have been studying. The church has actually participated in the "disenchantment of the world" anticipated by Weber. Anxious to stimulate a voluntary and conscientious faith, the church attempted to reduce and even to suppress everything that seemed to contradict this trend towards the rationalization of life that has been characteristic of modernity: the festive aspects, the aesthetic dimension, the identity-conferring role of its practices and rites. This concern for rationalizing church life neglected a number of things. First, the church has in fact never been able to control the popular meaning of its practices and rites. These rites and practices are inherently polysemic and lend themselves to multiple significations (Voyé 1973: 225-238), a characteristic that plays a unifying role as long as they remain unchanged. As Castoriadis has remarked, in relation to the symbolic, the form is relatively autonomous from its function: the "details" of rites and practices are not directly "useful" but their permanence guarantees their authenticity and their efficacy (Castoriadis 1989: 127-142). Moreover, the church probably did not perceive that the symbolic aspects of these rites and practices took on much more importance as they were eliminated from other social fields. The symbols were responding to a basic demand of existence, as Max Weber recognized when he commented that "the rational does not exhaust the human."

We can understand then why it is that some, no longer finding in "the church's offer" a satisfying response to this need for the symbolic with all its emotion and affectivity, have turned outside the church--towards sects, cults or Eastern religions. Or, as is the case in Belgium, they have developed small groups or networks on the fringe of the church through which they seek to compensate for this lack. Many of those interviewed have in fact underlined the importance that they attach to finding such expressions of the "re-enchantment of the world," to use another of Weber's terms. Thus, the idea of the feast, for example, is very much in evidence: "We call one another 'the table companions' because, for us it is essential to be united around a table for feasting! We spend a lot of time feasting: birthdays, holiday celebrations, reunions, etc. For us, to be together to feast, is to pray !" Similarly, the idea of the "setting" and of "decor" is important. Parents who have lost a child, for example, bring a photo or a possession of the child to the meeting in order to "feel through the concrete the Communion of Saints." Others build themselves a sort of hermitage in order to "live the solitude of prayer." Also important is the idea of the "miracle" which springs from an emotion and changes things abruptly: "He came and gave a talk," one member said of a meeting at which a particular speaker was present: "It always happens that way. There's always someone in the assembly who bites into [what he's saying]. And as it happened that time I bit. So I followed him, and he also felt this harmony. Ever since, we get together to listen to him, to discuss his books. It's spiritual. It's not a question of intelligence, but it is based on the humane." In the experience with this particular speaker, the contradiction with the church is affirmed: "He has had difficulties with the church because he's a man of the future."

These last two remarks are particularly interesting: the first opposes intelligence to the spiritual and to the humane; the second opposes the church to the future. In doing this they appear to sum up a last trait, characteristic of the groups analyzed which shows their immersion in post-modernity: that of calling into question rationality for the benefit of the humane and the emotional. One may detect as well an implicit questioning of the future of a church which does not make room for such dimensions.

Conclusion: Beyond Secularization?

All of this leads to a concluding question: What significance do these groups have, and how can they be located with regard to secularization and to that which is now sometimes called "the return of the religious"?

If Karel Dobbelaere's (1981) definition of secularization is used, it seems obvious that these groups contradict in no way the process of the loss of influence of the institutional church represented by secularization--Dobbelaere's primary emphasis. On the contrary, they confirm its culmination in two ways. First, these groups exist on the margin of the church, beyond all accountability (Delumeau 1983). Second, their members are not preoccupied with the question of consensus, either among themselves or with regard to the institution. The latter reflects their indifference to the church and its call for conformity.

This last point, however, merits further consideration. The call for conformity by the church seems, in fact, not to be suitable in many of concrete situations facing Christians: those, for example, that require that "the church's myth" be adapted to fit the diverse or changing circumstances. By ignoring such circumstances, church leaders avoid most of the risks of conflict, except in the case of a very small internal minority of "clerics" who are concerned *both* with a kind of universal coherence *and* with effective dialogue in the differing situations. For the most part, one finds a kind of surface unity, the superficiality of which little bothers those "clients" who seek the "services" of the church. The church, therefore, is able to maintain the power that allows it to be recognized as representing a significant part of the population.

The existence, therefore, of these "communities of Christian inspiration" in no way qualifies or diminishes secularization. Rather, it confirms its operation. The groups seem not to indicate a "return of the religious" for two reasons. First, the kind of religiosity exhibited in these groups, centered as it is on the concrete, the relational, and the emotional, has never been lacking. It merely became illegitimate in the eyes and discourse of some intellectuals, both clerical and lay. As such many viewed this religious style as being, in some ways, ruled out. Second, these groups' return to religion is far from a return to the institutional church and its power over individuals. For them, it is not a return of allegiance to the institution. To the contrary, it is a developing relationships that acquire significance beyond their concreteness in a quest for meaning. In their quests, group members use all existing means, including those they draw from the reservoir of the church and from childhood experiences.

The age of the majority of those involved in these groups (35-45 years of age) raises important questions about the younger generations. As we saw, for most of the group members, being in this age cohort has made it possible for many of them to experience, more or less directly, the changes in the church occasioned by Vatican II. Most also, no doubt, experienced a rather traditional, pre-Vatican II Christian education. One wonders, however, what will happen, and is already happening, to the younger generations for whom neither of these circumstances apply? Will a certain reference to the church survive, or will the "religious" become more and more autonomous from the institution, thus breaking away from practices which the church has long sought to impose on the religious? Can we, in the future expect to experience and express the sacred in many different forms and places (Zylberberg 1985)?

Must we conclude, therefore, that the church's social role will inevitably shrink? In my opinion, it is first of all a matter of a shifting social role. Indeed, even when its power over the behavior of individuals, especially in their private lives, seems to be shrinking, the "right of attention and of speech" granted to the church on the public stage seems to be expanding. This was recently confirmed by the Belgian results of the European Value Survey. The results showed that, the more distant the problems are from the personal lives of respondents, the more these respondents grant the church the right to make known its opinion on the problems--for example, on issues concerning the Third World. Conversely, the more questions concern one's private life, especially emotional and sexual issues (extramarital relations, abortion, and so forth), the less legitimacy is given to the opinion of the church. Must one then conclude that the church is becoming (or becoming again) a political actor at the very time when its authority over the individual is shrinking? This must be qualified, since the same survey shows that respondents believe that the church is least entitled to speak about matters of national governmental policy. Apart from the fact that this expresses an unquestioned conviction regarding the separation of church and state, it also confirms respondents' concern to keep the church at a distance from their concrete existence which governmental policy already regulates in many ways. The "right to speak" of the church thus seems to be restricted to those areas one considers, rightly or wrongly, to be distant from daily life. In addition, such freedom of speech is only allowed in situations where, given the magnitude of the problem, the church cannot be effective in the short term. One must not, however, minimize the overall importance of the renewed political dimension granted to the church: Although seemingly ineffective, the church's speech has a latent power. Survey responses concede the right of the church to be a legitimate social actor, independently of its loss of influence on the daily lives of people. Certainly, it no longer has a monopoly on all legitimate speech. It is one speaker among several. Yet, any recognition that others accord the church's opinions, even when they are beyond its own boundaries, assures it external support and compensates somewhat for the internal discords it is now experiencing.

Notes

1. Perhaps voluntary group members are less apt to leave daily life out of account than would be true if these groups were separated by sex--especially, for example,in the case of all male groups.

2. An important Christian community in France that has been a model to many other communities.

10

Religion and the Post-War Generation in Italy

Salvatore Abbruzzese[1]

The post-war generation grew up during a well defined period in Italy's national history. Born with the promise of affluence and modernization, this generation faced the new uncertainties resulting from the energy crisis in the early seventies and the conflicts and tensions brought about by the recent fall of political regimes in the East. Waves of immigration, uncertain economic development, and political conflicts have created a precarious situation for this generation. Having experienced both social progress and crisis (Habermas 1985), this generation has come to realize that self-sufficiency may not be achieved. Its history and experience, in other words, are interconnected with the modernization and development of society (Berger and Luckman 1966).

Looking at the generation's relationship with institutionalized religion (in the Italian case the Roman Catholic church), we see both progress and setbacks. Even though brought up in a traditional religious environment, the post-war generation emerged as the main carrier of secular values in the sixties and advocates for liberalizing the laws governing divorce and abortion in 1974 and in 1980. These reforms arising out of the modernization process bear directly upon the religious sphere. A generation's faith in modernization is shown in loss of credibility in the religious institutions. This does not necessarily indicate progress per se, but rather is a sign of cultural transformation.

In order to understand this process of transformation, we must consider what was happening generally in the post-Cold War era. In the aftermath of World War II the possibilities of economic growth were weakened due to political and social tensions. People were frustrated with the underlying tension as a result of political set backs, military failures, and frequent civil wars. Post-war Italy needed to be rebuilt not only as a country but also as a society with a new national identity. This development has been called the "post-war spirit" (Scoppola 1985; Ginsborg 1989).

The arrival of the generation born after 1945 to maturity coincided with a period of economic expansion beginning in 1961 and with a pacification in the political sphere: in 1962 the socialist party's entrance in the government initiated the long period of the center-left. At the same time, the Second Vatican Council sanctioned the opening of the church to modernity. The trauma of World War II and its post-war social conflicts which had been so meaningful for the fathers of this generation during the sixties were all discredited in the name of progress. Even though the concept of an ideal society existed in 1945, it was only with the end of the Cold War, the entrance of the center-left governments, and the opening of Vatican II that the hopes of economic modernization, already in progress, could be fulfilled.

While the processes of cultural and political renovation suggested that a real change occurred, they also served to obscure the costs and the contradictions brought on by economic development. In actuality, economic expansion during the sixties neither reduced emigration nor lessened the historical division between north and south in Italy. It is the discrepancy between a partial social and economic modernization and a cultural modernization based on faith in progress that helps us to understand the ambivalence of the post-war generation towards modernity. This modernity allowed for widespread social well-being and a social platform for economic emancipation and opportunity, all of which raised expectations. The willingness to endorse modernity was strongly tied to a moral expectation that society will provide the opportunity for economic and cultural promotion as well as the guarantee of democracy.

Let us turn to the modernization process in Italy itself. Only after analyzing this specific historical process of modernization can we reexamine (the second part of this chapter) the general detachment from institutionalized religion experienced by the post-war generation. Within this same process of modernization it is also possible to understand (this is the scope of the third part of the chapter) the post-war generation's attitude during the eighties, when a partial and fragmented recovery at the spiritual level is characterized in particular by the pontificate of John Paul II.

Economic Modernization and Cultural Modernity:
A Contradictory Development

The economic development in post-war Italy could not provide well-being for all. Even with the help of the United States and the efforts of the Italian government to bring the Italian economy to the level of the other

European countries, they could not prevent higher unemployment and increased emigration. Between 1951 and 1960, at the height of the crisis, almost three million Italian citizens left the country while only a little more than a million returned (Castronovo and Valerio 1975: 409). Nevertheless, unemployment did not decrease: in 1950 it reached 7.8%. Ten years later it was 7.3%, whereas the rest of Europe averaged 1.9%. Consequently, the cost of labor, a major element in economic development, did not increase notably. While industrial production between 1953 and 1960 increased by 89% and the production of each wage-earner increased by 62%, the actual industrial wages decreased by 0.6%. This low cost of labor made for an extremely competitive presence in the international economic market (Ginsborg 1989: 289).

Not until the sixties could one actually experience the beneficial results of the economic development in the standard of living and in the market place. By 1958 only twelve out of a hundred families owned a television, thirteen out of a hundred owned a refrigerator, and three out of a hundred owned a washing-machine. Only after 1965 did half of all Italian families acquire household appliances (Ginsborg 1989: 325). It would be incorrect, however, to assume that this was a mere case of slow economic development. In reality, this process of modernization was the same as that which had manifested itself in different forms throughout Europe.

First of all, in Italy the state played a specific role in the process of modernization. It provided services and assistance for the private sector of industry: expansion of the highway system, increased supply and distribution of energy, financial assistance and lowered taxes for industrialization in the South. Since 1957, the government-subsidized industries were required to invest 60% of their capital in Southern Italy[2], while in the North (especially the North East and Central Italy), where small industry was flourishing, the state guaranteed this region's development by means of tax breaks and little regulation.

In this way the state assumed a very particular role in the process of development, both by creating it where it has not existed and by leaving it unregulated where the industries have the highest profits. This apparently contradictory attitude of the government which combines intervention with deregulation leads to a total rejection of any planned development. Here in this paper it is not important to investigate how practical this program was for the economic development of Italy. What is important, however, is to understand the consequences of this strategy on the cultural development of its people. The economic modernization of Italy cannot be seen as the result of an intentional effort, which was then consequently legitimized by the state. Rather, modernization should be perceived as the result of a collaboration between various parts of the society. As such modernization does not have at its foundations cultural inspiration nor does it yield to values which would support it. The fundamental element in this process, with respect to the rest of Europe, is the detachment from any ideology of modernity. Obviously this is not true for all social groups. An ideological modernity (or an idealized view of it) is present only in the policies of the big industrial families of Italy who have been sending their children to Harvard and MIT since the 1950s, but is absent in all other institutions including the educational systems. For these young minds, molded in America, economic modernization does have indeed cultural significance. Alongside this highly specialized group it is possible to find yet another image of modernity: that of the young industrialists coming from the families of artisans and craftsmen. Here we can trace the age-old "ethos" of the artisan, steeped in traditional family ties, and insisting on commitment from its family members. This second group is also a believer in economic modernity but does not require any change in the preexisting social structures. The small business remains localized within the Italian provinces even though its operating market reaches as far as Asia and Africa (Ginsborg 1989: 321).

While economic modernity appears to be in conflict with and independent from the state, the psychological-cultural modernity is limited in this sphere as well. Varying factors prevent the individual from achieving modernization and from enjoying the luxury of free time, which combined represent one consequence of "social modernization." The uneven economic development, limited to Central-Northern Italy and unable to reduce general unemployment, is coupled with the absence of a catalyzing agent for the process of modernization capable of giving it cultural significance. From 1950 to 1970 the per-capita income increased more in Italy than in other European countries, but at the end of this documented development of the nation's economy in 1970, Italy showed an overall income that was 60% of that in France and 82% of that seen in U.K. (Ginsborg 1989: 325). In spite of all that had happened, at the end of the sixties Italians could not reach those standards of living necessary to equate them with other European countries. The deficit of Southern Italy by itself was enough to completely overturn the national budget (Graziani 1971).

This partial modernity, which affected only certain geographical areas, mostly those where a select set of established families promoted traditional productivity, and who acknowledged and accepted government regulation, was itself insufficient to produce its own culture. Neither the late development of a consumer society, nor the radical change in the standard of living resulting from the decline of the rural collectives and widespread urbanization, permited individualism as the decisive value for cultural modernity. This was due not only to the weak and partial process of economic modernization but to the peculiar idiosyncrasies of the Italian context.

The main component is the family process of saving as well as the stability of the family as an economic agent. The central position of the family in the process of economic modernization is not without its consequences. First of all, family size is reduced to two parents and one or two children at most. In 1951 the average family size was four, but by 1961 it had shrunk to 3.6, and by 1971 the average family size was 3.3 (Ginsborg 1989: 381). However, this reduction in size of the nuclear family is a result more of the new problems brought about by a consumer society than due to the increasing number of women entering in the market place. From 1961 to 1966 the number of women in the work force actually dropped by 17%. Paradoxically, if in 1959 the unemployment rate was more or less the same for both sexes (6.1% for men and 8.8% for women), in more recent years the gap has only widened: 3.3 to 6.8 in 1966; 3.7 to 9.6 in 1970; and 4.8 to 13.1 in 1980. The number of women regularly employed however remains constant: in 1985 the unemployment rate for women is three times that for men, 7% to 20.9% (See Table 10.1).

These work-related patterns are not only relevant from an economic point of view, but also because they modify the process of social change. The fact that women stay at home retards development of the state-funded social welfare system (which has noticeably increased its costs in other European countries), some of these services being nursery schools, nursing homes for the elderly, and assistance for the handicapped. As massive emigration frees the state from the explosive problem of unemployment, so does keeping women at home eliminate the need for expensive social services. This has its cultural consequences as well: it allows for both a parallel income free from fiscal and legal regulation, and for the continuity of education within the family institution. This central economic and educational position of the family, so dependent on keeping the woman in the home, is in conflict with the state which does not provide economic and formative assistance.

TABLE 10.1: Percentage of Men and Women Seeking Employment Out of the Total Workforce

Year	Males	Females
1959	6.1	8.8
1960	4.8	7.4
1965	4.3	8.0
1970	3.7	9.6
1975	3.8	10.6
1980	4.8	13.1
1985	7.0	20.9

Source: ISTAT, 1986. *Sommario di Statistiche storiche, 1926-1985.*

Thus Italy enters the modernization process bringing with it "anti-modern" contradictions. At the economic level we see unemployment and emigration. At the political level we see both a weak and generous central government, and at the social level the central role of the family both at the individual and the institutional level. Modernity thus manifests itself through its *gadgets* rather than by desiring to build a new society. Even though education becomes more accessible (from 387,000 enrolled in secondary school in 1950, to almost twice that amount in 1960), this increase nevertheless does not influence the market place. In 1970, while the secondary education already opened its doors to a 1,400,000 students, the market place could only employ 8.9% of them and 55.5% of the total number of workers only had an elementary education (Sylos-Labini 1974: 188). Though the educational system can accept a very high number of young people, it is extremely inefficient. Basically schools play the role of a parking lot for students, a fact which is evident both in the absolute lack of regulation of the number of enrolled and the consequent low number of graduates (Ispes 1989).

Modernization and Secularization in Italian Post-War Society

This partial and incomplete modernization process in Italy has been continually stressed because it is so important for understanding the social-cultural context in which the post-war generation has matured. This generation grew up in a consumer society built on the promise of upward mobility and social well being guaranteed to all with the rise of the welfare state[3]. But this generation also experienced a barrier to upward mobility as a result of the central position of the family. The opposing ideologies that went into forming fascism and the post-war political conflicts dissolved and were replaced by a disenchanted pragmatism which prohibited the development of a well-formulated ideology of modernity. Thus the post-war generation experienced a modernity based on different and sometimes opposing factors than that linked with consumerism brought on by an intense industrialization. Furthermore, this generation matured during a time characterized by the decline of ethical and moral references which, since the end of the Cold War has eroded the credibility of the various ethical institutions. The advent of mass consumption was almost immediately followed by an erosion of political and religious organizations claiming to advance society according to some prescribed plan for developing the modern world. Beginning with the early sixties there was a notable drop off in organizations such as *Azione Cattolica* as well as in the political parties of the Christian Democrats and the Communist Party (De Antonellis 1987; Ginsborg 1989; Istuto 1968).

Religious practice lost importance along with the role played by the church, especially in the post-war period, as the implementor of social identity. While in 1956, 69% of Italians regularly attended church, by 1962 the number reduced to 53% and in 1969 only 40% went to church with any regularity (Burgalassi 1968). This decline was not only due to the modernization process but was the result of specific events that characterized Italian society and its culture during the 1950s. The Roman Catholic church played a major role in determining these events.

Since the mid-1950s the church has gradually withdrawn from the political arena. Before this time the Italian Episcopate was very influential. After World War II Pope Pius XII represented a strong figure of authority for a population worn from military conflicts, as well as promising to insure political balance (Scoppola 1987). Regarding the conflict between East and West the choice of the Christian Democrats to enter into the NATO pact was totally approved by Pius XII. In the same political arena he completely opposed an agreement between the Catholic party and the socialist left. The participation of the church in politics was encouraged by the previous generation (Poggi 1963). Thus the post-war generation was the immediate heir to an uncertainty created by a Catholic movement steeped in the conflicts surrounding the end of the Cold War (and thus of the communist threat) and the agreements between Christian Democrats and the Socialist Party. The transition from collateralism to Vatican II and thus to the religious choice of the *Azione Cattolica* at the end of the 1950s, caused big changes in the Catholic movement. A widely dichotomized society that felt threatened only by the East has been replaced by a pluralist society where the communist threat no longer exists and where conflict runs the risk of being more detrimental to society. The Catholic organizations, which formerly opposed any form of injustice and which were used to supporting the political leadership legitimized by the church, are now losing their internal cohesion. At the same time the church becomes more and more cautious regarding those specific social issues which the economic modernization has begun to impose upon society.

The caution employed by the church in dealing with the social problems is more clearly understood if we recognize that the ability to deal with those problems has become a bone of contention between a technocratic pro-modernity power which is viewed as necessary and positive and an opposing political power which claims the need for strong political regulation of development and which contests the claims of modernity. In other words the church is at a dead end: if it takes a stand in solving social problems, it will loose political support. On the other hand, if it endorses modernization it will eventually exclude itself from any intervening role in this world. The difference between these two options is that the first one will have immediate effects at the political level, whereas the second will have long term effects at the cultural level. Thus the Italian church has tried to compromise by not involving itself in political problems and by adopting a cautious and moderate optimism regarding development (Moro 1968: 625-716). Such a compromise puts the church on the track of an internal secularization (Luckman 1963) which will inevitably limit its role in the modern world.

The church's caution can have immeasurable effects the moment it merges with the formative elements of the mass society. In effect the consumer society alone can not bring a true ideological foundation to the process of modernization, nor can it break down the family tradition. Nevertheless, it can conceal the sense of social uncertainty that exists in the post-war period. A consumer society founded on the limitless extension of enjoyment in everyday life has no place for a religion based on punishment and repentance. In such a society (one that enjoys the luxury of free time), the "education of the soul" looses its importance (Morin 1962), especially when it comes from an institution like the Catholic church that has traditionally been responsible for this function. Therefore, if the other institutions are able to transform themselves and can abandon their ethical principles in favor of a rising pragmatism (referring to the "secularization" of the political parties to the detriment of their ethical values), the church on the other hand cannot modernize according to the rules of society without compromising its message. Compromise results from the church's attempt to reduce as much as possible the idea of punishment, replacing it with a more religious message of individual freedom and self-realization.

The Italian church is caught between self-isolationism from that part of society which deals specifically with social and political tensions and the consumer society that disregards the idea of punishment and religious conversion. In other words, the religious message is doubly limited in its expression: at the social level it is forced into silence out of fear of political implications whereas at the cultural level it risks permanently loosing contact with a society that believes mainly in a happy ending. The price that is paid in adjusting to *this* world (Shiner 1967) is paid through a loss of those more specific religious values in favor of a natural ethic of tolerance and human respect.

The post-war generation finds itself in an abundant society whose mere existence marks an unbridgeable gap between the present and an immediate past characterized by scarcity of goods and party conflicts. This rapid distancing from the past does not occur without a loss of credibility in those institutions responsible for the crisis during that period, and which is now buried by a triumphant affluence and by international détente. This loss of credibility is even more defined as the two main political parties seem to ignore the internal contradictions within modernity itself. While the Catholic party in power tends to minimize the tensions and maximize the advantages, and thus legitimates modernization per se, the political opposition interprets every critical analysis of modernization according to the model of the true socialist countries characterized by opposition to consumerism in favor of equal distribution of goods. Both tendencies underestimate the importance of cultural development in the process of modernization and consider it an empty glass ready to be filled with any ethical element; they see it as a state of grace able to support any set of values.

In such a context, the post-war generation needs to create on its own both a new analysis of the limits and contradictions of modernization. Needed as well are new interpretations of modernity not limited to just consumerism and which can provide the means for achieving promotions and social opportunities all too often taken for granted in the modernization process. This interpretation of the spirit of modern times is manifested in the different religious and lay movements which are the basis of the political and ethical commitment characterizing and defining the post-war generation during the sixties.

In Italy this ethical and political commitment took on a very specific form. Italy did not experience those elements of mass protest which occurred in the United States nor the attack on the establishment which occurred elsewhere in Europe (Touranine 1972). Alongside an Italian society homogenized by mass media and consumer industry, the preexisting social problems long obscured now begin to reemerge. Here we see a new marginality: that of the Southern Italian immigrants who have populated the ghettoes of Milan, Turin, and Rome (Ferraotti 1974). We see the price of mass education which is in theory open to all, but in reality encourages widespread social exclusion[4]. We ultimately see the unaltered forms of social inequality existing between different geographical areas, economic classes, and between men and women.

In this protest against modernity born of consumerism (but ignoring the process of cultural, economic, and political growth of the individual), the post-war generation borrows a bit from everywhere for its elements of analysis. All this creates a form of ideology in response to the loss of credibility in the institutions. The crisis of religious practice is coupled with the decline of people choosing religious vocations, and this cannot be separated from the crisis of Catholic affiliation: thus the Italian church looses credibility on more than one front. Put at the margins of a growing affluent society, the church progressively looses touch with those who are politically and ethically committed and who see the church retreating in the face of the crisis of contemporary Italy. The merciless analysis that considers the Italian church an *instrumentum regni* (latin: tool of the state), however historically insubstantial, characterizes the general opinion of the post-war generation regarding the church. In fact, in 1981, the post-war generation was one of the least active groups in the church. In this year the degree of religious practice for this generation (age 25 to 34) was 17%, notably inferior to the older age group (age 35 to 44) at 36%, but which is still lower than the younger age group (age 18 to 24) which was 26%[5]. The loss of credibility in the religious institutions seems to go hand in hand with that happening in other institutions. The political parties today are merely seen as representing special interest groups who only try to maximize their influence. It is in connection with the loss of credibility in the various institutions that the radical protests characterizing the period from 1968 to 1978 would develop. The post-war generation, both culturally educated and economically consolidated, opened the way for a difficult path towards modernization of the political and economic institutions of an Italy already modernized some important social groups were concerned: from the laborers to new marginal groups appearing at the outskirts of the metropolitan areas.

The decline of the political protest movement and the radicalization of its most extreme margins, have left the post-war generation with a completely new horizon. At this point the process of modernization is in its utopian dimension while the failing economy resulting from the energy crisis of 1973 regenerates political awareness from all levels of society. A modernity characterized by unequal distribution of goods is replaced by a society full of political and economic uncertainty. Some predictions formulated during the sixties seem to be proving true: the parties based on ideologies are disappearing in favor of the "catch-all" coalition parties. Faith in powerful and self-sufficient technology is dying out, and the number of marginalized people is increasing in spite of a growing middle class. Nevertheless, unlike the sixties, the solutions today seem to be more unreliable while the country's leadership admits the difficulty in solving the problems. During the sixties modernity was triumphantly attacking the problems left unresolved from previous generations as well as those created by modernity itself: a decade later the incomplete and ambiguous character of progress is admitted by a modernity that now understands its limits.

1975-1985

During the post-crisis years the state attempted to save the beneficial elements of the social system without reducing the necessary political control or public spending. This goal has been constantly pursued, but the political system responded by showing its weaknesses. The different center-left governments which alternately led the country during the eighties were more and more unable to operate efficiently while they looked for the broad consensus necessary for a parliamentary democracy.

Improving the country's governability increasingly becomes the main objective of the political debate. But this goal can only be achieved through institutional reforms. Thus, on the eve of the 1993 European agreement, it is this same modernization process that finds itself at a turning point in its development.

A Generation at the Crossroads

The post-war generation, after the period of political unrest, has become one of the most influential groups in Italy. This generation now plays a major role in maintaining the political and social equilibrium. It would be simple to say that behind certain changes in thinking and in behavior, a mere process of adaptation and integration within the Italian society had occurred. But in reality it was a much broader process which included cultural change involved in the integration of a generation in the society.

Thus the integration of the post-war generation into the economic-professional context occurred simultaneously with the crisis of the 1970s. Many people consider the years between 1973 and 1978 to be the darkest period of the Italian economy; many institutions rapidly abandoned the hopes of triumph and well-being predicted in the 1960s (Ginsborg 1989: 597). The first measures of energy rationing were clear signs (in Italy as well as in the other Western countries) of the collapse of any notion of unlimited well-being and the myths connected to it. Certainly one aspect of modernity, the one of growing consumerism, looses credibility in the face of the increasing economic crisis.

These years were also characterized by a growing political ferment. The post-war generation could not show enthusiasm for the economic world in which it operated, nor could it identify with the urban protest (characterized by the poorest student populations). These years are characterized by the explosion of both terrorism and extreme violence between political parties. The assassination of the prime minister in 1978 shows the other side of a phase in the country's history with respect to the optimistic and enthusiastic sixties.

Clearly then, the post-war generation finds itself in a political and economic context which has been substantially and irreparably changed. Along with the declining hope of unlimited well-being, we can see a disillusionment and detachment from political activism and economic advancement. Economic development and political commitment cease to be inherently positive elements of modern society. Such modernization is seen as resulting in uncertainties at the political and economic levels, and in preserving the social-economic status quo as well as simultaneously transforming it. The 1970s therefore mark a period of confusion and crisis when the post-war generation could no longer rely on a productive modernity now in crisis nor on the outcome of a general protest with whose methods it could not identify. At the same time turning to institutional religion seems to be implausible. The encyclical *Humanae Vitae* has, since the 1960s, isolated itself because of its ethical stand on sexuality. The defeats suffered by the Catholic organizations with the referendum on divorce in 1974 and with the referendum on abortion in 1981 paint a clear picture of the post-war generation's widespread loss of faith in the religious institution[6].

During this time the divorce rate also greatly increased: in 1971 one out of 34 marriages sought separation, whereas by 1981 the number was one out of ten. The modernization founded on the permanent role of the housewife created a situation completely unacceptable for post-war generation women. The contests of the late sixties ended with severe repercussions in the revision of the family roles, a phenomenon totally new to the Italian culture which had been based on the stability of the marital institution. The same mechanism that kept women in the house in the 1960s lost its decisive influence during the 1970s. Starting from 1973 the number of women in the work place begins to grow: after having declined during the 1960s to about 28% of the total work force, female employment begins to increase consistently. In 1981 women represented 32% of the total work force, and by 1985 they reached 33%.

The seventies were not only the years of crisis but also the years when the state took on the role of social pacifier. Between 1971 and 1981 the government infrastructure and public service raised their employment rate by 22% while in the same decade the overall employment rate rose only 6.5% (Istat 1986: 132). The post-war generation found itself in an ambivalent situation. It was a time both of crisis for the political platform as well as a period of more direct ties to the state which guaranteed protection from civil unrest. Yet at the same time the decade marked a change in the internal structure of the family because of the rising number of women entering the work force (Table 10.2). After having anticipated a political and economic modernization the post-war generation faced a social modernization born out of crisis rather than development. It is within this context that we can understand this generation's relationship with the Catholic church. In 1981 the relationship between these two remained in conflict: 52% of Italians between the ages of 25 and 34 believed that the church did not offer satisfactory answers to the moral problems of the individual; 50% also believed the church's action to be inadequate in treating family issues, whereas only 36% felt that the church did not respond adequately to the spiritual needs of the individual. This age group also predicted, more concretely than the other groups, a general decline of religion: 40% of this group stated that religion would become less and less

TABLE 10.2: Female Employment in Italy

Year	Total Number Employed	Percentage out of total number of employed
1959	6,363,000	31.3
1960	6,147,000	30.2
1965	5,477,000	28.1
1970	5,322,000	27.5
1971	5,336,000	27.6
1972	5,102,000	26.9
1973	5,338,000	27.9
1974	5,548,000	28.4
1975	5,612,000	28.6
1976	5,764,000	29.2
1977	6,045,000	30.3
1978	6,086,000	30.4
1979	6,260,000	30.9
1980	6,449,000	31.5
1981	6,498,000	31.7
1982	6,524,000	31.8
1983	6,597,000	32.1
1984	6,676,000	32.3
1985	6,756,000	32.6

SOURCE: ISTAT, *Somario di Statistiche Storiche*, 1926-1985, Roma, 1986.

important for Italians. Of all the age groups this one in particular had the highest percentage of disbelief: the younger age group (18-24) interestingly was not as pessimistic (Calvaruso and Abbruzzese 1985). Another poll conducted as recently as 1987 confirms how far the sentiment of the post-war generation has spread. When asked how close they felt to the church, men between 31 and 40 showed the lowest levels of faith with respect to the other age groups (Garelli 1991). Even in 1991 Italians between the age of 30 and 49 showed the lowest level of religious practice in comparison to the other age groups (ISPES 1991). It would be imprudent to classify the post-war generation as secularized. The religious dimension is not necessarily opposed. In a recent survey (1991), this younger generation is characterized more by a simple discordance rather than a true opposition to religion. Those who are "indifferent" represent only 12% of the generation. Those members of the post-war generation who proclaim their faith in God are only slightly higher in numbers than the rest of the entire population: 33.8% versus 33.3%. Whereas this percentage is slightly less than for those who declare themselves "Catholic" (27% for the post-war generation versus 28% for all those interviewed) or for "active Catholics,"

TABLE 10.3: Attitude Towards Religion by Age

	Age 18-29	*Age 30-49*	*Age 50-69*	*Over 69*	*Average*
Indifferent	11.6	12.9	7.0	3.5	10.6
Believe in God	34.8	33.8	30.8	31.7	33.3
Catholic	27.6	26.8	31.7	28.2	28.3
Practicing Catholic	17.9	13.0	24.4	28.2	18.0

Source: Survey ISPES, 1991.

13% versus 18%. (See Table 10.3). Even though the post-war generation at present is not as religious as its predecessors, it is not entirely separated from the religious sphere. Above all what we see emerging is a decline of active church participation in favor of an individual and inner spirituality. The true detachment of this generation is not from the religious beliefs but from the institutions representing them: it is not a decline of the sacred as much as a decline of the church's authority as a moral guide.

Ultimately the overall cultural development of the post-war generation marks the affirmation of individualism, which is the heart of modernity, more than of secularization. While belief in the sacred is still plausible it is evident that the ecclesiastical institutions have lost authority in the domain of private life. The religious dimension is still present as an ethical reference, as an all encompassing criterion, which is absolute and sublime, but whose interpretive keys are now in the hands of the individual and will not be easily returned to the church authorities.

This form of religious individualism is grafted to a partial modernization and ends up as its only appropriate expression. The economic modernization and the development of consumerism are neither based on nor have ever been involved in a process of institutional secularization. Because the Catholic Party has been in control of Italian politics for some 45 years, including such institutions as the Ministry of Interior and the Ministry of Public Education, religious instruction in the public schools was mandatory up until the mid-1980s. The referenda on divorce and abortion represent a victory more for individual autonomy than for secularization at the cultural level (Scoppola 1987: 137). The right of church intervention is never seriously debated and now non-Catholics are free from such intervention. While the institutions are tending towards a process of secularization, this is happening very gradually and with many second thoughts. When the state is faced with economic and political crises and organized crime any conflict with the religious institution seems to be irrelevant compared to the true problems of the country. The institutional and cultural secularization is formed in the mold of a partial modernization, of an unfulfilled development of recurring crises. The church loses its power of intervention in the private sphere but no one, not even the post-war generation, attempts to discredit its religious domain.

Within the span of 30 years, from 1960 to 1990, the post-war generation in Italy has chosen a critical detachment and an absolute autonomy from both the various religious and lay authorities and from the structural elements of cultural modernity. Since the beginning the path towards modernization has been marked by a consistent disintegration from institutional ties as well as from cultural references. Formed within an Italy that completely emphasized the expansion of consumerism and free time, the post-war generation now only partially experiences the increasing opportunities which guarantee cultural promotion and social mobility. Externally, modernization is developed more in the technological sphere than in the cultural one. The partial development of institutional secularization supports this theory. Throughout the 1960s and the 1970s the church remained an important force in maintaining political balance even though it did not play the same role that it played in the 1940s and 1950s. The process of modernization does not imply a secularization of the institutions: church-state relations continued to be regulated by the 1929 Concordat as late as the mid-1980s. Therefore the decline in religious practice gradually took place and the loss of credibility in religious institutions occurred simultaneously with the failing of the developmental system. This system, with its emphasis on productivity and consumerism, and thus undermining complete individual development, came under scrutiny in the 1960s.

Because the church is unwilling and cannot objectively support the anti-establishment protest, the post-war generation progressively detached itself from the religious institution. Divorce as sanctioned in the *Humanae Vitae* forced the post-war generation into indifference towards institutions. But it would be the crisis of the political ideologies in the 1970s, unable to cope with both the economic productive development and with the more profound cultural-personal metamorphosis (i.e. the marriage crisis), which would influence a growing disillusionment and global secularization in the post-war generation or at least in its ideal model represented by the highest levels of education and professionalism. This secularization involves all the dimensions of social ethos (religious, political, traditional) and is not limited to any single institution.

Members of this generation embrace a strong ethical relativism based on a cautious suspension of judgment towards ethical values. Heirs to the war generation who knew war's horrors but also had passionate political hopes for the post-war period, they teach their children none other than pragmatic disenchantment and recentering around the concerns of the individual. The cultural system that is taking shape in the 1980s and 1990s is the direct consequence of such views. The ecological movement represents a direct relationship between the individual and the environment while the new religious movements developing at the periphery of the institutional religions offer, in the same way, a direct and personal experience of the divine and the renewal of life because of it. The disillusionment of the post-war generation is thus transmitted. After this each attempt at social planning can only be presented on the *rational* level based on concrete, practical experience, and one can no longer theorize about utopian social transformation.

The post-war generation has, to an extent, exhausted the ethical and developmental potential of modernity through experiencing its ineffectiveness in the renewal and transformation of society. As a result young Italians have laid down the foundation for a new idea of "utopia": from the theoretical, expressed in its formal coherence, to the practical experience of the *here* and *now*; in other words from the idealized utopia to the practiced utopia.

The disillusionment progressively experienced by the post-war generation moves utopia into a new realm where at least two substantial transformations occur. On the one hand, every principle of authority which legitimized and rendered plausible a theory of change, leaving it merely as a guide or point of reference, radically disappears. On the other hand, as the imagined utopia fails, with it an optimistic view of the world disappears. An emphasis upon concrete experiences shows the absence of faith in a future that should guarantee what is only dreamed of today. The *realistic* choice through which this generation organizes and stores its social conception of the world is translated, with the next generation, into the desire for immediacy and practical plans.

Ultimately this choice results in a radical change of attitude towards institutional religion. The church moves from the role of savior and regulator of beliefs and practices necessary for the well being of the soul, to becoming more and more a model institution with the role of setting a good example. While the doctrinal and regulative function of the church seems to remain at a low level of credibility, the exemplary function is more and more emphasized. No longer challenged at the social planning level (i.e. construction of the "city") but at the level of the practical experience (striving for solidarity and human advancement), the church must now tackle the development and implementation of concrete projects. While in the 1960s the church was applauded or contested for its statements, today it is increasingly judged for its actions. An exemplary religion based on the testimony of actions, it is the manifestation of a society no longer inspired by utopian ideals and which has no insurance or guarantees for the future.

Notes

1. Translated from the Italian by Isotta Poggi.

2. The state will advance 20% of the costs while an additional 70% will be guaranteed in credit for 15 years with a interest rate of 4%.

3. Ispes, *Rapporto Italia*. Roma: Ispes, 1989: Between 1951 and 1960 the funds for government programs reached 1,278 billion lire. During the following decade the number increased to 4,633 billion while from 1971 to 1980 it reached 22,194 billion lire.

4. One of the most influential books during the students' protest in that period was *Lettera ad una Professoressa*, edited by the students of Don Lorenzo Milani and published by the Libreria Editrice Fiorentina.

5. Data collected in the survey conducted by the European Values System Study Group and interpreted, in the Italian context by C. Calvaruso and S. Abbruzzese, *Indagine sui Valori in Italia*. Turin: S.E.I., 1985

6. The proposal by the Catholics to repeal the existing law on divorce was rejected in the referendum of May 12, 1974 by 59.1% of the voters. On May 17, 1980 the Catholics' proposal to repeal the abortion laws was rejected by 68% of the voters.

11

The Orthodox Church and the Post-War Religious Situation in Greece

Vasilios N. Makrides

Introduction

Discussing establishment religion in modern Greece does not seem to be a matter of great complexity. At first glance, it seems to be an easy task. Aside from the spiritual influence of the Ecumenical Patriarchate of Constantinople on Greece, the Greek Orthodox Autocephalous Church, founded in 1833, is constitutionally recognized as the dominant, established church of the Greek state. Furthermore, Orthodoxy as a specific religious tradition is similarly accepted as the official faith of the state. There are several reasons (e.g., historical and socio-political) for the unquestioned coexistence of and close collaboration between church and state in modern Greece (Makrides 1991a). It is therefore evident from the outset that in the Greek case we encounter neither a society characterized by religious pluralism including various churches and denominations, nor a society with an unofficial religious establishment (as in the United States). Greek society is compact and cohesive, and offers fertile ground for the existence of such a religious establishment which claims, as all Orthodox churches generally do, to possess the complete religious truth. Not surprisingly, this rather unique situation implies that some restrictions are consequently imposed on the free circulation of non-Orthodox religious ideas within Greece's "religious market." Therefore, although there was some liberalization in the 1975 constitution (Frazee 1979: 95-97), the issue of religious freedom remains a controversial one in a number of ways.

The cohesiveness of Greek society is clearly reflected in its extraordinary religious homogeneity and Orthodox omnipresence. According to the 1951 census, 97.9 percent of the Greek population belonged to the Orthodox church, whereas only 0.4 percent was Roman Catholic and 0.1 percent Protestant.[1] It is interesting to note that the percentage of those speaking Greek was 95.6 percent, namely almost equal to the number of those classified as Orthodox. This can be used as an additional indicator of the fact that the notions of "being Greek" and "being Orthodox" are inextricably intertwined among modern Greeks. Although in later censuses (the latest in 1991) questions regarding religious affiliation were omitted, it is generally believed that the aforementioned percentages have not changed radically since 1951.

Nonetheless, the religious homogeneity of Greece should not be overstated. It does not mean that there are no fluctuations or variant tendencies within the Greek Orthodox body. In fact, there exist more diverse, subjective and even controversial interpretations of the Orthodox tradition than one would ever expect to find within such a closed religious system. These interpretations very often deviate from the established standards and policies of the official church. As a result, the concept "Orthodoxy" is usually construed as an all-encompassing category incorporating the various "Orthodoxies" that exist. The main objective of this paper is to examine this phenomenon based on post-war religious developments. According to a foreign observer, "to some of us, arriving in the newly-liberated Athens in October, 1944, it seemed as if, for the first time in our life, we were in a Christian city" (cited in Ware 1980: 146). Ware added: "Alas! This could not be said of Athens thirty-five years later" (Ware 1980: 146). What actually are the changes and how can they be described and analyzed?

Post-War Social Changes: An Overview

Before proceeding with our main objective, it is important to begin with an overview of the massive, structural social changes of the post-war period. It should be kept in mind that Greek society suffered not only from World War II but also from an ensuing, dramatic civil war (1946-1949), which in fact polarized the whole country and left nearly incurable wounds in the consciousnesses of modern Greeks up to the present. This had an immediate negative impact on the church and its activities, since hundreds of priests were killed, many parishes, especially in northern Greece, were left vacant, and ecclesiastical property was largely destroyed (Frazee 1977: 145-146; Stavrou 1988: 199). Nevertheless, the overall development of the country from the early 1950s onwards was undoubtedly impressive and led to its complete transformation.

First, there was a rapid economic upswing due to an infusion of foreign capital, with a concomitant improvement in living standards and the potential for better education and upward mobility, mainly in the urban areas. For example, average annual income was 4,775 drachmae in 1951 compared to 12,926 drachmae in 1962 (McNeill 1978: 104).

Second, there was a considerable increase in internal migration and urbanization. In 1907 the urban population was only 24 percent of the total population, by 1920 it was 26.8 percent, in 1940 it was 33.3 percent. By 1971 it was 53.2 percent, and in 1985 it was 66.9 percent. According to the 1971 census, between 1951 and 1971 the population in the major urban centers (Athens, Thessaloniki) increased by over 70 percent--71.5 and 72.2 percent respectively (Stylios 1980: 56; Leontidou 1990: 127-171). The demographic changes, even between 1951 and 1961, produced a destabilization of the traditional balance between the cities and the countryside. This had an impact not only on the metropolitan Athens area, where about one-third of the Greek population currently resides, but also on other parts of the country as well (Kayser 1968: 37-45).

Third, there was a considerable increase in external migration (e.g., towards Western Europe), a trend which severely affected the population of the countryside (McNeill 1978: 106-107).

As could be expected, these changes did not leave the social life and the culture of Orthodox Greeks unaffected. For example, the interpersonal and communal way of life in the villages (Stylios 1980: 95-96) was destroyed when localism and village isolation broke down in the wake of contact with cosmopolitan, urban-based ideas, despite the fact that the urban-rural cleavage was never a very significant factor in forming cultural and political attitudes (Dimitras 1987: 75). The close connection between the decline of community and the process of secularization has been emphasized in several theories (Dobbelaere 1987: 111-113).

In addition, the degree of personal material consumption increased dramatically and, together with an increase in leisure time and activities, produced a widespread spirit of consumerism as well as an individualist, utilitarian culture among the middle-class, affluent citizens. These profound social changes seriously affected Greece's historically collectivist culture. They transformed its traditional collectivist structure to an individualist one, evident when family values in small rural communities are compared with those in urban centers. Acculturation of the small communities to the new value systems has not always occurred, a fact indicating that traditional values and forms of behavior are still deeply entrenched in many areas (Georgas 1989; cf. Kiefl and Marinescu 1986).

Additionally, it should not be overlooked that, due to Greece's commitment to the Western alliance, Greek society experienced a wholesale adoption of Western ways during the immediate post-war period. This produced, on the one hand, widespread mimicry of foreign lifestyles (e.g., through the influence of the mass media, especially TV), but, on the other hand, some fanatical reactions against the "Westtoxication" of the country. Greece still agonizes between the Scylla of xenomania and the Charybdis of blind traditionalism without finding a median between these two extremes. This brief description of the social changes of the post-war period reveals a country in transition and a dramatic oscillation between tradition and modernity.

The Post-War Religious Situation:
A Multifaceted Distancing from the Official Church

The social metamorphosis of Greece necessarily attracted the attention of the official church. The post-war period began for the church as a period of massive reconstruction to successfully address the new challenges. For example, an organization named *Apostoliki Diakonia* (Apostolic Service) was entrusted with the task of developing an expansive internal as well as external mission. The Church of Greece was present and active on the international level, for example, through participation in the Ecumenical Movement. Nevertheless, the entire structure of the church, which was based for the most part on traditionalistic patterns of thought and did not favor social action, was not in a position to fully adapt to the new situation and to address the concomitant challenges. There was also the grave problem of illiteracy among the clergy which had been prevalent for several centuries. As late as 1919, only one percent of the clergy (i.e., 43 out of a total of 4,433) had a university degree (Stavrou 1988: 200). This problem was not completely resolved even in the post-war decades, although there was a clear improvement (i.e., in 1975 about eight percent, or 589 out of 7,413, had university degrees; in 1979, about 650 had them (Stavrou 1988: 200; Frazee 1979: 100)).

There also exists a significant rift between the clergy and a great number of lay theologians (Jioultsis 1987), the latter traditionally better educated and employed by the state in educational roles (e.g., in secondary education). In contrast, priests were traditionally intended for the role performing religious rituals. Although this division has begun to change, it has functioned as a major barrier to priests in their struggle for better education and upward mobility. Statistical research has shown that the majority of the clergy ordained in the period 1950 to 1969 were from rural backgrounds, of an advanced average age and uneducated, and therefore totally inappropriate for appealing to the growing urban population and the younger generations (Gousidis 1975).

It should also be remembered that there have been many scandals (moral and financial), especially among the top leadership of the church, and that there exist various competing factions within the church hierarchy. It goes without saying that such dynamics do not advance the church's societal standing (Ware 1983: 213-218).

Finally, the church, despite its relative autonomy, remained dependent on the state and therefore vulnerable to changes occurring on the turbulent Greek political scene (Clogg 1979: 166-225). This has been a persistent source of problems for the church's overall image and social appeal. The seizure of power by the colonels in 1967, for example, and subsequent changes in the church hierarchy marked the beginning of a major situation that continues to wrack the entire church (Frazee 1977: 147-151; 1979: 91-95).

As could be expected, these developments have had serious consequences for numerous believers, contributing to breaks with the official church body, especially observable in the post-war period.

These developments do not mean, however, that post-war Greek society fell victim to secularism to such a degree that there was a complete loss of Orthodox influence, especially in the urban centers. The degree of religiosity remains high as recent public opinion surveys (October 1979; March and November 1980) show. To the question of whether they believed in the existence of God, 70 to 72 percent of respondents answered that they believed, 16 to 17 percent said they sometimes had doubts, and only 11 to 12 percent said they did not believe (Wenturis 1990: 24). A more recent Gallup poll carried out in the greater Athens area in October 1989 shows 93 percent of Athenians considered themselves Orthodox, while only six percent called themselves atheists (Dimitras 1991: 61). In another context, D. Martin called Greece "the most 'believing' of European nations" (1978: 277).

However, the general religiousness of the Greek people is somewhat misleading. It does not accurately reveal various individual attitudes and trends that have developed towards the official church during the post-war period, developments that are examined below.

Generational Cleavages: Some Data

Important changes can be observed in the religious outlook of the post-war generations. According to Dimitras (1987: 76-78), survey data show a deep generational cleavage on almost all public attitudes and not only in the religious domain. First, there is the older one-third of the electorate--people over 50 years-old today who were older than 30 in the mid-1960s--who display a social conservative profile reflecting those years (e.g., anti-communist, pro-Western, pro-capitalist, pro-business). At the religious level, they prefer the predominance of the Greek Orthodox tradition and oppose easy divorces, abortions, availability of contraceptives and premarital sex. They trust religion, the Greek Orthodox church, the bishops and the priests. They regularly go to church on Sundays and believe that religion has great value for humankind.

Second, there is the younger one-third of the electorate--those under 35 years-old who "matured" politically in the later junta and post-junta period (after 1974). The dictatorship (1967-1974) and its traumatic collapse have proven to be a catalyst in the emergence of a radically different political culture that has persisted in the 1980s. This generation was radically opposed to its older compatriots (e.g., it was anti-right, anti-Western, pro-leftist, anti-traditionalist) and had distinctly opposing opinions on the aforementioned religious issues.

Between these two groups lies the middle one-third of the electorate, people between 35 and 49 years old--the young generations of the turbulent 1960s. In all attitudes, they appear to be less radical than the youngest generation and less conservative than the oldest one, although in most cases they are closer to the younger group. These generational cleavages are evident in Table 11.1.

Fairly consistent data, especially concerning the issue of "religion," are found in four 1989 surveys of the greater Athens area that examined the rule of the socialist party PASOK (1981-1989) and its consequences (Dimitras 1990: 26-30). Survey respondents were divided into three age groups. First, there was the "war generation" (over 45 years-old), which maintained more or less the attitudes of the aforementioned older generation. On the issue of "religion," this generation preferred the prevalence of the Greek Orthodox tradition in the future evolution of the country (61 percent) instead of the European mentality (29 percent), went to church fairly regularly (53 percent), and believed that religion has great value for humankind (89 percent). The "junta generation" (28-45 year-olds) was more moderate overall, including on the issue of "religion" (e.g., 19 percent attended church regularly, 55 percent believed religion has great value for humanity and 38 percent preferred the continued predominance of Greek Orthodox tradition). The youngest generation (18-27 year-olds), which voted for the first time after the PASOK came to power (the "PASOK generation"), lies between the two previous groups politically. On the issue of "religion," however, it surpasses even the "junta generation" in its detachment. Although 55 percent believed that religion has great value for humanity, only 8 percent went to church regularly and only 26 percent preferred the Orthodox tradition's continued predominance in the future (67 percent preferred the dominance of the "European mentality").

It is evident that there are deep differences in the religious outlooks of these generations, not only with regard to the official Church of Greece, but also with regard to the Orthodox tradition in general.

TABLE 11.1: Greater Athens Surveys

	Survey date	Total	Age Under 35	35-49	Over 49
Trust religion	3/86	67%	42%	73%	89%
Trust the Greek Orthodox church	3/86	64	38	68	86
Trust priests	3/86	64	42	70	83
Trust "metropolites"	3/86	49	28	49	70
Religion has great value for the man	1/85	50	16	50	83
Go to church every, or often on, Sundays	1/85	18	1	10	42
Prefer European mentality to prevail	1/85	50	69	55	28
Prefer Greek Orthodox tradition to prevail	1/85	40	16	34	69
Church played a positive role historically	9/82	76	62	80	88
Road to socialism through our religious heritage	9/82	53	34	61	66
Stronger ties between Orthodoxy and nation	9/82	52	28	54	76
Without Orthodoxy we cannot remain Greeks	9/82	51	27	53	75
Oppose separation of the church from the state	9/82	50	30	51	69
Christianity and socialism are compatible	9/82	46	41	53	46
Opposed automatic divorce	11/80	43	24	43	64
Opposed abortions	11/80	46	28	44	68
Opposed contraceptives	11/80	32	15	31	51
Opposed premarital sex	11/80	31	7	32	56

SOURCE: Dimitras, 1987: 81, 83.

Although the data indicate a dissatisfaction with or distancing from the official church among the younger generations, this should not be equated with its complete rejection, as will become evident below.

Beyond the Conventionalism of the Official Church: Spiritual Renewal

If we take a closer look at some of the principal "religious" changes of the post-war period, we first notice a strong tendency to detach the Orthodox tradition from its common, contemporary manifestations, particulary that of the official church establishment, and to reconstruct it on the basis of its authentic and rich heritage. In order to understand this quest, one has to take into consideration the implications of "Orthodoxy" within the Eastern Christian world and specifically in Greece. In this milieu, the term does not imply a religious conservatism or simply anti-liberal trends. Rather, it signifies a deeply rooted conviction that Orthodoxy is the most true faith in the entire world and that the Orthodox church is its sole guardian. This conviction has had crucial social consequences in the historical evolution of the Orthodox world up to the present. In Greece there was a widespread perception starting in the early nineteenth century (cf. Campbell and Sherrard 1968: 207-209; Frazee 1969) that the official church was not fulfilling its mission to preserve the integrity of Orthodoxy. There were several reasons for this: first, the church's subjugation to and later alliance with the interests of the state, which cared for the church mainly out of political expediency; second, the church's ineffectiveness in proclaiming the Orthodox message in the country, its decorative role in dealing with social problems, and its consequently waning social image and significance; third, the church's bureaucratization, legalism and despotism in handling religious issues in general, which obstructed the expression of the rich Orthodox spirituality and its relational, communal character; and fourth, the church's overall conservatism, in exchange for which the state supported the church not only economically but also by granting it its customary honors (cf. Stavrou 1988: 186). All these factors contributed in a decisive way to the conviction that the official church had lagged behind, and that new, alternative ways had to be found both to overcome present defects and to protect against similar crises in the future.

Divergences from the official church can be traced to the pre-war period if the brotherhood of theologians, "Zoi," is taken into account (Makrides 1988). Zoi and other similar groups, although later founded, persisted into the post-war period. It cannot be shown, however, that they played a crucial role in the religious orientation of Greeks during that time. This is especially true after the 1960s when these brotherhoods began to wane, losing strength and influence. Nevertheless, many of their members deserted and paved a new path in search of an authentic Orthodox identity beyond the authoritarianism, moralism and pietism of the brotherhoods, as well as beyond the conventionalism, stagnation and sclerosis of the official church.

Their quest coincided with a rediscovery and reevaluation of the dynamics of Orthodox spirituality as expressed in various forms. New emphasis was placed, for example, on the rich Patristic tradition and on the Orthodox mystics of the "Byzantine" period, as well as on the liturgical heritage of the East. The fundamental features distinguishing the Orthodox tradition from the Roman Catholic and Protestant ones were also stressed. Academic theologians were sharply criticized as custodians of arid, dead knowledge. Although this multi-dimensional, disorganized reform current diverged from the general standards of the official church, its interaction with the church was far more fruitful than that of the brotherhoods since it triggered a useful debate which influenced many church officials. The appeal of this current persisted throughout the 1970s and the 1980s, in both latent and more open forms (e.g., the current of "Neo-Orthodoxy" (Makrides 1989)).

It is not accidental that monasticism on Mount Athos, a traditional center of Orthodox spirituality for centuries, reached a peak beginning in the 1970s, after a long period of gradual decline, particularly in the number of monks. In 1972, for example, there was a small increase in the total number of monks (from 1,145 to 1,146) for the first time in decades. The upward trend continued with insignificant exceptions until 1984. Of particular importance is that in the period 1972-1984, 725 young men became monks. Important in this development were "spiritual fathers" who went to Mount Athos with their "pupils" and contributed to a reorganization of monastic life, particularly focussing on its public image and appeal. The educational level of the monks also increased. Monks were traditionally viewed as hostile towards mundane, secular knowledge. In the period 1960-1964, only three new monks (representing 2.8 percent) had a university degree. In 1984, out of a total of 1,266 monks, 119 (9.3 percent) had a university degree in theology and 75 (5.9 percent) had a degree in some other discipline. One can easily guess that these young men were attracted to Mount Athos' monasticism for special reasons, since they could have stayed in the world and been successful in their careers. Among these reasons one must stress the aforementioned crisis in the official church establishment (Mantzaridis 1975; 1985: 284-291; Ware 1983: 223-225). The monasticism on Mount Athos was considered a culmination of personal freedom, an unpredictable, uncontrollable, "anarchist way of life" beyond all rules, prescriptions and totalitarian patterns. These perceived qualities are the exact opposites of the perceived conventionalism, rigidity and inflexibility of the official church structure.

The Intensification of Orthodox Fundamentalism

Another important deviation from the standards of the official church can be observed in the multi-dimensional current which, in the author's view, may properly be called "Greek Orthodox fundamentalism" (Makrides 1991a). We should be careful not to consider this current an exclusively post-war phenomenon. In fact, facets of a fundamentalist mentality can be detected in earlier periods. Factors both internal and external to the Greek Orthodox church gave rise to this current. Of particular relevance here is the fact that fundamendalist trends became increasingly manifest in the post-war period. Although we cannot point to a general mass movement characterizing Greek society as a whole, fundamentalism constitutes an important feature of modern Greek religious life. The proponents of fundamentalism are often quite separate from one another. One can find them, for example, among monks on Mount Athos (the so-called "Zealots") or among other religious organizations such as the Panhellenic Orthodox Union. Tension and conflict between fundamentalist factions are not unusual. Although their influence, especially on official church policies, has not been particularly significant in the past, it would be a mistake to overlook the pressures they have exerted (cf. Vassiliadis 1991: 41).

What are the reasons for the intensification of this fundamentalist current during the post-war period? An important one is the general status of the official church. Its accumulated problems and scandals contrast sharply with the ideal conception fundamentalists have of the ecclesiastical organism. Since fundamentalists tend to judge the present situation by reference to an elapsed "Golden Age" (cf. Riesebrodt 1990: 19-21) in which the principles of the ideal church were embodied, they are critical of the "pseudo-Orthodox" policies of the present church hierarchy. They wish to restore the old, pristine order. They view the present symbiosis of church and state in Greece as hypocritical and fallacious and as serving profane goals. In their view the primary goal must be the preservation of Orthodoxy, the most true faith in the entire world, which is in turn not only the crucial prerequisite for reward in Heaven, but also for the overall success and development of the Greek nation. In short, fundamentalists are convinced that the official church has strayed from its Orthodox moorings and that some "therapeutic measures" must be imposed.

In addition, fundamentalists feel jeopardized by the Orthodox church's involvement in the Ecumenical Movement, which they scornfully call the "culmination of heresies." In their opinion this involvement will inevitably lead to the relativization and loss of the Orthodox faith, and their opposition is evident even beyond Greek frontiers. For instance, during the recent Seventh General Assembly of the WCC in Canberra (February 7-20, 1991) there were anti-ecumenical demonstrations on the part of some "True Orthodox" (cf. Lossky 1991: 212). Among them were several Greeks living in Australia who had been influenced by the fundamentalists. Also, the rapprochement instigated by the Patriarch Athenagoras I (1886-1972) between the Patriarchate of Constantinople and the Roman Catholic church, traditionally the most feared enemy of Orthodoxy, was seen by fundamentalists as a betrayal of the Orthodox struggles to avoid any contact with the "heretics of the West."

The fact that Greece is a part of today's world-system (e.g., through its full membership in the EEC) also contributes to the intensification of the fundamentalist current. The globalization process, in Robertson's analysis (1985), inevitably implies dangers for the preservation of specific national, cultural and religious identities within the global melting pot. Greek fundamentalists are afraid that their claims to be a "chosen people" with a unique comprehension of truth will vanish within a syncretistic context, and they vehemently oppose the internationalizing tendencies of the state and the "Orthodox anemia" of some church officials. Reactions against the influence of the EEC on Greece's cultural and religious heritage, therefore, have been quite regular since the 1980s (Makrides in press).

Finally, it must be noted that fundamentalists do not uniformly support the aforementioned attempts to restore the "genuine" Orthodox tradition and spirituality, and they often strongly disagree with one another, reflecting the different premises on which they base their specific interpretations of the Orthodox heritage. In addition, fundamentalists are usually far more militant and fanatical in imposing their ideas on the church and society, a fact that often creates strong tensions between them and the surrounding society. Recent, violent conflicts between fundamentalists and the official church in the diocese of Larissa (1990-1992) showed the fundamentalists' unexpected vigor and ability to mobilize, and demonstrated that they could not be overlooked as a factor and force shaping future Greek religious life. Previously marginalized and insulated within their strict Orthodox lifestyle enclaves, fundamentalists may begin to demand more access to positions of influence in order to realize their visions concerning the ideal Greek Orthodox state.

"Diffused Religion": Religious Individualism
Within the Frame of the Orthodox Church

The phenomenon of people distancing themselves from the church establishment points to an increase in religious individualism among people still ostensibly aligned with the Greek Orthodox church. Cipriani (1988) coined the term "diffused religion" in his discussion of politics and religion in modern Italy, where Catholicism can be considered the main religious establishment. The concept also is applicable to the Greek situation. Kokosalakis (1987: 41) provides a short discussion of the analogies between Greece and Italy in this regard. Although the concept "diffused religion" requires further elaboration, especially in relation to the process of secularization (cf. Dobbelaere 1987: 124-125), it is still useful in describing certain phenomena within modern Greece. Briefly, the term "diffused religion" pertains in a closed and homogeneous religious system with one established church and a dominant, fideistic form of religion (cf. Cipriani 1989: 29). In such a milieu ongoing cultural differentiation and societal evolution produces subjective tendencies and tastes beyond the limits of the official church and its main doctrinal or practical precepts. Nevertheless, because the church has been closely connected to the historical consciousness of the population, and because its influence has permeated the entire national and cultural ethos, the rise of religious subjectivism is not coterminous with total rejection of the pre-existing religious establishment nor with that establishment's disappearance from the public sphere. Although some individuals prefer to follow their own beliefs on certain disputed matters regardless of the official church's teachings, they still maintain an open or latent link with the church which can be observed at different levels, and which is reinforced by other societal institutions such as the family, the educational system, the mass media, and even the state as a whole. Moreover, many non-overtly religious persons exhibit behavior influenced by the dominant religious tradition.

This paradigm clearly applies to Greece. The Orthodox church, apart from occasional lapses, has been inextricably intertwined with the historical struggles and aspirations of the Greek people. The Orthodox tradition has also had an abiding impact on the formation of Greek national and cultural identity. It is therefore no accident that the Orthodox church still enjoys the status of a religious monopoly in Greece and is considered an indispensable element in the functioning and integration of the Greek social system. However, deviations from this religious establishment have appeared in the form of "diffused religion."

Although one can detect these tendencies earlier (cf. also in Italy-- Cipriani 1989: 30), this phenomenon is primarily a characteristic of the post-war period. By rapidly moving from an essentially peasant society to an urbanized environment during the post-war period, and because of the concomitant increase in affluence, thousands of Greeks have been influenced not only by their own religious tradition and culture through primary and secondary socialization, but also have been exposed to a wide range of foreign beliefs, ideas and lifestyles. This was made possible by the pro-Western orientation of the state and more generally by the globalization process which did not leave the Greek social system unaffected nor find it immune to foreign influences. The result was the relativization of the preexisting religious status quo which proved to be ineffective in successfully meeting all the post-war challenges. However, "diffused religion" in Greece is not just a simple manifestation of the collision of traditional and modern influences, but also is continually influenced by the country's religious past.

It is crucial not to equate "diffused religion" with the phenomenon of "believing without belonging." Greeks practicing "diffused religion" are not unchurched and, despite their religious idiosyncrasies, still consider themselves members of the Greek Orthodox church. One even can find atheists who think of themselves as belonging to the Greek Orthodox church (Ware 1983: 208). There are manifestations of "Sheilaism" (Bellah et al. 1985:221) in Greece, to be sure. However, in the Greek milieu even this sort of highly personal, self-centered faith has not led, at least up to now, to a complete rejection of the religious establishment. It is still influenced by the predominant Orthodox tradition, because within such a closed religious system there are few alternatives by which to be influenced or from which to choose. Religious individualism exists in Greek society, but individuals cannot arrive at their own religious beliefs completely independent of the official church.

Empirical data illustrates the operation of "diffused religion" at various levels in Greece. First, Table 11.2 shows that church attendance in the great urban centers has declined considerably from the 1960s to the 1980s. Although church attendance in the villages appears to be higher (Ware 1983: 219), the urban 1980s percentages have been corroborated by other public opinion surveys (Wenturis 1990: 24).

It is evident that although the percentage of Greeks categorized as "believers" is high, the percentage of those attending church every Sunday for various reasons (Frazee 1979: 104-105) is significantly less. However, the percentages of those going to church on the Great Feasts (Christmas, Easter) or for various ceremonies (baptisms, weddings) remain high. In these phenomena one can discern a facet of "diffused religion." Although certain occasions have acquired broad social and cultural significance in Greece, they are still not completely detached from the religious contexts from which they originated. All Greeks attending church on Great Feasts are not necessarily believers, nor do they necessarily care much about religious issues. Nonetheless, they are reluctant to sever their superficial attachment to the originally religious rituals which have become indispensable parts of their cultural ethos.

TABLE 11.2: Church Attendance in the Athens Area, 1963-1980

Question: How often do you go to church?			
September 1963:		Spring 1980:	
- Every Sunday	31%	- Every Sunday	9%
- Two or three times a month	32	- Fairly often	20
- Once a month	15		
- On Great Feasts	14	- Only for Great Feasts or special occassions such as weddings	60
- When I have time	3		
		- Never	11

SOURCE: Ware, 1983: 218.

Of course, there are few non-ecclesiastical rites of passage available, notwithstanding the recent constitutional introduction of civil marriages. According to Savramis (1968: 162), the cultural symbols and traditional notion that the church, by virtue of its sacramental functions, can permeate every domain, give the church the power to continue playing a crucial role in modern Greece. Therefore, the presence of clergymen at national celebrations, local feasts, and ceremonies is deemed absolutely necessary. This is why, as Savramis points out, the Greeks, though not strict churchgoers, are distinguished by a "distanced church-boundedness" (*distanzierte Kirchlichkeit*). It is no accident that the percentage of those selecting a civil instead of a religious marriage has been extremely limited so far. In 1984, 52,684 (91.4 percent) religious marriages were performed in Greece compared to only 4,987 (8.6 percent) civil ones; in 1985, 56,831 (90.9 percent) religious marriages were performed compared to 5,716 (9.1 percent) civil ones; and in 1987, 57,078 (90.7 percent) religious marriages were performed compared to 5,821 (9.3 percent) civil ones (Tomara-Sideri 1991: 65).

It cannot be argued, however, that Orthodoxy in Greece survives solely because of its popular rituals. The principal underlying cause for its survival is the fact that the great majority of Greeks consider their

Orthodox tradition as a *condition sine qua non* of their overall identity and existence. For them, being Greek means, among other things, being Orthodox.

Although the social image of the church generally is not particularly appealing, especially among the younger generations (see Table 11.1), Orthodoxy is still considered a basic component of modern Greek identity that must be kept intact. The negative attitudes among the "PASOK generation" towards the Orthodox church should not be equated, for example, with the generation's complete secularization. The negative attitudes have more to do with the aforementioned crises in the official church. Surveys repeatedly show that in the Greek case negative views and critiques of the official church, and even declining church attendance, do not obscure the strong influence that Orthodoxy (often as an abstract category closely linked to Hellenism) exerts on the broad population (Dimitras 1990: 24-25). This does not mean complete adherence to the directives of the religious tradition and its hierarchy but rather a loose boundedness to them which preserves certain principles influenced and promoted by Orthodoxy and its culture.

Another aspect of "diffused religion" is found in the attempt of many Greeks to transform the primary religious function of the Orthodox church into something not overtly religious. There is also evidence showing a preference for keeping the church out of one's private, daily life and allowing it to speak only on more general and abstract issues, either national or international. The main reason for this is that Orthodox teachings are not generally compatible with the modern lifestyles and preferences of many Greeks. To be more specific, in March, 1987, there was a serious conflict between the church and the state over the proposed nationalization of ecclesiastical property. In a survey in May, 1987 of the greater Athens area people showed many of the above characteristics of "diffused religion." Sixty-seven percent of the respondents identified the church with the Greek people and said that without Orthodoxy they could not remain Greeks. Eighty-three percent considered the role of the church in the past as positive. Yet, only 28 percent were satisfied with the way the church fulfilled its mission currently and only 33 percent were satisfied with its adjustment to the modern world. They also advocated changing the priorities of priests by putting more emphasis on their non-religious functions. Sixty-two percent wanted the priest to counsel and help people generally whereas only 25 percent wanted them to teach the will of God (Dimitras 1991: 63).

What we see are lifestyles based on a kind of "voluntary principle" under which obedience to church directives (e.g., in sexual matters) becomes a matter of personal choice, and a more selective religiosity operates within a "diffused" Orthodox milieu which does not completely reject the institutional authority of the church. According to some data, only 34 percent of Greeks think that the church should give advice on sexual matters, only 46 percent think that abortion should be condemned, and only 32 percent think that contraceptives should also be condemned (means of the years 1979-1985, Wenturis 1990: 151).

Finally, "diffused religion" is starkly apparent in the attitudes of the political parties towards the Orthodox church and the articulation of the parties' ideologies and policies. This is true even for the allegedly atheist, communist parties. All consider the concept "Orthodoxy," defined idiosyncratically, very important for their purposes (see the data provided by Wenturis 1990: 153-176). Even among the traditionally pro-Soviet communist party, various surveys show that, although only 3 percent of its members go to church regularly on Sundays, 36 percent still attend church for the Great Feasts and 52 percent attend for various ceremonies while only nine percent never attend at all (means of the election years 1977, 1981 and 1985, Wenturis 1990: 174). There is a plethora of similar data which corroborate our initial assumption that Orthodoxy is present in a diffused form in the minds and lives of vast numbers of Greeks, a phenomenon characterizing post-war Greek society.

Concluding Remarks

The aforementioned data and analysis show in a schematic way the main characteristics of the post-war religious situation in Greece, especially the multi-faceted distancing from the established Orthodox church within this closed religious system. A few observations and my cautious prediction for the future conclude this paper.

Although predictions are hazardous at best, I would venture to suggest that the existing data do not corroborate the assumption that distancing from the official church will vanish in the near future. The church is still wracked by major internal and external problems and will not easily regain its old, historical role of church for the whole nation in such a functionally differentiated society. As a result, it is reasonable to suppose that the divergences mentioned above and the overall differentiation of individual religiosity from the institutional church will intensify in the future.

However, the more critical question is whether it will ever be possible to reject the Orthodox religious establishment or, at least, to marginalize it by rendering it virtually insignificant. Will the predominant Orthodox culture remain viable in the future as an influence in Orthodox individualism and "diffused religion?" Though tradition still persists, Greek society and culture is becoming more and more vulnerable to syncretism. Foreign ideas, values and lifestyles are observable everywhere.

The general identity crisis affecting modern Greeks regarding their history abets the intrusion of external influences which present a serious challenge to traditional value systems and ways of life. Up to now, Orthodoxy as a specific religious tradition (and not always due to the policies of the official church) has been able to maintain its monopoly status and to remain dominant. However, since the 1980s one observes the growing importation of foreign religious ideas, which, despite countermeasures taken by the Orthodox establishment, are steadily expanding. In a few decades the Orthodox religious establishment may be seriously challenged by this influx of new ideas. This may also be compounded if the called for (even by some bishops) separation of the church and the state occurs. Such a development will have far-reaching, indeed disastrous, repercussions for the Orthodox establishment. It will lose its privileges as "the official religion of the state," namely, its monopolistic hegemony. This would probably promote more pluralism and tolerance than the current non-multicultural conditions allow. Such a situation might also give rise to a stronger religious individualism and subjective spirituality, much of which could take the form of "Sheilaism" in its ideal form, totally beyond the influence of religious institutions. The Orthodox tradition would probably play less of a role in the formation of such personal religious perspectives.

In closing, it should be stressed that the preceding scenario, though possible, seems highly speculative at present. Recent events (e.g., the radical changes in the former Eastern Bloc) which emphasize the role that religion can play in the "new world order" indicate that an imminent separation of church and state in Greece is unlikely. On the contrary, we should expect that recent political developments will promote a greater church-state alliance to implement various policies in Eastern Europe, a part of the world where Orthodoxy has traditionally been firmly rooted. This also reminds us of the crucial, multi-dimensional and polysemic role that Orthodoxy can play in the operation of the Greek social system, which differs fundamentally from Western European societies. The radical changes that have affected the socio-religious evolution of the West since the Middle Ages and that have been stressed by secularization theories (Dobbelaere 1987) affected Greece and the Eastern Orthodox world more as *exogenous* than endogenous factors. One cannot find in the Orthodox East the type of society which intended to sever all relationships with its ecclesiastical institutions, such as there was in the West in its relationship with the Roman Catholic church. For instance, the phenomenon of *laicité*, as it appears in modern France, is practically unknown in Greece. Orthodoxy remains for the Greeks a *national religion* of utmost importance. Even the sharp criticism of it comes almost exclusively from within, i.e., from its members, without implying a separation from it (cf. Stavrou 1988: 186). Strangely enough, many theorists have paid only tangential attention to this fundamental difference between East and West and its great consequences. Thus, although we have traced in this paper a growing dissatisfaction with and a distancing from the official church, this by no means signifies a separation of modern Greek culture and Orthodoxy in general. Even if nothing can be precluded for the long-term, all current indicators suggest that, whatever the problems of the official church, Orthodoxy is not condemned to inevitable eclipse but will linger on and play a distinct role in articulating the dimensions of modern Greek society.

Notes

1 . The Orthodox numbered 7,472,559 out of a total population of 7,632,801, while Roman Catholics numbered only 28,430, and Protestants and other Christians numbered 12,677. There were also 112,665 Muslims, 6,325 Jews, and 121 persons with no religious affiliation.

12

Conclusion:
The Post-War Generation - Carriers of a New Spirituality

Wade Clark Roof, Jackson W. Carroll, and David A. Roozen

What have we learned from these cross-national probes into the religion of the post-war generation and its implications for religious establishments in the several countries represented? As we have reflected on what we have learned, we have found that the following paragraph from the journalist Thomas Friedman's account of the Middle East crisis (1990: 50-51) provides a somewhat analogous description of our experience in trying to draw together our insights about the religious trends:

> What made reporting so difficult from Beirut was the fact that there was no center--not politically, not physically; since there was no functioning unified government, there was no authoritative body which reporters could use to check out news stories and no authoritative version of reality to either accept or refute; it was a city without 'officials.' After the civil war broke out in 1975, the center in Lebanon was carved up into a checkerboard of fiefdoms and private armies, each with its own version of reality, which it broadcast through its own radio station and its own spokesmen. . . . Rarely did you ever have the satisfaction of feeling that you really got to the bottom of something. It was like working in a dark cave with the aid of a single candle. Just when you thought you had spotted the white light of Truth, you would chase it, only to discover that it was someone else, also holding a candle, also looking for the light.

The religious situation that has concerned us in this book is clearly not as chaotic as the conditions in Beirut that Friedman describes. His account, nevertheless, serves as a useful analogy, pointing to two major themes to which our research has drawn attention: *(1) Religious establishments--official or authoritative versions of religious reality--have, to varying degrees, broken down or at least have substantially weakened in influence in the years since World War II, with the relative non-involvement of the post-war generation among the leading indicators of decline. (2) In their place a variety of alternative versions of religious reality have emerged, most of them reflected in the religious or spiritual styles of the post-war generation.*

Before considering these two themes--especially the second--we acknowledge that differences in the historical trajectories and experiences of each of the countries have created important variations in the ways that established religions have fared and the post-war generation has involved itself in religion. For one thing, different patterns of cultural and/or legal establishment of religion are significant--for example, the contrast between the United States ("cultural" establishment) and Greek (official/legal) patterns of establishment, to take the most extreme cases, or the difference between the "pillars" in Belgium and the Netherlands in contrast to France's "parochial civilization." Likewise, most nations that we considered have lacked the strong anti-clericalism that France, for example, has experienced. Also important are national differences in historical and economic development. Where a particular country was in terms of social, economic and political modernization prior to World War II has affected its subsequent post-war development, including developments in the role of the religious establishment and also how the post-war generation has related to religion. The chapters on Italy and the former West Germany provide clear examples of these differences. These and other national and historical variations are of considerable importance in understanding the patterns that our authors have observed. Since they defy easy summarization, we will not pursue them further here. Rather we simply acknowledge their significance for understanding the differences that exist and note that they serve as a caution against over-generalization about common patterns.

At the same time, however, as is clear from our research, *something* occurred during the 1960s and early 1970s--the formative years for the post-war generation--that crossed international boundaries and profoundly affected this generation. We refer to the social unrest and turmoil generally characteristic of all modern societies during this period. Many of our authors have remarked on these years. This "period" effect helped decisively to shape the post-war cohort. While some of their rejection of establishment religion may, at the time, have been the result of life-cycle issues--the rebellious attitudes of youth--that appears not to have been the decisive factor shaping the responses to religion of this generation. What shaped them more decisively were the characteristics of the period. As our authors have shown, these changes have continued to set this generation off from preceding generations and, perhaps also, from the one that has followed.

In what follows, we wish to draw together some of the commonalities that our research suggests, both of the impact of this generation on religious establishment and some of the common themes regarding baby boomer spirituality. In the latter case, we ask especially whether these themes reflect an emerging late- or post-modern form of spirituality.

The Turn Away from Established Religion

As we emphasized above, almost all of the authors in this book sound a common theme: religious establishments--whether legal or cultural--have substantially weakened if not collapsed in most of the nations that we have considered. The primary exception is Greece, where Orthodoxy retains its role as a major source of Greek identity and a force in Greek social life. Even there, the traditional relation of church and state is undergoing redefinition, and individual Greeks are increasingly choosing how they will be religious within the bounds of Orthodoxy.

In all countries, Greece included, involvement in established religions has eroded as measured by attendance as church services. Membership declines are also evident in most of the countries. While these trends began in some cases prior to the post-war period--for example, formal church membership among the Dutch has been falling since the mid-nineteenth century, and in France and England since the 1930s--the declines have been especially pronounced among the post-war generation and accelerated dramatically during the late 1960s and 1970s, reflecting their decreasing participation. Even in Greece, where membership in the Orthodox Church has remained quite high, younger generations (especially the post-war cohort) participate much less frequently than older Greeks. In the United States, some older baby boomers have returned to church involvement, though not always to the "mainstream" or "culturally established" denominations, and those that have returned to more traditional forms of church participation are a minority.

Not only has participation declined, but the number claiming to have no religion has grown. Recall Laeyendecker's report of the survey in which 50 percent of the population in the Netherlands claim no religious affiliation--a figure unprecedented in Europe. Again, this trend is most marked among the post-war generation. Several authors attribute this phenomenon in large part to the failure of agencies of religious socialization, especially the family. In some instances, as in Sweden, the separation of church and state and the consequent shifting of "confessional" (Lutheran) religious education from the schools to the family, played a role. Yet, in Sweden, as elsewhere, families have been ill-equipped to assume this role. In Australia, where denominational switching, including switching out of any religious identification is low, Bouma and Mason speculate that many of these individuals were raised with no religion and no religious education.

The erosion of support for established religions has also taken place at the level of beliefs and moral teachings. Acceptance of orthodox beliefs and morality is on the decline in all the countries that we have surveyed, and the post-war generation is once again at the leading edge, questioning or rejecting many traditional beliefs and moral teachings. Even where identification with the church remains strong, as in Greece, there is increased subjectivism with regard to beliefs and morality. Where traditional beliefs in God and in the divinity of Christ are still held by the majority, as in France, they are often held in conjunction with such non-Christian beliefs as reincarnation. This denotes a "mixing of codes" to which we will return below. Moral relativism (Belgium and Italy) and ethical opportunism (Belgium) are on the rise. In Scandinavia, the national church is accepted as having a legitimate role in the definition of social morality (even if its guidance is often ignored), but the church is not looked to for guidance in personal morality.

These various changes have not brought about the total collapse of religious establishments. In this sense, the Beirut analogy overstates the case. In several instances established religions continue to play a civil religious role in helping to define national cultural identity. The Church of England, for example, continues to play the role of a partial upholder of a wider British sacred identity, and the same is true for the established church in Sweden; in Belgium, the Catholic Church is a continuing participant in national rituals; and, as noted, the Greek Orthodox Church is a key contributor to Greek national and cultural identity. Likewise, in the area of important life cycle changes, religious organizations, including the established churches, are looked to for rites of passage. The post-war generation is no exception in this regard. They, along with older generations, turn to the church for marriage, baptism, confirmation and, especially, funerals. In this sense, as Dobbalaere notes, the churches are adapting to a "service role" whereby families use the church, if only for brief periods, to promote family togetherness. Even here, however, the post-war generation seems less likely than older generations to turn to the church for these services.

To sum up, while religious establishments have not collapsed, their role and influence have been substantially weakened, and much of the change seems to be reflected in the post-war generation's pattern of religious involvement. A multitude of factors, some specific to individual countries and others attributable to global processes associated with modernity, lie behind these changes. It has been in and through the experiences of the post-war generation, however, that these changes have come to a head, and this generation's changing involvement in religion has decisively affected the established churches.

Elements of Late- or Post-Modern Spirituality

Although our cross-national surveys point to the weakening of most religious establishments, they also make equally clear that religion is not in danger of disappearing, and this includes the post-war generation's involvement in religion. Their participation in more traditional forms of religion may have declined, but many baby boomers--perhaps the majority--have not rejected religion. Instead, they appear to be reshaping religion, providing alternative definitions of religious reality and forms of involvement. Such reshaping of religion into a variety of alternative and often competing definitions is a correlate to the weakening (if not collapse) of the regulatory power of religious establishment. The diversity makes description and analysis difficult, much as was the case for the news reporters in Lebanon. When taken together, however, the preceding chapters begin to point to some commonalities that exist across the variegated religious landscape that the authors have described.

These common themes, taken together, give us a picture of what might be called a late- or post-modern[1] spirituality of which the post-war generation is the principal "carrier," to use Max Weber's helpful concept. Weber (1968: 468-518) maintained that each of the major religious systems found affinity with a particular status group that became its primary carrier in its time of formative development--for example, Buddhism with contemplative and mendicant monks, Islam with a stratum of disciplined warriors, post-exilic Judaism with a group of pariah people, Christianity with itinerant artisans. Each of these carrier groups helped to give shape to the religion. We are not suggesting that the post-war generation is the carrier of a *new* religion; rather, we are arguing that this generation is the carrier of a distinctive form of spirituality that is reshaping existing patterns of faith and practice in important ways in the several countries we have examined. What, in spite of marked differences in religious involvement cross-nationally, is common to this generation's religious style? Based on our research, five characteristics in particular stand out.

Individual Choice

The first and perhaps the most striking common characteristic of late-modern spirituality is that of the emphasis on individual *choice*. In previous chapters, several authors have had occasion to use Canadian sociologist Reginald Bibbey's (1987) apt phrase, "religion a la carte." The phrase describes the way that members of the post-war generation involve themselves "cafeteria" style in religion. They reject a fixed menu and pick and choose among religious alternatives, including the alternative to disaffiliate altogether from religion. Without exception, from Greece and Italy, to the Nordic countries, to Belgium, France, Germany, Holland, England, the United States and Australia, our authors commented how members of this generation involve themselves selectively in religion. They reject the authority of religious traditions and institutions to prescribe from the top down what one should believe, how one should practice his or her religion, or how one should live morally as a religious person. Instead, they view these matters in much the same way that they view choice of life-style and consumption patterns: as affairs of individual prerogative. As Dobbelaere expressed it, "'*Cogito ergo sum*' may [now] be understood as *I* think and *I* choose my practices to express *my* religious feelings and *my* beliefs and norms."

This highly selective, instrumental approach to religion bespeaks what Roof and McKinney (1987) call the "new voluntarism," or what Bellah and his associates (1985) refer to as "expressive individualism" in their analyses of American religion and culture. Bellah et al. (p. 47) argue that expressive individualism reveals a culture "whose center is the autonomous individual, presumed able to choose the roles he will play and the commitments he will make, not on the basis of higher truths, but according to the criterion of life-effectiveness as the individual judges it." This recalls Hervieu-Léger's characterization of the "diffuse and private religiosity" of French baby boomers, who are "oriented toward the immediate gratification of the psychological needs of the individual."

While choice in matters religious is clearly not a new phenomenon, its widespread, cross-national diffusion is new, dominating as it does the religious style of such a large cohort as the post-war generation. And as the dominant religious style, it has important consequences for religious establishments in particular and religious institutions generally, marking a significant erosion of their capacity to secure compliance with traditional definitions of beliefs and morality. In her chapter, Voyé refers to Lyotard's analysis of post-modernity as involving "the end of the Great Narratives," which she believes applies also to the "Great Narrative" of the church. The Church of England bishop that Barker cites could well speak for all late-modern societies: "We've moved from where Christianity is a culture to where Christianity is a choice." If this is the case--and our research suggests that it is so--then religious institutions and their leaders are unlikely to influence the beliefs, values and moral practices of their adherents, especially those from among the baby boom generation, by resorting to authoritative, top-down pronouncements. Much more likely to gain a hearing will be reasoned persuasion and appeals to a larger common good that both includes and transcends individual self-interest.

A Mixing of Codes

As a consequence of the growth of choice, a second common theme is that of faith exploration among diverse religious traditions or what some have called *a mixing of codes*. As they move in and out of religious involvement, baby boomers explore and experiment with various religious and spiritual possibilities, and they often construct their own personal form of spirituality, drawing from a variety of often disparate sources. In his study of U. S. baby boomers, Roof (1993) asked his interviewees if one should explore the teachings of various religions or stick to a particular faith tradition, less than a third of those interviewed said that a person should stick to one tradition. Sixty percent said one should explore other possibilities, and, as his analysis of their beliefs and practices revealed, they engaged in considerable exploration. In France, as previously mentioned, beliefs such as reincarnation overlay orthodox Christian beliefs, such as belief in the divinity of Christ, without any apparent sense of contradiction. Hervieu-Léger also notes the rise of belief in the occult, especially among the better educated segments of the population.

Such mixing of codes results in "multi-layered" meaning systems that several of our authors found to be commonplace among the post-war generation. That is, many draw their religious beliefs and practices from a variety of sources, both religious and quasi-religious--for example, Eastern spiritual practices, various forms of New Age spirituality, witchcraft, the ecology movement, psychotherapy, feminism, as well as more traditional Judeo-Christian elements. In the United States, Native American spirituality is also a source for constructing one's religion. The result is often a kind of pastiche, a religious pluralism *within* the individual, a personal "collage" rather than a "received one," to use Karel Dobbelaere's words. Eileen Barker's young Catholic hairdresser, exploring New Age spirituality and consulting with Jehovah's Witnesses, is perhaps paradigmatic of the code mixing that appears so characteristic of the religion of the post-war generation in late- or post-modern societies.

As with the growth of choice, this mixing of codes reflects what Hervieu-Léger has called the "deregulation" of the religious world. It is a further instance of the erosion of the authority of religious establishments and their leaders to define religious reality and practices in terms of their version of a "Grand Narrative."

New Religious Movement *and* Evangelical Christian Religious Involvement

Several, though not all, of our authors point to a third characteristic of baby boomer religiosity: When they choose religious involvement members of this generation frequently choose groups that seem, at least on the surface, to reflect the opposite ends of a theological spectrum. Some, as we noted above, are drawn to various new religious movements, especially religious expressions that can loosely be called "New Age"; others, however, are drawn to groups that represent conservative Protestant Christianity, especially pentecostal or charismatic expressions.[2] Many conservative Christians often strongly oppose New Age thinking on theological grounds.[3]

These two religious expressions that appeal to some of the post-war generation are, in fact, quite different. To use Ernst Troelstch's categories, New Age spiritualities represent a more mystical type of religion, while conservative Christian groups reflect sect-type religion. More traditional churchly forms of religion fare less well among baby boomers, though they do attract some returnees. Another way of contrasting these groups, following Roozen, Carroll and Roof (above), is in terms of forms of imagination: *mystical* imagination (New Agers and new religious movements that draw on Eastern spirituality) versus *dialectical* (conservative Christian) imagination.

New Age and new religious movement spirituality ranges from the use of crystals, to astrology, to "earth religion," to some expressions of the occult, and (especially in the United States) to numerous "twelve-step," self-help groups patterned after Alcoholics Anonymous. Forms of Eastern spirituality are also incorporated into many New Age religious expressions. As previously noted, many baby boomers draw eclectically on such traditions to construct a personal spirituality. It might also be argued that the growing popularity of folk Catholicism or "festive" religion among the post-war generation, noted both by Dobbelaere in Belgium and Hervieu-Léger in France, also reflects the more mystical approach to religion.

But there is also the apparently opposite appeal of various conservative Christian groups: fundamentalist and other evangelical Protestant groups, as well as Protestant and Catholic pentecostals or charismatics. Such groups both retain a higher proportion of their baby boom members and gain more of those who switch religious affiliation numbers of baby boomers find a spiritual home in the growing number of conservative "mega-churches" such as Willow Creek Community Church near Chicago, to mention what is perhaps the best known example. Such churches offer multi-media worship and a wide range of programs, including numerous small groups. The groups, for single young adults as well as married couples, vary from Bible study to conservative Christian versions of "twelve step" groups. Why are two such seemingly opposite religious expressions appealing? It is not difficult to understand the attraction of New Age and other similar forms of spirituality, especially in light of the high premium placed on individual choice and the tendency of young persons to mix the codes of diverse religious traditions in their quest for spiritual growth. Also, some New Age religious forms continue themes popular in the counter-culture of the late 60s and early 70s. But why the appeal of conservative Christian groups which are, on the face of it, the mirror opposite of the eclectic New Age spirituality? It may well be that conservative groups are appealing because they *limit* choice, or at least they contain choices within a fairly narrow theological framework. They also offer unambiguous and authoritative teaching about difficult moral and lifestyle issues. Such clear-cut answers are appealing to many among the post-war generation who are confused and turned off by the erosion of clear standards and the pluralism characteristic of late modernity. Mary Jo Neitz (1987), in her study of Catholic charismatics, found that many whom she interviewed were attracted to the movement precisely because they were frustrated by a society that offered too many choices.

There is also another likely reason that makes the two contrasting alternatives appealing.

Religious Experience and Personal Growth

Although New Age spirituality and conservative Christianity have strongly opposite theological tendencies and modes of religious discourse, they share at least one important characteristic--which we cite as a fourth characteristic of the newer religious styles: *Both place a high premium on religious experience and growth.* In spite of their differences, both traditions speak to concerns for wholeness, healing, personal transformation and direct spiritual experience. God is not remote, not wholly other, not talked about in abstract doctrinal formulae. Rather, God or the divine spirit is immediate and personal and can be experienced directly. This is especially true for many conservative Christians, not only those who are pentecostal or charismatic, but also non-pentecostal evangelicals whose spiritual style reflects a kind of personalistic, informal popular piety. For these Christians, God is a friend who intervenes in the events of one's life. Jesus is a "trusted brother." Furthermore, for both New Agers and evangelical Christians, it is permissible to "feel" and "express" one's religion without being embarrassed about it. Thus, for all their real differences, both groups place a high premium on experiential religion. This makes them attractive options for many in the post-war generation.

Such an argument, in so far as it stresses God as personal and near, seems counter to Dobbelaere's argument about declining belief in a personal God as a result of an increasingly rational society where humans control much of what once was thought to be mysterious and uncontrollable. Dobbelaere's contention may, in fact, be true for many of the post-war generation, but not for all, including those for whom the celebrative occasions of the church--a kind of popular Catholicism--is still important, even when they reject most of the church's official teachings and practices.

Personal, experiential religion also appears to be a major attraction of the "communities of inspiration"--the small groups that have attracted a number of the post-war generation in Belgium. In them, it will be recalled, Voyé found that the center of religious life is in concrete life experiences, not in "the bureaucratic and cold character of the church." Only in such experiences is God to be found. Also in France, as noted above, Hervieu-Léger has observed the growing popularity, especially among the post-war generation, of what she calls "festive religion"--pilgrimages, feast days, and other celebratory occasions. Such festive experiences provide participants with "peak moments" or "peak experiences" that stand in sharp contrast to the more ordinary, routine religious observances in which only a small percentage of the population participates. In Greece, perhaps the most traditional society included in our research, Makrides notes that celebratory experiences are also important aspects of the post-war generation's spirituality. They are, however, more likely to be tied to traditional ritual occasions of the church than is the case in France or Belgium.

Anti-Institutional and Anti-Hierarchical

A final characteristic of the post-war generation's spirituality is that it is generally *anti-institutional and anti-hierarchical*. This should not be surprising when one considers the countercultural emphases of the late 1960s and early 1970s when the majority of this generation came to maturity.

Anti-institutionalism and anti-hierarchicalism do not reflect so much overt hostility to institutional forms of religion as indifference-- especially in the United States, but also in Australia and England, for example. This differs significantly from some European nations with strong anti-clerical traditions, where anti-institutionalism goes beyond indifference, and where participation of the younger generation in institutional religion has reached an all-time low--for example three percent among younger boomers in Finland. As the U. S. statistics show, in contrast, regular church attendance has remained remarkably high--even for baby boomers.

At the same time, in a nation such as the United States, where there are multiple options for membership, boomers' loyalty to particular denominations is quite low. The data on religious "switching" reported by Roozen, Carroll and Roof make this clear. Furthermore, their research shows that the organizational forms that matter to baby boomers are primarily local, ones with which they have immediate personal contact and which address their particular needs. Loyalty to such organizations is both voluntary and instrumental. You belong "if it helps you." You drop out if it doesn't. This anti-institutional localism also characterizes the "communities of inspiration" that are attracting young people in Belgium.

What, then, are we to make of all of this? While many of the post-war generation have simply opted out of religious involvement altogether, many others--perhaps even the majority--have not totally abandoned religious or spiritual pursuits. These pursuits, however, are taking several characteristic forms that we have considered: a high premium on choice in whether and how one is involved in religion; an eclectic mixing of codes as many construct their own way of being religious; an attraction to both New Age spiritual forms and to conservative Protestant groups; the appeal of religious expressions that emphasize emotions and experience; and a negative attitude toward hierarchy and institutions. With some differences, most of these characteristics are true of all the countries we have examined.

Although we have painted with a rather broad brush and have said little about the minority of boomers whose religious involvement is more traditional, these five characteristics provide a window into what seems to be an emerging form of religion in late- or post-modern society, with many the post-war generation as its primary carriers. Contrary to the assumptions of some secularization theorists, religion is not withering away. Instead, as Robert Wuthnow (1988) has suggested, it appears to be undergoing a significant restructuring, a redefinition of its symbolic boundaries and meanings. It becoming increasingly privatized and pluralistic, and it clearly poses a distinct challenge to more traditional religious establishments and their institutional forms. How these religious establishments and other traditional forms of religion respond to this challenge is, we believe, of considerable importance for the future. Social theorist Anthony Giddens has, in recent works (1990, 1991), written about the possibilities and perils of late-modern society. He argues that the characteristics of high modernity, especially what he calls its "reflexivity," "propel social life away from the hold of pre-established precepts or practices." Certainty is undermined; doubt is institutionalized; everything, including science itself, seems open to revision. Consequently, many individuals experience the world as bereft of the all-encompassing traditions and certainties that sustained earlier generations. We are increasingly thrown back on ourselves, on our own subjective choices to deal with doubt, uncertainty, stress, fragmentation, and the threat of meaninglessness characteristic of high modernity. In many ways, the religiosity of the post-war generation that we have described can be understood as a response to these perils.

But is this highly subjective, individualistic kind of religiosity what is required? Giddens argues that to confront these perils we need "a remoralization" of social life. Such remoralization challenges the fragmenting, corrosive forces of modernity by bringing moral/existential problems into public debate. While Giddens does not consider the role that religion might play in the remoralization of public life, this has clearly been one of its roles in the past. At its best, religion has fostered and sustained moral communities grounded in transcendent norms of justice and love that have pushed individuals and groups beyond narrow self-interest.

It remains to be seen whether the religion of the post-war generation is capable of playing such a role. One possibility is that it may not be capable of doing so, that its tendencies to individualism, anti-institutionalism and pragmatic absorption with the self will be corrosive of any broader social concern. To revert to the analogy with Beirut with which we began this chapter, there may be no authoritative version of reality capable of overcoming such tendencies and holding them in check. Another possibility, however, is that those of the post-war generation, many of whom were nurtured in the crucible of social action in the 1960s, will forge new ways of balancing self interest and commitment to social institutions that will assist the remoralization of social life by bringing a new and vital balance of spirituality and social concern. That this may be a possibility is suggested in the following quote from one of Roof's baby boomer interviewees, a member of a United Church of Christ congregation in Colorado:

> [T]here is a tension here in this congregation between the heritage of our tradition which is outward looking and all of this inward reflection that's new to this tradition. I think it's a needed corrective. But we haven't lost our commitment to public morality. There is still a very strong sense that this church is part of the broader community and that in what it does it sets an example. But I think we needed that corrective because

I think we got so outward oriented that we weren't sure what
was holding that together (Roof 1993: 260).

The challenge to religious institutions, therefore, is not that of
holding on to their privileged positions. In most cases, it is too late for that.
Nor is it simply discovering the techniques and programs that will attract
baby boomers into back their folds. Of considerably more importance is
what happens when this post-war generation does participate: how they
are helped to shape their religious interests in ways that combine the
individual and the communal, right self-love with neighbor love, a concern
for personal well-being with a passion for justice.

Notes

1. While the term "post-modern" has gained considerable currency as a description
of the historical period to which most technologically advanced societies have
come, others (e.g. Giddens, 1991) argue that "late modern" is a more appropriate
designation. Since there is little agreement over the precise meaning of either
term, we are not inclined to try to settle on one or the other descriptor. We believe,
however, that both point to fundamental changes in the ways that we experience
the world and our own lives as a result especially of technological changes that
have altered our relation to both time and space.

2. While both fundamentalists and pentecostals/charismatics can both be referred
to as evangelical or conservative Christians, and while both hold to a high view of
scriptural authority (often viewing the Bible as inerrant), they are quite different in
many respects and should not be conflated.

3. See, for example, Campolo (1992). The title of his book, *How To Rescue the
Earth Without Worshipping Nature*, reveals his, and many evangelical Christians'
antipathy towards various forms of New Age and "creation" spiritualities.

About the Editors and Contributors

Salvatore Abbruzzese is a sociological researcher at the University of Trento and Professor of Sociology at Angelicum University in Rome. He is currently writing a book on changing values in Italy.

Eileen Barker is Professor of Sociology with Special Reference to the Study of Religion at the London School of Economics. Her main research interests are new religious movements and contemporary Armenians.

Gary D. Bouma is Professor of the Sociology of Religion at Monash University, Melbourne, Australia. He has recently completed a book on *Mosques and the Settlement of Muslim Migrants in Australia*, and is pursuing further research on the role of religion in multicultural and post-modern societies.

Jackson W. Carroll is Ruth W. and A. Morris Williams, Jr. Professor of Religion and Society and Director of the J. M. Ormond Center for Research, Planning and Development in the Divinity School of Duke University. His most recent book (co-edited with W. Clark Roof) is *Beyond Denominationalism: Protestant Identity in a Post-Protestant Age*. He is currently completing a book on seminary cultures and their role in the formation of theological students.

Karel Dobbelaere is Professor of Sociology at the Catholic University of Leuven and at the University of Antwerp (UFSIA). He currently works on religion and ethics.

Karl Gabriel is Professor of Sociology at the Catholic School of Social Work in Osnabrük/Vechta. He is the author of the book *Christentum zwischen Tradition und Postmoderne*, Freiburg 1994. He is working on a study of Christian "Third World Groups" in Germany.

Danièle Hervieu-Léger is Director d'Etudes at Ecole des Hautes Etudes en Sciences Sociales (Paris) in the Centre d'Etudes Interdisciplinaires des Faits Religieux. She is currently preparing a book on the problem of religious transmission in modern secularized societies.

Leo Laeyendecker is Professor in General Sociology in the State University of Leiden, The Netherlands.

Vasilios N. Makrides holds a D.Phil. degree from the University of Tübingen and a Ph.D. degree from the University of Athens.

Michael Mason is chair of the Department of Moral and Practical Theology at the Yarra Theological Union, one of the Associated Teaching Institutions of The Melbourne College of Divinity. He is currently writing a book on the Catholic Church in Australia.

Wade Clark Roof is the J. F. Rowny Professor of Religion and Society at the University of California at Santa Barbara. His most recent book is *A Generation of Seekers: The Spiritual Journeys of the Baby Boom Generation*, published in 1993.

David A. Roozen is Director of Hartford Seminary's Center for Social and Religious Research, Hartford, Connecticut, U. S. A. His recent books include: *Church and Denominational Growth* (Abingdon Press, 1993); *The Globalization of Theological Education* (OrbisBooks, 1993); and *Rerouting Mainstream Protestantism* (Abingdon Press, 1994).

Susan Sundback has worked for many years at the Department of Sociology at Åbo Akademi University, Finland. She is now Associate Professor of Sociology at Bergen University, Norway. Her present research concerns the return of the Roman Catholic church in Scandinavia.

Liliane Voyé is Professor of Sociology at the Catholic University of Louvain. She currently works and writes on religion and culture and on urban society.

References

Ahern, Geoffrey and Grace Davie. 1987. *Inner City God: The Nature of Belief in the Inner City*. London: Hodder and Stoughton.

Ahlstrom, Sydney E. 1972. *A Religious History of the American People*. New Haven, CT: Yale University Press.

Albanese, Catherine L. 1988. Religion and the American Experience: A Century After. *Church History* 57: 337-351.

Alestalo, Matti. 1986. *Structural Change, Classes and the State. Finland in a Historical and Comparative Perspective, Research Group for Comparative Sociology, Research Reports 33*. Helsinki: University of Helsinki.

Alestalo, Matti and Stein Kuhnle. 1984. *The Scandinavian Route, Research Group for Comparative Sociology, Research Report 31*. Helsinki: University of Helsinki.

Allardt, Erik. 1991. Den nordiska identitetens sociologi. *NORD* 25: 33-46.

ALLBUS. 1982 *Allgemeine Bevölkerungsumfrage der Sozialwissenschaften*. Cologne: Zentralarchiv für Empirische Sozialforschung.

American Association of Theological Schools. 1972. Voyage: Vision: Venture. Report of the Task Force on Spiritual Development. *Theological Education* 8: 152-205.

Australian Bureau of Statistics. 1980. *Population and Dwellings, 1976: Summary Tables, Bulletin No.1. Ref. 2409.0--2417.0*. Canberra: ABS.

———. 1983. *Census of Population and Housing, 1981. Small Area Summary Data, Full Format (22-page printout), Table 21, for Australia and States*. Canberra: ABS.

_____. 1988. *Census of Population and Housing, 1986. Small Area Data, Format CSD (21-page), Table C06, for Australia.* Canberra: ABS.

Australian Gallup Polls. 1946-1970. *Australian Public Opinion Polls (Bulletins-- irregular).* Melbourne: Australian Gallup Polls.

Bäckström, Anders. 1989. Från institution till rörelse. *Religion och samhälle* 12 (50).

Balandier, Georges. 1985. *Le détour.* Paris: Fayard.

Barker, Eileen. 1985. And So To Bed: Protest and Malaise among Youth in Great Britain. In *Concilium,* John Coleman and Gregory Baum (eds), 74-80. Cambridge: T and T. Clarke.

_____. 1987 The British Right to Discriminate. In *Church-State Relations: Tensions and Transitions,* Thomas Robbins and Roland Robertson (eds), 269-280. New Brunswick: Transaction.

_____. 1989a. *New Religious Movements: A Practical Introduction.* London: HMSO.

_____. 1989b. Tolerant Discrimination: Church, State and the New Religions. In *Religion, State and Society in Modern Britain.* Paul Badham (ed.), 185-208. Lewiston and Lampeter: Edwin Mellen Press.

Barna, George. 1990. *The Church Today.* Glendale, CA: Barna Research Group.

Beck, U. 1983. Jenseits von Stand und Klasse. In *Soziale ungleichheiten.* R. Krechel (ed.), 35-73. Göttingen: Schwartz.

_____. 1986. *Risikogesellschaft. Auf dem Weg in eine audere Moderne.* Frankfurt a M.: Suhtkamp.

_____. 1991. *Politik in der Riskogesellschaft.* Franfurt a M.: Suhtkamp.

Becker, H. 1990. Generations in Contemporary Society. Paper presented to the XXIInd World Congress of Sociology, Madrid.

Bellah, Robert N. et al. 1985. *Habits of the Heart: Individualism and Commitment in American Life.* Berkeley, CA: University of California Press.

Bennett, John C. 1946. *Christian Ethics and Social Policy*. New York: Scribner.

Berger, Peter. 1961. *The Noise of Solemn Assemblies: Christian Commitment and the Religious Establishment in America*. Garden City, NY: Doubleday.

_____. 1969. *The Social Reality of Religion*. London: Faber.

_____. 1979. *The Heretical Imperative: Contemporary Possibilities of Religious Affirmation*. New York: Anchor Press/Doubleday.

Berger, Peter and Thomas Luckman. 1966. *The Social Construction of Reality*. Garden City, NY: Doubleday & Co.

Berkel-van Schaik, A. B. van and L. B. van Snippenburg. 1991. Sociaalhistorische generaties, verbeelding of empirische werkelijkheid? Een toets van een generatiethese. *Sociologische Gids*, 38:227- 248.

Bessière, G. et al. 1985. *Les volets du presbytère sont ouverts. 2000 prêtres racontent*. Paris: Desclée.

Bibby, Reginald W. 1987. *Fragmented Gods: The Poverty and Potential of Religion in Canada*. Toronto: Irwin Publishing.

Billiet, J. and J. Vanhoutvinck. 1991. Het stemgedrag van de Vlaamse bejaarden nu en morgen: Een onderzoek naar de relatie tussen stemgedrag, leeftijd, kerkelijke betrokkenheid en niveau van onderwijs. In *Tussen sociologie en beleid*, F. Lammertijn and J.C. Verhoeven (eds.), 41-71. Leuven/Amersfoort : Acco.

Black, Alan. 1990. The Sociology of Religion in Australia. *Sociological Analysis* 51: 527-541.

_____. 1991. *Religion in Australia: Sociological Perspectives*. Sydney: Allen and Unwin.

Blombery, 'Tricia. 1989a. *God Through Human Eyes*. Melbourne: Christian Research Association.

_____. 1989b. *Tomorrow's Church Today*. Melbourne: Christian Research Association.

Bonnet, Serge. 1973. *A hue et à dia: Les avatars du catholicisme sous la Ve République*. Paris: Cerf.

Boulard, F. and J. Remy. 1968. *Pratique religieuse et régions culturelles*. Paris: Ed. Ouvrières.

Bouma, Gary D. 1983. Australian Religiosity. In *Practice and Belief*, Alan Black and Peter Glasner (eds.), 15-24. Sydney: Allen and Unwin.

_____. 1988. *The Sociology of Religion in Australia*. Australian Religious Studies Review 1(2):44-49.

_____. 1991. By what authority? An analysis of the locus of ultimate authority in ecclesiastical organisations. In *Religion in Australia: Sociological Perspectives*, Alan Black (ed.), 121-132. Sydney: Allen and Unwin.

_____. 1992. *Religion: Meaning, Transcendence and Community in Australia*. Melbourne: Longman Cheshire.

Bourdieu, P. 1964. *Les Héritiers*. Paris: Minuit.

_____. 1970. *La Reproduction*. Paris: Minuit.

Boy, D. and G. Michelat. 1986. Croyances aux parasciences: dimensions sociales et culturelles. *Revue Française de Sociologie* 27: 175-204.

Braudel, F. 1969. *Écrits sur l'histoire*. Paris: Flammarion.

Brierley, Peter. 1980. *Prospects for the Eighties: From a Census of the Churches in 1979*. London: The Bible Society.

_____. 1988. *UK Christian Handbook: 1989/90 Edition*. Bromley: Marc Europe.

_____. 1991a. `Christian' England: What the English Church Census Reveals*. London: Marc Europe.

_____. 1991b. *Prospects for the Nineties: Trends and Tables from the English Church Census*. London: Marc Europe.

Burdick, Michael A. and Phillip E. Hammond. 1991. World Order and Mainline Religions: The Case of Protestant Foreign Missions. In *World Order and Religion*, Wade Clark Roof (ed.), 193-213. Albany, N.Y.: SUNY Press.

Burgalassi, Silvano. 1970. *Le Cristianità Nascoste. Dove Va la Cristianità Italiana?* Bologna, Italy: Dehoniane.

Calvaruso, Claudio and Salvatore Abbruzzese. 1985. *Indagine sui Valori in Italia. Dai Post-Materialismi alla Ricerca di Senso*. Turin: S.E.I.

Campbell, John and Philip Sherrard. 1968. *Modern Greece*. London: Ernest Benn.

Campolo, Tony. 1992. *How to Rescue the Earth Without Worshipping Nature*. Nashville: Thomas Nelson.

Carroll, Jackson W. 1991. *As One With Authority*. Louisville: Westminster/ John Knox.

Carroll, Jackson W. et al. 1979. *Religion in America: 1950 to the Present*. New York: Harper and Row.

Castronovo, Valerio. 1975. Il "miracolo economico." In *Storia d'Italia*, Vol. IV-VI: 399-439. Torino: Einaudi.

Castoriadis, Cornelius. 1975. *L'institution imaginaire de la societe*. Paris: Seuil.

Central Office of Information. 1967. *Britain: An Official Handbook*. London: HMSO.

Central Statistical Office. 1972. *Facts in Focus*. Harmondsworth: Penguin.

Chadwick, Owen. 1975. *The Secularisation of the European Mind in the Nineteenth Century*. Cambridge: Cambridge University Press.

Champion, F. 1989. La nébuleuse mystique-ésotérique. In *De l'émotion en religion*, F. Champion and D. Hervieu-Léger (eds.), 17-69. Paris: Cerf.

Charles, F. 1986. *La géneration défroquée*. Paris: Cerf.

Church of England. 1985. *Faith in the City: The Report of the Archbishop of Canterbury's Commission on Urban Priority Areas*. London: Church House Publishing.

Cipriani, Roberto. 1988. *La religione diffusa*. Teoria e prassi. Roma: Borla.

———. 1989. 'Diffused Religion' and New Values in Italy. In *The Changing Face of Religion*, James Beckford and Thomas Luckmann (eds.), 24-48. London: Sage.

Clogg, Richard. 1979. *A Short History of Modern Greece*. Cambridge: Cambridge University Press.

Cohen, M. 1986a. *Le Renouveau charismatique en France ou l'affirmation des catholicismes*. Christus 131, Juillet: 261-279.

———. 1986b. Vers de nouveaux rapports avec l'institution ecclésiastique: l'exemple du Renouveau charismatique en France. *Archives de Sciences Sociales des Religions* 62(1) Juillet- Decembre: 61-77.

Commonwealth Bureau of Census and Statistics. 1965. *Census of the Commonwealth of Australia*. Vol. 8 Australia Canberra: Commonwealth Bureau of Census and Statistics.

———. 1974. *Census of Population and Housing, 1971. Summary of Population, Bulletin No.1, Parts 1- 9. Old ref. no. 2.83.1--2.83.9. New ref. no. 2221.0--2229.0.* Canberra: Commonwealth Bureau of Census and Statistics.

Cottrell, Melanie. 1976. *Everyday Life Meaning Systems: A Test of Thomas Luckmann's Invisible Religion*. Unpublished PhD. dissertation, University of Oxford.

CREDOC. 1989. *Religion et comportements sociaux*. Consommation et modes de vie 44, Decembre.

Cupitt, Don. 1984. *Sea of Faith: Christianity in Change*. London: British Broadcasting Corporation.

Currie, Robert et al. 1977. *Churches and Church-goers: Patterns of Church Growth in the British Isles since 1700*. Oxford University Press.

Dahlgren, Curt. 1985. Sverige. In *Religiös förändring i Norden 1930- 1980*, Göran Gustafsson (ed.), 196-237. Malmö: Liber.

Daiber, K.-F. 1988. Religiöse Orientierungen und Kirchenmitgliedschaft in der Bundesrepublik Deutschland. In *Religion, Kirchen und Gesellschaft in Deutschland. Gegenwartskunde Sonderheft* 5, F. X. Kaufmann and B. Schäfers (eds.), 61-73. Opladen: Leske.

Davie, Grace. 1990a. Believing without Belonging: A Post-Modern View of Religion in Britain? Paper delivered to the Sociology of Religion and Theory Study Groups Conference, University of Bristol.

———. 1990b 'An Ordinary God': the Paradox of Religion in Contemporary Britain. *The British Journal of Sociology* 41 (3): 395-421.

———. 1990c. Believing without Belonging: Is This the Future of Religion in Britain?. *Social Compass* 37 (4):455- 469.

———. 1992. `You'll Never Walk Alone': The Anfield Pilgrimage. In Pilgrimage in *Popular Culture*, I. Reader and A. J. Walter (eds.). London: Macmillan.

de Antonellis, Giacomo. 1987. *Storia dell'Azione Cattolica*. Milano: Rizzoli.

Decker, G. and J. Peters. 1989. *Gereformeerden in meervoud*. Kampen: Kok.

de Certeau, M. 1968. *La prise de parole. Pour une nouvelle culture*. Paris: Desclée.

de Certeau and J. M. Domenach. 1974. *Un christianisme éclaté*. Paris: Seuil.

de Vaus, David A. and Ian McAllister. 1987. Gender Differences in Religion: A Test of the Structural Location Theory. *American Sociological Review* 52:72-481.

De Moor, Ruud. 1987. Religieuze en morele waarden. In *Traditie, secularisatie en individualisering: Een studie naar de waarden van de Nederlanders in een Europese context*, Loek Halman (ed.), 15-49. Tilburg: University Press.

Delumeau, Jean. 1983. *Le péché et la peur. La culpabilité en Occident (13e-18e siècles)*. Paris: Fayard.

Dimitras, Panayote. 1987. Changes in Public Attitudes. In *Political Change in Greece. Before and After the Colonels*, Kevin Featherstone and Dimitrios K. Katsoudas (eds.), 64-83. London: Croom Helm.

_____. 1990. Greek Public Attitudes: Continuity and Change. *Greek Opinion* 7 (12):10-33.

_____. 1991. *Politikos Perigyros, kommata kai ekloges stin Ellada*, Volume 1. Athens: Lychnos.

Dobbelaere, Karel. 1966. *Sociologische analyse van de katholiciteit*. Antwerpen/Leuven: Standaard Wetenschappelijke Uitgeverij.

_____. 1981. Secularization : A Multi-Dimensional Concept. *Current Sociology* 2 (29):1-213.

_____. 1984. Godsdienst in België. In *De stille ommekeer: Oude en nieuwe waarden in het België van de jaren tachtig*, J. Kerkhofs and R. Rezsohazy (eds.), 67- 111. Tielt: Lannoo.

_____. 1985. Secularisation theories and sociological paradigms: A reformulation of the private-public dichotomy and the problem of societal integration. *Sociological Analysis*, 46: 377-387.

_____. 1987. Some Trends in European Sociology of Religion: The Secularization Debate. *Sociological Analysis*, 48:107-137.

_____. 1988a. *Het "Volk-Gods" de mist" in Vover de Kerk in Belgie*. Leuven/Amersfoort: Acco.

_____. 1988b. Secularization, Pillarization, Religious Involvement, and Religious Change in the Low Countries. In *World Catholicism in Transition*, T. Gannon (ed.), 80-115. New York/London: Collier Macmillan.

_____. 1992. Church Involvement and Secularization: Making Sense of the European Case. In *Secularization, Rationalism and Sectarianism*, Eileen Barker et al. (eds.), 19-36. Oxford: University Press.

Dobbelaere, Karel and Jaak Billiet. 1978. Community-Formation and the Church. A Sociological Study of an Ideology and the Empirical Reality. In *Faith and Society*, M.Caudron (ed.)., 211-259. Gembloux: Duculot.

Dobbelaere, Karel and Liliane Voyé. 1991. Western European Catholicism since Vatican II. In *Religion and The Social Order: Vatican II and U.S. Catholicism*, Helen Rose Ebaugh (ed.), 205-231. Greenwich, Connecticut: Jai Press Inc.

Dobbelaere, K. et al. 1976. Dimensies in de houding van professoren tegenover het katholieke karakter van hun universiteit. *Kultuurleven* 43 (10): 873-884.

Donegami, J.-M. 1984. L'appartenance au Catholicisme Français: Point de vue sociologique. In *Regards sur le Catholicisme Français*, J. Gellard et al. (eds.), 44-65. Paris: Cahiers Recherches - Débat.

Doorn, P. and Y. Bommeljé. 1983. *Maar...men moet toch iets wezen. Nieuwe gegevens over ontkerkelijking in Nederland*. Utrecht: Humanistisch Verbond.

Douglass, H. Paul and Edmund de S. Brunner. 1935. *The Protestant Church as a Social Institution*. New York: Russell and Russell.

Duclos, P. 1983. *Les prêtres*. Paris: Seuil.

Dumont, Louis. 1983. *Essais sur l'individualisme. Une Perspective Anthropologique sur l'Idéologie Moderne*. Paris: Seuil.

Durkheim, Emile. 1912. *Les formes élémentaires de la vie religieuse: le systéme totémique en Australie*. Paris: Presses Universitaires de France.

_____. 1960. *De la division du travail social*. 7éme edition. Paris: Presses Universitaires de France.

Economist, The. 1990. *Book of Vital World Statistics*. London: Hutchinson.

Eichelberger, H.-W. 1989. Konfession und Ethik am Beispiel der Einstellung zum Schwangerschaftsabbruch. In *Religion und Konfession. Studien zu politischen, ethischen und religiösen Einstellungen von Katholiken, Protestanten und Konfessionslosen in der Bundesrepublik*

Deutschland und in den Niederlanden, K.-F. Daiber (ed.), 72-92. Hanover: Lutherisches Verlaghaus.

Elchardus, Mark et al. 1990. *Soepel, flexibel en ongebonden: Een vergelijking van twee laat-moderne generaties*. Brussel: VUB-Press.

Featherstone, Mike. 1988. In Pursuit of the Postmodern. An Introduction. *Theory, Culture and Society* 5:2-3

Feige, A. 1990. *Kirchenmitgliedschaft in der Bundesrepublik Deutschland*. Gütersloh: G. Mohn.

Felling, A. et al. 1982. Identitätswandel in den Niederlanden. *Kölner Zeitschrift für Soziologie und Sozialpsychologie* 38: 26-53.

_____. 1983. *Burgerlijk en onburgerlijk Nederland: Een nationaal onderzoek naar waardenoriëntaties op de drempel van de jaren tachtig*. Deventer: Van Loghum Slaterus.

_____. 1986. *Geloven en leven: Een nationaal onderzoek naar de invloed van religieuze overtuigingen*. Zeist: Kerckebosch.

Ferrarotti, Franco. 1970. *Roma, da Capitale a Periferia*. Bari, Italy: Laterza.

Finke, Roger and Rodney Stark. 1992. *The Churching of America 1776-1990*. New Brunswick, N.J.: Rutgers University Press.

Francis, John G. 1992. The Evolving Regulatory Structure of European Church-State Relationships. *Journal of Church and State* 34, Autumn: 775-804.

Frazee, Charles. 1969. *The Orthodox Church and Independent Greece, 1821-1852*. Cambridge: Cambridge University Press.

_____. 1977. Church and State in Greece. In *Greece in Transition: Essays in the History of Modern Greece*, John T. A. Koumoulides (ed.), 128-152. London: Zeno.

_____. 1979. The Orthodox Church of Greece: The Last Fifteen Years. In *Greece: Past and Present*, John T. A. Koumoulides (ed.), 89-110. Muncie, Indiana: Ball State University Press.

Friedman, Thomas. 1990. *From Beirut to Jerusalem*. London: Fontana.

Friedrich, W. 1990. Mentalitätswandlungen der Jugend in der DDR. *Aus Politik und Zeitgeschichte* B 16-17: 25-37

Gabriel, K. 1988. Lebenswelten unter den Bedingungen entfalteter Modernität. *Pastoraltheologische Informationen* 8: 93-108.

_____. 1990. Von der `vordergründigen' zur `hintergründigen' Religiosität. Zur Entwicklung von Religion und Kirche in der Geschichte der Bundesrepublik. In *Die Bundesrepublik. Eine historische Bilanz*, R. Hettlage (ed.), 255-279. Munich: Beck.

Gabriel, K., and F. X. Kaufmann (eds.) 1980. *Zur Soziologie des Katholizismus*. Mainz: Mathias- Grunewald-Verlag.

_____. 1988. Der Katholizismus in den deutschsprachigen Ländern. In *Religion, Kirchen und Gesellschaft in Deutschland. Gegenwartskunde Sonderheft* 5, F. X. Kaufmann and B. Schäfers (eds.), 31-60. Opladen: Leske.

Gadourek, I. 1982. *Social change as Redefinition of Roles*. Assen: Van Gorcum.

Galland, O. 1991. *Sociologie de la jeunesse*. Paris: Armand Colin.

Gallup. 1984. *Attitudes of Laity, Clergy and Bishops towards the Church of England*. London: Gallup.

_____. 1990. *European Values Study Group: Tabulated Results of U.K.* London: Gallup.

Garelli, Franco. 1991. *Religione e Chiesa in Italia*. Bologna, Italy: Il Mulino.

Gay, John D. 1971. *The Geography of Religion in England*. London: Duckworth.

Georgas, James. 1989. Changing Family Values in Greece. From Collectivist to Individualist. *Journal of Cross- Cultural Psychology* 20: 80-91.

Gerard, David. 1985. Religious Attitudes and Values. In *Values and Social Change in Britain*, Mark Abrams et al, (eds.), 50-92. London: Macmillan.

Giddens, Anthony. 1984. *The Constitution of Society: Outline of the Theory of Structuration..* London: Polity Press.

_____. 1991. *Modernity and Self-Identity: Self and Society in the Late Modern Age.* Cambridge, England: Polity Press.

Ginsborg, Paul. 1989. *Storia d'Italia dal Dopoguerra a Oggi,* 2 Vols. Turin: Einaudi.

Glock, Charles Y., and Rodney Stark. 1965. *Religion and Society in Tension.* Chicago: Rand McNally.

Goddijn, W. 1973. *The Deferred Revolution.* Amsterdam: Elsevier.

Goddijn, W. et al. 1979. *Opnieuw: God in Nederland.* Amsterdam: De Tijd.

_____. 1986. *Pastoraal Concilie 1965-1970.* Baarn: Nelissen.

Gousidis, Alexandre. 1975. Analyse statistique et sociographique des ordinations dans l'Eglise de Grèce entre 1950 et 1969. *Social Compass* 22:107-147.

Graziani, Augusto (ed). 1971. *L'Economia Italiana: 1945-1970.* Bologna, Italy: Il Mulino.

Greeley, Andrew M. et al. 1976. *Catholic Schools in a Declining Church.* Kansas City: Sheed and Ward.

_____. 1990. *The Catholic Myth: The Behaviour and Beliefs of American Catholics.* New York: Scribner.

Greer, Bruce. 1993. Denominational Strategies for Evangelism, 1965-1990: The Ambivalence of Saints. In *Church and Denominational Growth,* David A. Roozen and C. Kirk Hadaway (eds.), 87-111. Nashville: Abingdon Press.

Gustafsson, Göran. 1983. Demografiska och socioekonomiska data om kyrkfolket. In *Aktiva i Svenska kyrkan - en livsstilsstudie* 23-47. Stockholm:Verbum.

_____. 1984. Civilreligionsbegreppet och civilreligion i dagens Sverige. *KISA-rapport.* 21:7-21.

_____. 1985. Utvecklingslinjer på det religiösa området i de nordiska länderna - en jämförelse. In *Religiös förändring i Norden 1930-1989*, Göran Gustafsson (ed.), 238-265. Malmö: Liber.

_____. 1987. Nationellt och lokalt - två perspektiv på kyrka och religion. In *Religion och kyrka i fem nordiska städer*, Göran Gustafsson (ed.), 376-386. Malmö, Oslo: Liber.

_____. 1988. Religiös kultur och vardaglig religiositet. In *Sverige-vardag och struktur*, Ulf Himmelstrand and Göran Svensson (eds.), 461-488. Stockholm: Norstedts.

Habermas, Jürgen. 1985. *Der Philosophische Diskurs der Moderne: 12 Vorlesungen*. Frankfurt am Main: Suhrkamp Verlag.

Hadden, Jeffrey K. and Anson Shupe (eds.). 1989. *Secularization and Fundamentalism Reconsidered: Religion and the Political Order, Volume III*. New York: Paragon House.

Halman, L. 1991. *Waarden in de Westerse wereld*. Tilburg: University Press.

Halman, L. et al. 1987. *Traditie, secularisatie en individualisering*. Tilburg: University Press.

Hamberg, Eva. 1990. Stabilitet och förändring i religiositet. In *Religion och samhälle* 11 (61).

_____. 1991. On Stability and Change in Religious Beliefs, Practice, And Attitudes: A Swedish Panel Study. *Journal for the Scientific Study of Religion* 30 (1):63-80.

Hannemann, B. and H. Franke. 1990. Kirchenmitglieder wollen schnelle Einheit. *Übergänge* 16: 139-143.

Hanselmann, J., H. Hild, and E. Lohse (eds.). 1984. *Was wird aus der Kirche? Ergebnisse der zweiten EKD-Umfrage über Kirchenmitgliedschaft*. 2nd ed. Gütersloh: G. Mohn.

Harding, Stephen et al. 1986. *Contrasting Values in Western Europe: Unity, Diversity and Change*. Basingstoke: MacMillan.

Hart, J. J. M. de. 1990. *Levensbeschouwelijke en politieke praktijken van Nederlandse middelbare scholieren*. Kampen: Kok.

Hébrard, M. 1979. *Les nouveaux disciples, voyage à travers les communautes charismatiqués*. Paris: Centurion.

_____. 1987. *Les nouveaux disciples, dix ans après*. Paris: Centurion.

_____. 1989. *Révolution tranquille chez les catholiques. Voyage au pays des synodes diocésains*. Paris: Centurion.

Heek, F. van. 1954. *Het geboorteniveau der Nederlandse Rooms-Katholieken*. Leiden: Stenfert Kroese.

Heikkilä, Markku. 1982. Kyrkobegreppet och kyrkopolitik i mellankrigstidens Finland. In *Kirken, krisen og krigen*, S.U. Larsen and I. Montgomery (eds.), 20-28. Bergen, Oslo: Tromso.

Heino, Harri. 1988a. Uskonnollisuuden ja kirkollisuuden muutoksia toisen maailmansodan jälkeisessä Suomessa. *Kirkon tutkimuskeskus* B:56.

_____. 1988b. *Finnish Christian Handbook. Part 1: Churches*. Helsinki, Kent: MARC Europe.

Herberg, Will. 1960. *Protestant--Catholic--Jew*. New ed. Garden City, New York: Doubleday.

Hervieu-Legér, Danièle. 1986. *Vers un nouveau christianisme? Introduction à la sociologie du christianisme occidental*. Paris: Cerf.

_____. 1987. Charismatisme catholique et institution. In *Le retour des certitudes*, P. Ladriére and R. Luneau (eds.), 218-234. Paris: Centurion.

_____. 1989. Renouveaux èmotionnels contemporains: fin de la sécularisation ou fin de la religion?. In *De l'emotion en religion*, F. Champion and D. Hervieu- Léger (eds.), 217-248. Paris: Centurion.

Hogan, Michael. 1987. *The Sectarian Strand: Religion in Australian History*. Melbourne: Penguin.

Hoge, Dean R. 1974. *Commitment on Campus: Changes in Religion and Values Over Five Decades*. Philadelphia: Westminster Press.

_____. 1979. National Contextual Factors Influencing Church Trends. In *Understanding Church Growth and Decline: 1950-1978*, Dean R. Hoge and David A. Roozen (eds.), 94-122. New York: Pilgrim Press.

_____. 1986. Interpreting Change in American Catholicism: The River and the Floodgate. *Review of Religious* Research 27: 289-299.

Hoge, Dean R. and David A. Roozen (eds.). 1979. *Understanding Church Growth and Decline: 1950-1978*. New York: Pilgrim Press.

Hornsby-Smith, Michael P. 1989. *The Changing Parish: A Study of parishes, Priests and Parishioners After Vatical II*. New York: Routledge.

_____. 1991. *Roman Catholic Beliefs in England: Customary Catholicism and Transformations of Religious Authority*. Cambridge University Press.

Hout, Michael and Andrew M. Greeley. 1987. The Center Doesn't Hold: Church Attendance in the United States, 1940-1984. *American Sociological* Review 52: 325-345.

Hughes, Philip. 1989. *The Australian Clergy*. Melbourne: Christian Research Association.

Hughes, Philip and 'Tricia Blombery. 1990. *Patterns of Faith in Australian Churches*. Melbourne: Christian Research Association.

Hunter, James Davison. 1983. *American Evangelicalism: Conservative Religion and the Quandary of Modernity*. New Brunswick, NJ: Rutgers University Press.

Inglehart, Ronald. 1977. *The Silent Revolution: Changing Values and Political Styles Among Western Publics*. Princeton, NJ: Princeton University Press.

_____. 1981. Post-Materialism in an Environment of Insecurity. *American Political Science Review* 75: 880-900.

_____. 1990. *Culture Shift in Advanced Industrial Society*. Princeton: Princeton University Press.

Institut für Demoskopie Allensbach . 1986. Das Kirchenverständnis der Katholiken und Protestanten. Repräsentativbefragung im Auftrag der Redaktion Kirche und Leben des ZDF. Allensbach. Unpublished paper.

_____. 1989a. Vertrauenskrise der Kirche? Eine Repräsentativerhebung zu Kirchenbindung und-kritik. Allensbach. Unpublished paper.

_____. 1989b. Das Glaubensbekenntnis. Repräsentativebefragung im Auftrag der Zeitschrift P. M. Perspektive. Allensbach. Unpublished paper.

INSEE. 1985-86. *Donnees Sociales*. Paris: INSEE.

Ireland, Rowan. 1988. *The Challenge of Secularisation*. Melbourne: Collins Dove.

Isambert, F. A. and J. P. Terrenoire. 1980. *Atlas de la pratique religieuse des catholiques en France*. Paris: FNSP/CNRS.

ISPES. 1989. *Rapporto Italia*. Rome: Ispes.

ISTAT. 1986. *Sommario di Statistiche storiche, 1926-1985*. Rome: Istituto centrale di statistica.

Jessen, Arne Todal. 1990. Ungdommen har snart ikke respekt for noe. *Tidsskrift for samfunnsforskning* 31:341-365.

Jioultsis, Basile. 1987. Les Théologiens laïcs dans l'Eglise orthodoxe contemporaine. Approche sociologique, pastorale et théologique. *Irénikon* 60:177-192.

Johnson, Douglas W. and George W. Cornell. 1972. *Punctured Preconceptions: What North American Christians Think About the Church*. New York: Friendship Press

Kaldor, Peter. 1987. *Who Goes Where? Who Doesn't Care? Going to Church in Australia*. Sydney: Lancer.

Kaufmann, F. X. 1989. *Religion und Modernität*. Tübingen: Mohn.

Kaufmann, F. X. et al. 1986. *Ethos und Religion bei Führungskräften.* Munich: Kindt.

Kayser, Bernard. 1968. *Anthropogeografia tis Ellados,* trans. by T. Tsaveas-M. Meraklis. Athens: Ethnikon Kentron Koinonikon Ereunon.

Kerkhofs, J. and R. Rezsohazy (eds). 1984. *De stille ommekeer: Oude en nieuwe waarden in het België van de jaren tachtig.* Tielt: Lannoo.

Kiefl, Walter, and Marina Marinescu. 1986. Zwischen Überlieferung und Wandlung. Modernisierungstendenzen der Familie in Griechenland. *Südosteuropa-Mitteilungen* 26:51-63.

Klages, H. 1985. *Wertorientierungen im Wandel.* Frankfurt: Campus Verlag.

Köcher, R. 1987. Religiös in einer säkularisierten Welt. In *Die verletzte Nation,* E. Noelle-Neumann and R. Köcher (eds.), 164-281. Stuttgart: Deutsche Verlags- Anstalt.

_____. 1990. Gottlos. *Rheinischer Merkur/Christ und Welt* 39 (28), September: 25-26.

Kokosalakis, Nikos. 1987. The Political Significance of Popular Religion in Greece. *Archives de Sciences Sociales des Religions* 64:37-52.

Kruijt, J. P. 1933. *De onkerkelikheid in Nederland.* Groningen: Wolters.

Kühr, H. 1985. Katholische und evangelische Milieus. Vermittlungs instanzen und Wirkungsmuster. In *Wirtschaftlicher Wandel, religiöser Wandel und Wertwandel,* D. Oberndörfer, et al. (eds.), 245- 261. Berlin: Duncker and Humblot.

Laermans, Rudi. 1992. *In de greep van 'De Moderne Tijd'.* Leuven: Acco.

Laeyendecker, L. 1989. Beweging binnen de R.K. Kerk in Nederland. In *Sociale bewegingen in de jaren negentig,* L. W. Huberts and W. J. van Noort (eds.), 117-136. Leiden: DSWO Press.

Lambert, Y. 1985. *Dieu change en Bretagne. La religion à Limerzel de 1900 a nos jours.* Paris: Cerf.

Lambert, William et al. 1959. Some Correlates of Beliefs in the Malevolence and Benevolence of Supernatural Beings: A Cross-cultural Study. *Journal of Abnormal and Social Psychology* 58:62-169.

Lechner, Frank J. 1989. Catholicism and Social Change in the Netherlands: A Case of Radical Secularization? *Journal for the Scientific Study of Religion* 28: 136-147.

Leege, David C. 1990. Leadership in the Contemporary Catholic Parish. Unpublished.

Lenski, Gerhard. 1963. *The Religious Factor*. Garden City, New York: Doubleday.

Leontidou, Lila. 1990. *The Mediterranean City in Transition. Social Change and Development*. Cambridge: Cambridge University Press.

Lipovetsky, Gilles. 1983. *L'ère du vide. Essais sur l'individualisme contemporain*. Paris: Gallimard.

Lipset, Seymour Martin. 1959. Religion in America: What Religious Revival? *Columbia University Forum II*, Winter.

_____. 1963. Three Decades of the Radical Right: Coughlinites, McCarthyites, and Birchers. In *The Radical Right*, Daniel Bell (ed.), 373-446. Garden City, New York: Doubleday.

Listhaug, Ola. 1990. Macrovalues: The Nordic Countries Compared. *Acta Sociologica* 33 (3):219-234.

Livingstone, E. A. (ed.). 1977. *The Concise Oxford Dictionary of the Christian Church*. Oxford University Press.

Long, John C. 1990. *Presbyterians: A New Look at an Old Church. Progressions: A Lilly Endowment Occasional Report* 2: 1-3.

Lossky, Nicolas. 1991. The Promise and the Outcome. *The Ecumenical Review* 43:211-216.

Lotti, Leila. 1983. *Some Aspects of the Religiousness of the Finns, 1951 and 1984. Suomen Finnish Gallup Oy Report 11*. Helsinki: Suomen Gallup.

Luckmann, Thomas. 1963. *The Invisible Religion. The Transformation of Symbols in Industrial Society*. New York: Macmillan and Co.

_____. 1967. *The Invisible Religion*. London: Macmillan.

_____. 1977. Theories of Religion and Social Change. *Annual Review*, 1:1-27.

_____. 1990. Shrinking Transcendence, Expanding Religion? *Sociological Analysis* 51: 127-138.

_____. 1991. *Die unsichtbare Religion*. Frankfurt: Suhtkamp.

Luhmann, Niklas. 1977. *Funktion der Religion*. Frankfurt: Suhrkamp Verlag.

Lukatis, I., and W. Lukatis. 1987. Jugend und Religion in der Bundesrepublik Deutschland. In *Jugend und Religion in Europa*, U. Nembach (ed.), 107-144. Frankfurt: Lang.

Lundby, Knut. 1985. Norge. In *Religiös förändring i Norden 1930- 1980*, Göran Gustafsson (ed.), 154-195. Malmö: Liber.

_____. 1988. Closed Circles. An Essay on Culture and Pietism in Norway. *Social Compass* 35:1:57-66.

Lyles, Jean Caffey. 1990. *The Fading of Denominational Distinctiveness*. *Progressions: A Lilly Endowment Occasional Report* 2: 16-17.

Lyotard, Jean-François. 1984. *The Postmodern Condition*. Minneapolis: University of Minnesota Press.

Maitre, J. 1988. Les deux côtés du miroir. Note sur l'évolution actuelle de la population française par rapport au catholicisme. *L'Année Sociologique* 38 (3): 31-48.

Maitre, J. et al. 1991. *Les Francais sont-ils encore catholiques?* Paris: Cerf.

Makrides, Vasilios. 1988. The Brotherhoods of Theologians in Contemporary Greece. *The Greek Orthodox Theological Review* 33:167-187.

_____. 1989. Neoorthodoxie - eine religiöse Intellektuellenströmung im heutigen Griechenland. In *Die Religion von Oberschichten: Religion - Profession- Intellektualismus*, P. Antes and D.Pahnke (eds.), 279-289. Marburg: Diagonal.

_____. 1991a. Aspects of Greek Orthodox Fundamentalism. *Orthodoxes Forum* 5:49-72.

_____. 1991b. Orthodoxy as a conditio sine qua non: Religion and State/Politics in Modern Greece from a Socio-Historical Perspective. *Ostkirchliche Studien* 40:281-305.

_____. 1993. Le rôle de l'Orthodoxie dans la formation de l'antieuropéanisme et l'anti-occidentalisme grecs. In *Religions et transformations de l'Europe*, G. Vincent and J.-P. Willaime (eds.), 103-116. Strasbourg: Presses Universitaires de Strasbourg.

Mannheim, K. 1952. *Essays on the Sociology of Knowledge*. London: Routledge & Kegan Paul.

Mantzaridis, George. 1975. *New Statistical Data Concerning the Monks of Mount Athos*. Social Compass 22:97-106.

_____. 1985. *Koinoniologia tou Christianismou*, 3rd ed. Thessaloniki: Pournaras.

Marler, Penny Long and David A. Roozen. 1993. Increasing Church Consumerism: The Gallup Surveys of the Unchurched American. In *Church and Denominational Growth*, David A. Roozen and C. Kirk Hadaway (eds.) Nashville: Abingdon Press.

Martin, Bernice and Ronald Pluck. 1976. *Young People's Beliefs. Research Report for the General Synod Board of Education*. London: General Synod Board of Education.

Martin, David. 1967. *A Sociology of English Religion*. London: Heinemann.

_____. 1978. *A General Theory of Secularization*. New York: Harper & Row.

Marty, Martin E. 1976. *A Nation of Behavers*. Chicago: University of Chicago Press.

_____. 1979. Foreword. In *Understanding Church Growth and Decline: 1950-1978*, Dean R. Hoge and David A. Roozen (eds.), 9-16. New York: Pilgrim Press.

Marty, Martin et al. 1968. *What Do We Believe?* New York: Meredith.

Mason, Michael. 1983. *Pastoral Leadership for Tomorrow.* Australasian Catholic Record 60 (1):9-45.

_____. 1991. Australian Catholics and Religious Pluralism. In *Christianity in a Multicultural Society. Working Papers on Migrant and Intercultural Studies*, No. 7, Radha Rasmussen (ed.), 9-25. Melbourne: Centre for Migrant and Intercultural Studies, Monash University.

_____. In press *Australian Catholics Today and Tomorrow.* Melbourne: Collins Dove.

McCallum, John. 1987. Secularization in Australia between 1966 and 1985: A research note. *Australian and New Zealand Journal of Sociology* 23:7-422.

McLoughlin, William G. 1966. Is There a Third Force in Christendom? In *Religion in America*, William G. McLoughlin and Robert Bellah (eds.). Boston: Beacon Press.

McNeill, William. 1978. *The Metamorphosis of Greece since World War II.* Oxford: Basil Blackwell.

Mickey, Paul A. and Robert L. Wilson. 1977. *What New Creation.* Nashville: Abingdon.

Mol, J. J. (Hans). 1971. *Religion in Australia.* Sydney: Nelson.

_____. 1972. *Western Religion: A Country-by-Country Sociological Inquiry.* The Hague: Mouton.

_____. 1985. *The Faith of Australians.* Sydney: Allen & Unwin.

Mooser, J. 1983. Auflösung der proletarischen Milieus. Klassenbindung und Individualisierung in der Arbeiterschaft vom Kaiserreich bis in die Bundesrepublik Deutschland. *Soziale Welt* 34:270- 306.

Morin, E.   1962.   *L'Esprit du Temps*. Paris: Grasset.

_____. 1968. *Mai 1968. La brêche*. Paris: Cerf.

Moro, Renato.   1968.   Il "modernismo buono." La "modernizzazione"
cattolica tra fascismo e post-fascismo come problema storiografico.
Storia Contemporanea 19 (4), Augusto, 1988: 625-716.

Munck, Henrik.   1986.   Danmarks officielle kirkstatistik 1974-1984. In
Kirke og folk i Danmark, H.R. Iversen and A.P. Thyssen (eds.). Århus:
Århus University Press.

Murnion, Philip J.   1990.   Constructing a Parish Spirituality and
Ecclesiology. Unpublished paper.

Neal, Sister Marie Augusta.   1966.   Catholicism in America. In *Religion in
America*, William G. McLoughlin and Robert Bellah (eds.), 312-338.
Boston: Beacon Press.

Neitz, Mary Jo.   1987.   *Charisma and Community*. New Brunswick, NJ:
Rutgers University Press.

Nora, P.   1984.   *Entre mémoire et histoire: la problèmatique des lieux
(Introduction) La République, vol. 1, Tome 1, Les lieux de mémoire*. Paris:
Gallimard.

O'Dea, Thomas F.   1970.   Five Dilemmas in the Institutionalisation of
Religion. In *Sociology and the Study of Religion*, Thomas F. O'Dea, 201-
220. New York: Basic Books.

Ottosen, Knud.   1986.   *A Short History of the Churches of Scandinavia*.
Århus: K. Ottosen.

Pannet, Robert.   1974.   *Le catholicisme populaire: 30 ans après "La France,
pays de mission."* Paris: Le Centurion.

Parsons, Talcott.   1960.   *Structure and Process in Modern Societies*. Glencoe:
The Free Press.

Pastoraal Concilie van de Nederlandse . 1968. *Kerkprovincie, deel I*.
Amersfoort: De Horstink.

Peeters, Pascale. 1990. *Gezin en Kerk*. Unpublished M.A. dissertation, Katholieke Universiteit Leuven.

Perrin, L. 1989. *L'affaire Lefébvre*. Paris: Cerf.

Petitat, Andre. 1987. L'unique et ses institutions. Jalons dans l'émergence d'un multi-individualisme institutionnel. *Revue Eruopénne des Sciences Sociales* 25:74:109.

Pettersson, Thorleif. 1988. *Bakom dubbla lås*. Uppsala: University of Uppsala.

_____. 1991. Religion and Criminality: Structural Relationships between Church Involvement and Crime Rates in Contemporary Sweden. *Journal for the Scientific Study of Religion* 30 (3):279-291.

Petursson, Petur. 1985. Island. In *Religiös förändring i Norden 1930-1980*, Göran Gustafsson (ed.), 111-153. Malmö: Liber.

_____. 1987. Religiös förändring i fem nordiska städer sedan 1930. In *Religion och kyrka i fem nordiska städer*, Göran Gustafsson (ed.), 357-375. Malmö, Oslo: Liber.

_____. 1988. The Relevance of Secularization in Iceland. *Social Compass* 35 (1):107-124.

Pittkowski, W. and R. Volz. 1989. Konfession und politische Orientierung. Das Beispiel der Konfessionslosen. In *Religion und Konfession*, K.-F. Daiber (ed.), 93-112. Hanover: Lutherisches Verlaghaus.

Poggi, Gianfranco. 1963. *Il clero di reserva*. Milano: Feltrinelli.

Pollack, D. 1991. Integration vor Entsvheidung Zur Entwicklung von Religiosität und Kircklichkeit in der ehemaligen DDR. *Glauben und Lernen* 6 (2): 144-156.

Potel, Julien. 1977. *Les prêtres séculiers en France*. Paris: Centurion.

_____. 1988. Crises du clergé catholique ou nouvelle race de prêtres? *L'Année Sociologique* 38 (3): 63-78.

Princeton Religious Research Center (PRRC). 1991. *Emerging Trends.*
Princeton: Princeton Religious Research Center.

Reitinger, H. 1991. *Die Rolle der Kirche im politischen Prozeß der DDR 1970
bis 1990.* Munich: Tudur.

Rezsohazy, R. 1985. La religion des jeunes. In *La Belgique et ses Dieux:
Eglises, Mouvements Religieux et Laïques,* L. Voyé et al. (eds.), 271-283.
Louvain-la-Neuve: Cabay.

Riesebrodt, Martin. 1990. *Fundamentalismus als patriarchalische
Protestbewegung. Amerikanische Protestanten (1910- 1928) und iranische
Schiiten (1961-1979) im Vergleich.* Tübingen: Mohr.

Riesman, David et al. 1950. *The Lonely Crowd.* New Haven: Yale
University Press.

Riis, Ole. 1984. *Nya tendenser i den religiösa socialisationen.
Religionssociologiska institutet* 4. Stockhom: Religionssociologiska
instituet.

_____. 1985. Danmark. In *Religiös förändring i Norden 1930- 1980,*
Göran Gustafsson (ed.), 22-65. Malmö: Liber.

_____. 1989. The Role of Religion in Legitimating the Modern
Structuration of Society. *Acta Sociologica* 32:2:137-153.

_____. 1990. Folkekirken og folkereligiositet religionssociologisk
belyst. *Kritisk Forum for Praktisk Teologi* 39: 56-75.

Robbins, Thomas. 1988. Cults, Converts and Charisma. *Current
Sociology* 36 (1): 1-256.

Robbins, Thomas et al. 1978. Theory and Research on Today's 'New
Religions.' *Sociological Analysis* 39: 95-122.

Robbrecht, Paul. 1986. *Mariaverering te Scherpenheuvel: Proeve van een
hedendaagse pastoraal in een Mariaal bedevaartsoord.* Brussels: Lumen
Vitae.

Roberts, Keith A. 1984. *Religion in Sociological Perspective.* Homewood,
IL: The Dorsey Press.

Robertson, Roland. 1985. The Relativization of Societies: Modern Religion and Globalization. In *Cults, Culture and the Law*, T. Robbins, W. Shepherd and J. McBride (eds.), 31- 42. Chico, California: Scholars Press.

Robinson, John. 1963. *Honest to God*, London: SCM Press.

Roge, J. 1965. *Le simple prêtre, sa formation, son expérience*. Paris: Casterman.

Rokkan, Stein. 1977. Towards a generalized concept of 'Verzuiling': a preliminary note. *Political Studies* 25:4:563-570.

Roof, Wade Clark. 1990. Narrative and Numbers. Unpublished J.F Rowny Inaugural Lecture, May.

_____. 1991. Denominational Religion and the Voluntary Principle. *Religion and Social Order* 1: 225-238.

_____. 1993. *A Generation of Seekers: The Spiritual Journeys of the Baby Boom Generation*. San Francisco: Harper Row.

Roof, Wade Clark and Karen Loeb. Unpublished Baby Boomers and Religious Change. Unpublished paper.

Roof, Wade Clark, and Wiliam McKinney. 1987. *American Mainline Religion: Its Changing Shape and Future*. New Brunswick, NJ: Rutgers University Press.

Roozen, David A. 1979. The Efficacy of Demographic Theories of Religious Change: Protestant Church Attendance, 1952-68. In *Understanding Church Growth and Decline: 1950-1978*, Dean Hoge and David A.Roozen (eds.), 123-143. New York: Pilgrim Press.

Roozen, David A. et al. 1990. The 'Big Chill' Generation Warms to Worship. *Review of Religious Research* 31: 314-322.

Roozen, David A. and C. Kirk Hadaway (eds.). 1993. *Church and Denominational Growth*. Nashville: Abingdon Press.

Roy Morgan Research Centre. 1970, 1972. *Morgan Gallup polls. (Bulletins--irregular)*. 1976, 1981. Melbourne: Roy Morgan Research Centre.

Ryder, Norman B. 1965. The Cohort as a Concept in the Study of Social Change. *American Sociological Review* 30:43-61.

Savramis, Demosthenes. 1968. *Die soziale Stellung des Priesters in Griechenland.* Leiden: Brill.

Scheepens, Th. 1991. *Kerk in Nederland. Een landelijk onderzoek naar kerkbetrokkenheid en kerkverlating.* Tilburg: University Press.

Schilling, H. 1988. Reformation und Konfessionalisierung in Deutschland und die neuere deutsche Geschichte. In *Religion, Kirchen und Gesellschaft in Deutschland. Gegenwartskunde Sonderheft* 5, F. X. Kaufmann and B. Schäfers (eds.), 11-29. Opladen: Leske.

Schreuder, O. 1990. De religieuze traditie in de jaren tachtig. In *Religie in de Nederlandse samenleving*, O. Schreuder and L. van Snippenburg (eds.), 17-41. Baarn: Ambo.

Schreuder, O. and L. van Snippenburg (eds). 1990. *Religie in de Nederlandse samenleving.* Baarn: Ambo.

Scoppola, Pietro. 1987. *La "Nuova Cristianità" Perduta.* Rome: Studium.

SCS. 1989. *Statistics from the Church of Sweden 1989.* Stockholm. Unpublished.

SE 1991. 1991. Kirkestatistik, 1989. *Statistisk Efterretninger Uddannelse og kultur* 1991: 1. Copenhagen: Danmarks statistik.

Séguy, Jean. 1971. Les Sociétés Imaginées: Monachisme et Utopie. *Annales E.S.C.* 2:238-354.

Shiner, Larry. 1967. The Concept of Secularization in Empirical Research. *Journal for the Scientific Study of Religion* 6 (2): 207-220.

Sihvo, Jouko. 1988. Religion and Secularization in Finland. *Social Compass* 35 (1):67-90.

_____. 1991. The Evangelical Lutheran Church and State in Finland. *Social Compass* 38 (1):17-24.

Sillitoe, Alan F. 1971. *Britain in Figures: A Handbook of Social Statistics*. Harmondsworth: Penguin.

Skog, Margareta. 1989. *Antalet medlemmar i valda samfund 1975-1989. Religion och samhälle 1989: 9 nr.47*. Stockholm: Religionssociologiska institutet.

Smart, Ninian. 1987. *Religion and the Western Mind*. Albany, N.Y.: SUNY Press.

Smith, Peter. 1986. Anglo-American Religion and Hegemonic Change in the World System, c. 1870-1980. *British Journal of Sociology* 37: 88-105.

Smylie, James H. 1979. Church Growth and Decline in Historical Perspective: Protestant Quest for Identity, Leadership and Meaning. In *Understanding Church Growth and Decline: 1950-1978*, Dean R. Hoge and David A.Roozen (eds.), 69-93. New York: Pilgrim Press.

Sociaal en cultureel rapport. 1986. Den Haag: 1986. Staatsuitgeverij.

Statistisches Jahrbuch der DDR. Berlin (East): 1990. Staatliche Zentralverwaltung für Statistik.

Statistical Abstracts of Sweden 1990. 1990. Stockholm: Statistika Centralbyrån.

Staverman, M. 1954. *Buitenkerkelijkheid in Friesland*. Assen: Van Gorcum.

Stavrou, Theofanis. 1988. The Orthodox Church of Greece. In *Eastern Christianity and Politics in the Twentieth Century*, Pedro Ramet (ed.), 183-207. Durham and London: Duke University Press.

Stoffels, H. C. and G. Decker. 1987. *Geloven van huis uit*. Kampen: Kok.

Stylios, Efthymios. 1980. *To synchronon astikon perivallon os poimantikon problima. Meleti "poimantikis koinoniologias"*, Th.D. dissertation. Athens: privately published.

Sundback, Susan. 1985. Finland. In *Religiös förändring i Norden 1930-1980*, Göran Gustafsson (ed.), 66-110. Malmö: Liber.

_____. 1986. *Folkkyrkan och folkets passivering. Meddelanden från Ekonomisk-statsvetenskapliga fakulteten vid Åbo Akademi A:229.* Åbo: Åbo Akademi.

_____. 1987. Hur möter människorna religionen i de fem städerna? In *Religion och kyrka i fem nordiska städer,* Göran Gustafsson (ed.), 336-356. Malmö, Oslo: Liber.

_____. 1989. *Sekularisering och kyrkotrohet i Danmark. Acta Jutlandica LXV:2, Samfundsvidenskapbelig serie 18.* Århus: Aarhus universitatesforlag.

_____. 1991. *Utträdet ur Finlands lutherska kyrka.* Åbo: Åbo Akademi.

Suolinna, Kirsti. 1975. *Uskonnollisten liikkeitten asema sosiaalisessa muutoksessa. Institute of Sociology, University of Helsinki, Research Reports 203.* Helsinki: University of Helsinki.

Swanson, Guy E. 1960. *The Birth of The Gods: The Origin of Primitive Beliefs.* Ann Arbor: University of Michigan Press.

Swatos, William H., Jr. 1981. Beyond Denominationalism?: Community and Culture in American Religion. *Journal for the Scientific Study of Religion* 20:217-227.

SYF. 1990. *Statistical Yearbook of Finland 1990.* Helsinki: Central Statistical Office of Finland.

Sylos-Labini, Paolo. 1974. *Saggio Sulle Classi Sociali.* Rome: Laterza.

SYN. 1991. *Statistical Yearbook of Norway 1991.* Oslo-Kongsvinger: Statistik Sentralbyrå.

Thomas, Terence (ed.). 1988. *The British: Their Religious Beliefs and Practices 1800-1986.* London: Routledge.

Thung, Mady A. et al. 1985. *Exploring the New Religious Consciousness: An Investigation of Religious Change by a Dutch Working Group.* Amsterdam: Free University Press.

Thurlings, J. M. G. 1971. *De wankele zuil. Nederlandse katholieken tussen assimilatie en pluralisme.* Nijmegen-Amersfoort: Dekker & van de Vegt-De Horstink.

Tomara-Sideri, Matoula. 1991. Thesmikos eksynchronismos kai koinoniki dynamiki (I thespisi tou politikou gamou stin Ellada). *Synchrona Themata.* 46/47: 64-69.

Touraine, Alain. 1968, 1972. *Le mouvement de Mai ou le communisme utopique.* Paris: Seuil.

_____. 1984. *Le retour de l'acteur.* Paris: Fayard.

Towler, Robert. 1985. *The Need for Certainty: A Sociological Study of Conventional Religion.* London: Routledge and Kegan Paul.

Van Hemert, M.M.J. 1980. *"En zij verontschuldigden zich...": De ontwikkeling van het misbezoekcijfer 1966-79.* The Hague: Kaski.

Van Trier, Walter. 1986. *Een sociologisch onderzoek naar enkele facetten van de moderne landbouw.* Leuven: Departement Sociologie.

Van Molle, Leen. 1990. *Ieder voor allen : De Belgische Boerenbond 1890-1990.* Leuven : Universitaire Pers Leuven.

Vassiliadis, Petros. 1991. Greek Theology in the Making. Trends and Facts in the 80s - Vision for the 90s. *St. Vladimir's Theological Quarterly* 35:33-52.

Vigestad, Kjell. 1981. Baerpillarne uthules. In *Statskirke i etterkrigssamfunn,* Knut Lunby and Ingun Montgomery (eds.), 68-84. Oslo: Bergen-Tromso.

Voyé, Liliane. 1973. *Sociologie du geste religieux: De l'analyse de la pratique dominicale à une interprétation théorique.* Bruxelles: Les Editions Vie Ouvrière.

_____. 1985. Au-delà de la sécularisation. *Lettres Pastorales: Informations officielles du diocèse de Tournai* 1 (21): 253-274.

_____. 1988a. Prolongements et perspectives: le point de vue d'un sociologue. In *Le religieux en Occident: Pensée des déplacements,* J.P. Schlegel et al., 127-136. Bruxelles: Facultés universitaires Saint-Louis.

_____. 1988b. Approche méthodologique du sacré. In *Religion, Mentalité et Vie Quotidienne*, M. Cloet and F. Daelmans (eds.), 255-277. Bruxelles: Archives et Bibliothèques de Belgique.

_____. 1988c. Du monopole religieux à la connivence culturelle en Belgique. Un catholicisme "hors les murs". *L'Année Sociologique* 38:135-167.

_____. 1989. Godsdienst, Kerk en Samenleving. In *Geloven in de Samenleving*, Jef Stevens (ed.), 127-142. Helmond: Uitgeverij Altiora.

Voyé, Liliane and Karel Dobbelare. 1992. Le religieux: d'une religion institué á une religiosité recomposée. In *Belges, heureux et satisfaits. Le valuers des belges dans les annés 90*, Liliane Voyé, Bernadette Bawin, Karel Dobbelare, and Jan Kerkhofs (ed.), 159-238. Bruxelles: De Boeck-Wesmael.

Walker, Andrew. 1988. *Restoring the Kingdom: The Radical Christianity of the House Church Movement*. London: Hodder & Stoughton.

Walrath, Douglas Alan 1987. *Frameworks: Patterns of Living and Believing Today*. New York: Pilgrim Press.

Ware, Timothy [Kallistos]. 1980. *The Orthodox Church*. Harmondsworth: Penguin Books.

_____. 1983. The Church: A Time of Transition. In *Greece in the 1980s*, Richard Clogg (ed.), 208-230. London: Macmillan.

Weber, Max. 1968. *Economy and Society*. Guenther Roth and Claud Wittich (eds.), Ephraim Fischoff et al. (trans.). New York: Bedminster Press.

Wenturis, Nikolaus. 1990. *Griechenland und die EG*. Tübingen: Francke.

Westley, Frances. 1983. *The Complex Forms of the New Religious Life: A Durkheimian View of New Religious Movements*. Chico, CA: Scholars Press.

Wilson, Bryan. 1966a. Religion and the Churches in Contemporary America. In *Religion in America*, William G. McLoughlin and Robert Bellah (eds.), 73-110. Boston: Beacon Press.

_____. 1966b. *Religion in Secular Society*. London: Watts.

_____. 1976. Aspects of Secularization in the West. *Japanese Journal of Religious Studies* 3 (3/4):259-276.

_____. 1982. *Religion in Sociological Perspective*. Oxford: University Press.

_____ 1985. Secularization: The *Inherited Model. In The Secular in a Secular Age*, Phillip E. Hammond (ed.), 9-20. Berkeley: University of California Press.

Wiman, Ronald. 1978. The Impact of the Post-War Baby-Boom in Finland. *Yearbook of Population Research in Finland* XVI: 83-98.

Wolton, D. and J. L. Missika. 1987. *Le choix de Dieu. Entretiens avec le Cardinal Lustiger*. Paris: Ed. de Fallois.

Wuthnow, Robert. 1976. *The Consciousness Reformation*. Berkeley: University of California Press.

_____. 1978. *Experimentation in American Religion: The New Mysticisms and their Implications for the Churches*. Berkeley: University of California Press.

_____. 1988. *The Restructuring of American Religion: Society and Faith Since World War II*. Princeton, NJ: Princeton University Press.

_____. 1989. *The Struggle For America's Soul: Evangelicals, Liberals and Secularism*. Grand Rapids, MI: William B Eerdmans.

Yankelovich, Daniel. 1974. *The New Morality: A Profile of American Youth in the 70s*. New York: McGraw-Hill.

Yinger, Milton J. 1957. *Religion, Society and the Individual*. New York: Macmillan

_____. 1970. *The Scientific Study of Religion*. New York: Macmillan.

YNC. 1991. *Yearbook of the Norwegian Church/Årbok for den norske kirke 1966-1991*. Oslo: Den norske kirke.

YNS. 1980-1990. *Yearbook of Nordic Statistics 1980, 1988, 1989, 1990.*
Copenhagen: Nordiska rådet.

Yonnet, P. 1985. *Jeux, modes et masses: La Société française et le moderne,*
1945-1985. Paris: Gallimard.

Zander, H. 1988. Zur Situation der katholischen Kirche in der DDR. *Aus*
Politik und Zeitgeschichte B 4-5:29-38.

Zeegers, G. H. L. (ed.). 1987. *God in Nederland.* Amsterdam: Van Ditmar.

Zetterberg, Hans. 1983. Kyrkfolkets livsstilar. In *Aktiva i Svenska kyrkan-*
en livsstilsstudie. Hans Zetterberg, 11-22. Stockholm: Verbum.

Zylberberg, Jacques. 1985. Les transactions du sacre. *Sociétés* 1 (4): 9-11.

About the Book

For those who make up what we now call "the Baby-Boom generation," World War II is more than a backdrop to history: It signifies the beginning of a new world. Amidst dramatic changes in international political and economic systems, the advent of television, and cultural pluralism, this generation has come to take for granted new perspectives on the meaning and purpose of family, politics, education, and, most notably, religion.

This is the first book to offer a comparative analysis of the impact this post-war generation has had on Christianity around the world. Taking a cross-cultural approach, the contributors examine ten developed countries, including England, France, Germany, Australia, and the United States, and explore the ways baby boomers have helped reshape and redefine "establishment religions"—that is, the dominant, primarily Christian institutions.

Looking at the Church of England, the Catholic Church in France, the Lutheran Church in Sweden, and other institutions, the authors of the study find similarities with the ways baby boomers have affected religion in various countries. Yet the peculiar and historical context of each nation has fostered some striking differences as well. The researchers' conclusions are broad and far-reaching, shedding light on the fate of religion both in countries now modernizing and in those countries moving through the modern to the postmodern. Sociologists, historians, and scholars of religion will profit from the insights put forth here on religion in a postmodern context.

DATE DUE

GAYLORD			PRINTED IN U.S.A.